lone

OF TRAVEL

# FIJI

Rotuma
(600km)

Vanua Levu
& Taveuni
p140

Mamanuca &
Yasawa
p94

Ovalau &
Lomaiviti
p121

Nadi, Suva
& Viti Levu
p47

✪
SUVA

Kadavu & Lau
p167

**Anirban Mahapatra**

# CONTENTS

**Bull shark, Beqa
Lagoon (p70)**

## Plan Your Trip

Welcome ........................... 4

Map ..................................... 6

Our Picks ........................... 8

Regions & Cities ........... 24

Itineraries ...................... 26

When to Go ..................... 34

Get Prepared ................. 36

The Food Scene ............ 38

The Outdoors ................ 40

Action Areas .................. 42

## The Guide

Nadi, Suva & Viti Levu ..... 47
  Nadi ................................. 52
  Beyond Nadi ................. 57
  Natadola ........................ 61
  Beyond Natadola ......... 64
  Pacific Harbour ........... 69
  Beyond Pacific Harbour .72
  Suva ................................ 75
  Beyond Suva ................. 82
  Suncoast ........................ 88
  Beyond Suncoast ......... 91

Mamanuca & Yasawa .......... 94
  Mamanuca .................... 100
  Beyond Mamanuca ........ 104
  Kuata ............................. 106
  Beyond Kuata ............... 109
  Drawaqa ....................... 111
  Yaqeta ........................... 115
  Beyond Yaqeta ............. 118


Ovalau & Lomaiviti ............. 121
  Levuka ........................... 126
  Beyond Levuka ............. 130
  Leleuvia ........................ 133
  Beyond Leleuvia .......... 137


Vanua Levu & Taveuni ...... 140
  Savusavu ...................... 146
  Beyond Savusavu ........ 152
  Somosomo .................... 156
  Beyond Somosomo ...... 159
  Matei ............................. 163


Kadavu & Lau ...................... 167
  Great Astrolabe Reef ..... 172
  Beyond the Great
  Astrolabe Reef ............. 177
  Vanua Balavu ............... 180
  Beyond
  Vanua Balavu ............... 182

**Indigenous Fijian
dancers**

**Sri Siva Subramaniya
Swami Temple, Nadi (p53)**

## Toolkit

Arriving ............................. 186

Getting Around ............... 187

Money ................................ 188

Accommodation ............. 189

Family Travel .................. 190

Health & Safety .............. 191

Food, Drink & Nightlife .... 192

Responsible Travel ........ 194

LGBTIQ+ Travellers ....... 196

Accessible Travel ........... 197

Local Laws ....................... 198

Nuts & Bolts .................... 199

Language .......................... 200

## Storybook

A History of Fiji
in 15 Places ...................... 204

Meet the Fijians ............. 208

Voyages –
Past & Present ................ 210

Speak. Share.
Drink. Repeat. ................ 214

Towards a
Greener Future ............... 216

FROM LEFT: MARTIN PROCHAZKACZ/SHUTTERSTOCK ©, LEMB/SHUTTERSTOCK ©, HENRYK SADURA/SHUTTERSTOCK ©

IGNACIO MOYA CORONADO/SHUTTERSTOCK ©

Kuata (p106)

# FIJI
## THE JOURNEY BEGINS HERE

I came to live in Fiji at an epochal crossroads of time and tide. The COVID-19 pandemic was past its worst, and the country was once again calling out to visitors from around the world with its signature emphasis on community, happiness and the undiluted spirit of adventure. I plunged into the task of documenting innovative ways in which Fiji was using community-centric tourism to find answers to contemporary economic and environmental issues. Whether going on shark-awareness dives with conservationists in Kuata, or hiking the remote highlands to spend time with the community in Nabutautau village, it now brings me immense pleasure to see my tourism spend going directly into making a positive difference, both in the lives of people as well as the fate of the environment. The surf is now up for exploring this wonderland in the distant Pacific, and I am glad to have caught the wave just in time.

**Anirban Mahapatra**

Anirban is a travel journalist and conservation storyteller juggling critical issues such as climate change, sustainability and regeneration.

# MY FAVOURITE EXPERIENCE

Writer and expert Anirban Mahapatra chooses
the place which, for him, defines Fiji.

DANITA DELIMONT CREATIVE/ALAMY STOCK PHOTO ©

**Diver, Rainbow Reef (p160)**

My favourite experience in Fiji is to spend the day scuba diving – with the graceful manta rays in the untamed **Great Astrolabe Reef** (p173), and surrounded by psychedelic soft corals in the vibrant **Rainbow Reef** (p160).

## Anirban Mahapatra

*@i_mahapatra*

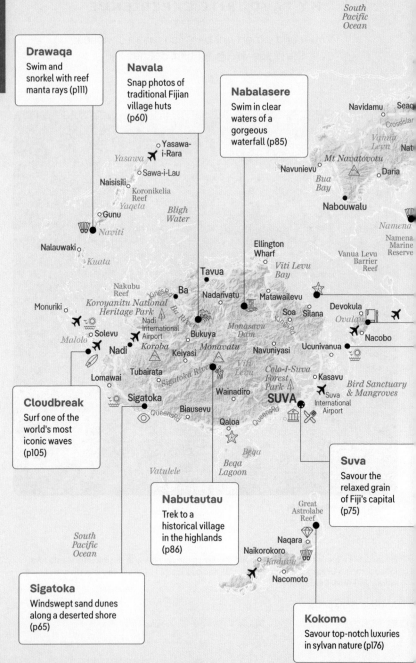

**Drawaqa**
Swim and snorkel with reef manta rays (p111)

**Navala**
Snap photos of traditional Fijian village huts (p60)

**Nabalasere**
Swim in clear waters of a gorgeous waterfall (p85)

**Cloudbreak**
Surf one of the world's most iconic waves (p105)

**Nabutautau**
Trek to a historical village in the highlands (p86)

**Sigatoka**
Windswept sand dunes along a deserted shore (p65)

**Suva**
Savour the relaxed grain of Fiji's capital (p75)

**Kokomo**
Savour top-notch luxuries in sylvan nature (p176)

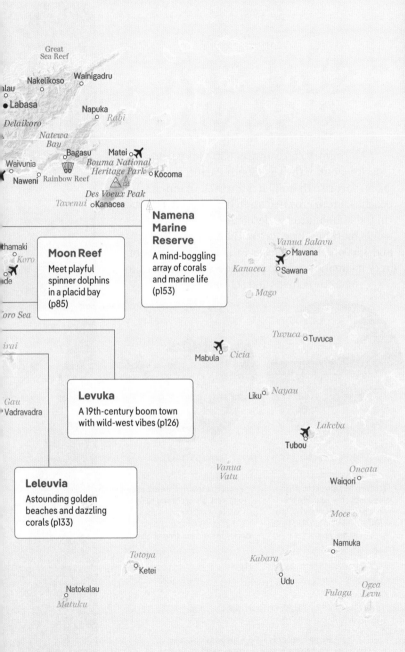

Great
Sea Reef

Nakelikoso    Wainigadru

alau
Labasa

Napuka

Delaikoro          Rabi

Natewa
Bay

Waivunia    Bagasu    Matei    ✈

Naweni    Rainbow Reef    Bouma National
Heritage Park    Kocoma

Des Voeux Peak

Tavenui    Kanacea

**Namena
Marine
Reserve**

A mind-boggling
array of corals
and marine life
(p153)

Vanua Balavu
Mavana

Kanacea    Sawana

Mago

thamaki

Koro
✈
ade

**Moon Reef**

Meet playful
spinner dolphins
in a placid bay
(p85)

oro Sea

Tuvuca    Tuvuca

irai

Mabula    Cicia

Gau
Vadravadra

Liku    Nayau

**Levuka**

A 19th-century boom town
with wild-west vibes (p126)

Lakeba
✈
Tubou

Vanua
Vatu

Oncata
Waiqori

**Leleuvia**

Astounding golden
beaches and dazzling
corals (p133)

Moce

Namuka

Totoya
Ketei

Kabara

Natokalau    Udu    Ogea
Matulcu    Fulaga    Levu

0        60 km
Ⓝ 0        30 miles

7

# SUN, SEA & SAND

As a country consisting of 330-plus islands peeking out of the vast South Pacific, it comes as no surprise that Fiji has a surfeit of top-notch beaches. From crowded stretches fronting resorts in the Mamanucas to desolate slivers of pristine sands marking the edges of the Yasawas, Kadavu and Taveuni, Fiji's beaches call out to travellers of every inclination – from partygoers and families to romantic couples and solitude seekers.

### Beach Season

Fiji's beaches attract tourists throughout the year, but the weather between May and August is more clement than at other times of the year.

### Beach Facilities

Resorts allow guests access to towels, showers and toilets while using their beaches. Nonmotorised sports gear is usually loaned out free of charge.

### Safety Protocol

There are no lifeguards in Fiji, especially on public beaches. Your safety is your own responsibility. Always ask locals for guidance before stepping into the water.

❸  ❺

❷

❶  ❹

## BEST BEACH EXPERIENCES

Flop around in style in **Natadola**, Viti Levu's showcase beach that offers activities and relaxation for the whole family.
❶ (p61)

Swim, snorkel, kayak and paddleboard in the azure waters off **Malolo**, a top island destination in Mamanuca.
❷ (p102)

Snorkel amid seagrass beds at **Blue Lagoon**, or relax under the row of emerald palms lining its pristine beach.
❸ (p116)

Frolic in the dazzling waters off **Leleuvia** island, while spotting diverse coral species, giant clams and colourful fish.
❹ (p133)

Hike the wilderness trail of **Lavena Coastal Walk**, exploring some of Fiji's most secluded beaches along the way.
❺ (p164)

# ROMANTIC ESCAPES

From private islands catering to a limited number of clients to elegant resorts pampering their guests with unending luxuries, Fiji is a dream getaway for honeymooners as well as couples looking to exchange their daily grind for some quality alone time. Shake off the world and slip away behind nature's veil to spend a memorable holiday in paradise.

### Adults-Only Resorts

These exclusive properties promise privacy, solitude and luxury in the serene lap of nature, and are often located in gorgeous island locations.

### Private Islands

To remove yourself by another degree from all social contact, stay at an upscale private island that hosts only a select few loners at a time.

## BEST ROMANTIC EXPERIENCES

Sleep in the overwater *bures* of **Likuliku Lagoon**, an absolute indulgence for romantics, lovebirds and newlyweds.
❶ (p101)

Enjoy quality quiet time at adults-only **Tadrai**, which offers a spot of privacy on an otherwise busy island in Mamanuca.
❷ (p101)

Switch off from the world on salubrious **Turtle Island Resort** in Yasawa, a private hideaway amid sapphire lagoons.
❸ (p116)

Treat yourself to a luxury escapade on serene and upscale **Wakaya** island, featuring its own exclusive marine-protected area.
❹ (p139)

Wallow in the lap of luxury on the lavish private island of **Kokomo**, hidden away in the far southern wilderness of Fiji.
❺ (p176)

**Family snorkelling, Vanua Levu (p140)**

# YOUNG EXPLORERS

Families and children have a special place in the hearts of Fijian people, and this is reflected in their signature hospitality. During your holiday here, you will never be short of experiences and opportunities that allow you to bond as a family, all while your kids play, learn and have a thrilling time.

### Courses & Lessons

Fix your children up for a certification in scuba diving, a beginner's lesson in surfing or a crash course in Fijian cooking.

### Rolling & Tumbling

Treat your kids to a a string of unique rides and safaris that introduce them to Fiji's magnificent outdoors and promise tons of fun.

## BEST CHILDREN'S EXPERIENCES

Explore the placid seagrass beds of **Blue Lagoon**, which hide a fabulous array of marine life for kids to discover.
**❶** (p116)

Hoot in excitement as you and your kids tumble down shark-themed rides at **Big Bula Waterpark** in Denarau.
**❷** (p56)

Grin back at spinner dolphins on a dolphin safari in **Moon Reef**, then snorkel amid sparkling hard corals.
**❸** (p85)

Ride a giant swing among treetops at **Kila World**, followed by a bunch of activities in this popular adventure park.
**❹** (p74)

Snorkel with harmless reef sharks in **Kuata**, which is both safe and fun and a unique experience for children.
**❺** (p106)

# DISCOVER THE DEEP

Fiji is one of the top destinations for scuba diving anywhere on this planet. Dubbed the soft-coral capital of the world, the oceans and lagoons here teem with hundreds of species of coral (both soft and hard), as well as a plethora of reef fish and pelagic megafauna. Underwater photographers would be doubly excited at the prospect of imaging coral seascapes of astounding beauty, and having rare encounters with sharks, rays, turtles and innumerable fish and invertebrate species.

**Where to Dive**

From lazy drifts in calm waters to gut-wrenching excursions in strong tidal currents, Fiji has various dive sites to suit your experience and ability.

**Getting Certified**

With a few days to spare, there's no better place than Fiji to combine an exciting diving experience with picking up your scuba certification.

**Dive Safety**

Never board an airplane within 24 hours of your last dive. Always follow dive safety protocol, and stay within the diving limit of your certification level.

**BEST DIVING EXPERIENCES**

Join the psychedelic party of vibrant soft corals in **Rainbow Reef**, an unforgettable display of the colours of nature.
❶ (p160)

Dive the protected waters of **Namena Marine Reserve**, home to a constellation of fish and invertebrate species.
❷ (p153)

Hover over stunning corals carpeting the slopes of **Great Astrolabe Reef**, fourth largest on the world's list of barrier reefs.
❸ (p172)

Fall under the arresting spell of a bull shark circling within arm's reach during a thrilling shark dive in **Pacific Harbour**.
❹ (p69)

Dive the conservation park of **Vatu-i-Ra**, home to stacks of coral reefs and marine life in the ocean passage of Bligh Waters.
❺ (p92)

# FLIPPING & FLOATING

For non-divers and swimmers, Fiji's undersea coral gardens can also effectively be enjoyed over a snorkelling session. Snorkelling opportunities abound, no matter where you are headed in the country, as long as there's a coast nearby. The water visibility is stunning from May to August, when you can see much deeper into the topography of coral reefs.

## BEST SNORKELLING EXPERIENCES

Snorkel with blacktip and whitetip reef sharks in **Kuata**, one of the few places in the world for this unique experience.
**①** (p106)

Meet migratory manta rays in the shallow passage off **Drawaqa** island, during the winter months from May to September.
**②** (p111)

Snorkel in **Blue Lagoon**, and amid nearby coral bommies, spotting curious ocean creatures like sea cucumbers and pipefish.
**③** (p116)

Swim in the shallows around **Leleuvia**, and access expansive coral gardens by literally wading into the water from the beach.
**④** (p133)

Duck-dive on the deeper coral expanses of **Great Astrolabe Reef** to witness the vastness of the world's fourth-largest barrier reef.
**⑤** (p172)

### Hard vs Soft Coral

Hard coral reefs are more easily explored while snorkelling, as they're located in shallower depths than soft corals, which grow in deeper waters.

### Essential Gear

Bring along your own mask, snorkel and fins if possible, as they will doubtless fit better than rental gear, and will also be more hygienic.

FLYSTOCK/SHUTTERSTOCK ©

**Surfing, Cloudbreak (p105)**

# SURF'S UP!

A cluster of reef breaks in southern Mamanuca has legendary status among surfers worldwide as the home of Cloudbreak, one of the world's most challenging waves. Several other waves in this cluster are surf-worthy, some more democratic than the others. Kadavu, in Fiji's far south, also has impressive waves that call out to daring surfers.

### Surfing Season

May to August is peak surfing season – the waves at Cloudbreak reach heights of up to 6m and it doubles as a venue for surfing competitions.

### Novices

While only the most experienced and daring surfers head to Mamanuca and Kadavu, first-timers can surf smaller and gentler waves in spots like Natadola.

## BEST SURFING EXPERIENCES

Surf the iconic **Cloudbreak**, a barelling left-breaking reef in Mamanuca that is routinely voted as one of the world's top 10 challenging waves.
❶ (p105)

Tackle Mamanuca's other famous left-hander, named **Restaurants**, which extends for up to 200m over a shallow stretch of reef.
❷ (p105)

Cruise the gentle waves breaking off **Natadola**, an ideal place for learners and newbies to perfect their surfing manoeuvres.
❸ (p61)

Take on a mix of powerful left and right breaks amid the waves at Kadavu's **Vesi Passage**, accessible from Matava.
❹ (p175)

Surf the tall right-hand break at **Naiqoro Passage**, a playfield for veteran surfers halfway down Great Astrolabe Reef.
❺ (p173)

15

# WALKS IN THE WILD

No trekker worth their salt can resist the raw appeal of lonesome walking trails that lead over the horizon into Fiji's great wild interior. Each trail takes you to a different destination, ranging from antique villages high in the savannas to lava-sculpted summits of ancient volcanic mountains. There are half-day trips, overnight walks and multiday jaunts to choose from, featuring unique experiences like waterfall swims, river crossings and overnight stays with village communities.

### Hiking Season

The dry, cool months of May through August are best for hiking. The wet months make trails slippery and bring flash floods in the hills.

### Difficulty Rating

Fiji's hikes can be as easy as a walk in the park, or as demanding as a scramble on all fours up near-vertical mountain slopes.

### Essential Gear

Remember to have your own pair of hiking shoes, sun shade, rain gear, insect repellent, first-aid and stash of dry snacks on a trek.

❺

❷❹ ❸
❶

## BEST HIKING EXPERIENCES

Embark on a three-day trek to **Nabutautau** village, passing through gorgeous hills, windswept savanna and deep river valleys.
❶ (p86)

Go for a challenging summit push on **Tomanivi** in the heart of Viti Levu, to set foot on the highest point in the country.
❷ (p93)

Hike to **Lovoni** in Ovalau's volcanic crater, hearing legends along the way and spotting native flora in the bushes.
❸ (p131)

Scale the volcanic plug of **Vatuvula**, looming above Wayasewa island, a fascinating half-day hike through wild terrain.
❹ (p110)

Stroll along the **Lavena Coastal Walk** in Taveuni, all the way to a picturesque waterfall hidden in the wilderness.
❺ (p164)

# CASCADES & POOLS

Viti Levu, Kadavu and Taveuni hide a few of Fiji's biggest and most spectacular waterfalls, flowing through virgin forests before crashing down sheer rock cliffs. Most waterfalls in Fiji come with a natural swimming pool carved into its rocky base, where joyous locals and tourists jump in and soak up nature's liquid bounties.

### Bushwalking Basics

Getting to most waterfalls requires hiking through wilderness. Come prepared for rough terrain, and hire a local guide to navigate the forests.

### Swimming Etiquette

It is not acceptable to go skinny-dipping in nature. Carry swimwear if you intend to swim at a waterfall (and a towel to dry yourself).

## BEST WATERFALL EXPERIENCES

Visit the towering waterfall of **Nabalasere** on Viti Levu, and explore a rock cavern hidden behind the curtain of falling water.
❶ (p85)

Hike through the enchanted Bouma National Park to meet the **Tavoro Waterfalls** cascading down a mountain in three stages.
❷ (p164)

Clamber up the twin waterfalls of **Naikorokoro** in Kadavu for an unforgettable swimming experience in hidden rock pools.
❸ (p179)

Discover the cascades of **Wainibau** on Taveuni, guarded by dense rainforest at the end of the Lavena Coastal Walk.
❹ (p164)

Swim in the deep pools formed by waterfalls in the rainforests of **Colo-i-Suva**, a favourite day-trip destination from Suva.
❺ (p83)

FROM LEFT: DON MAMMOSER/SHUTTERSTOCK ©, DON MAMMOSER/SHUTTERSTOCK ©

**View of Kuata from Wayasewa island (p109)**

# NATURAL MASTERPIECES

From windswept sand dunes overlooking ocean channels and limestone caves hewn by the sea, to coastal blowholes spouting rainbow mist and lava-sculpted volcanic outcrops, Fiji has a plethora of spectacular geological wonders that augment the primordial appeal of its scenery. Some of these natural splendours are now protected as national parks, yet open to tourists.

### Guided Tours

Hotels and resorts can arrange for guides to escort you to places of geological interest. Venturing into the wild alone is not recommended.

### Photo Tips

A GoPro is invaluable for photographing Fiji's natural beauty, thanks to its waterproof design that makes it usable in torrential rain and in water.

## BEST NATURAL WONDERS

Amble across the sand dunes of **Sigatoka**, known to history buffs as a settlement and burial site of the Lapita people.
❶ (p65)

Visit the limestone caves of **Sawa-i-Lau** in northern Yasawa, an astounding testament to the artistic powers of the ocean.
❷ (p119)

Gape in awe at the summit of **Vatuvula** looming above Wayasewa island, best viewed from Kuata across the ocean channel.
❸ (p110)

Go on a jaunt to Taveuni's forlorn **South Cape**, and photograph the rainbow-spewing blowhole in the black-rock volcanic coast.
❹ (p157)

Be stunned by magnificent stalactites and stalagmites in the ritualistic **Snake God Cave** in eastern Viti Levu.
❺ (p84)

19

# BLASTS FROM THE PAST

As a confluence of cultures and peoples who migrated through the Pacific over centuries, Fiji is home to old towns and villages that retain the quaint charm of their bygone heydays. History buffs will be delighted to potter around these settlements, rediscovering monuments and reliving legends that play a unique role in Fiji's history and culture. It is also a fantastic way of understanding and appreciating the cosmopolitan matrix that defines contemporary Fijian society.

### Walking Tours

Nothing beats a pedestrian excursion, preferably in the company of a local guide, when it comes to poking around old towns and villages.

### Museum Visits

Fiji doesn't have too many museums to write home about, but the historical collections in Suva, Levuka and Ba are definitely worth swinging by.

### Seasonal Tips

November through February can be hot, humid and rainy for walking tours. May to August affords fantastic daytime weather for ambling around.

④ ⑤

❷❶

❸

## BEST HISTORICAL EXPERIENCES

Imagine yourself as a 19th-century fortune seeker as you soak up the wild-west atmosphere of **Levuka** on Ovalau island.
❶ (p126)

Complement your hike to **Lovoni** by listening to a tale of deceit, betrayal and enslavement dating back to the 19th century.
❷ (p131)

Walk through downtown **Suva** and explore the relics from its complicated colonial history amid cosmopolitan neighbourhoods.
❸ (p75)

Experience a thriving nautical culture in the former trading post of **Savusavu**, harking back to the days of maritime exploration.
④ (p146)

Soak up the lazy grain of **Somosomo**, home to a spectacular Catholic mission founded during Fiji's colonial era.
⑤ (p156)

# FOLLOW THE FOOD TRAIL

Fiji's signature cuisine was born out of the intermingling of culinary histories and habits native to various migrants who settled in the country over time. The dominant food traditions are iTaukei, Chinese, Indian, Polynesian and European, with a number of fusion flavours in between. Topping it off are international fast-food and upmarket restaurants dabbling in fine dining.

## BEST DINING EXPERIENCES

Sample the diverse flavours of Fijian cuisine in **Suva**, a melting pot of culinary traditions introduced by several communities.
❶ (p75)

Relish top-notch Fijian and international dining on **Malolo** island, featuring a string of classy resort restaurants.
❷ (p102)

Bite into fresh seafood in **Kadavu**, where resorts source their day's catch from nearby reefs and plate it up within hours.
❸ (p173)

Wolf down a delicious vegan lunch prepared from vegetables sourced from **Ovalau's** forests on a day hike to Lovoni village.
❹ (p131)

Reserve a table in the restaurants of **Nadi and Denarau**, to get a sense of Fiji's take on contemporary fine dining.
❺ (p52)

### Vegan Options

There is no shortage of delicious vegan and vegetarian food in Fiji. Modern Fijian cuisine features copious amounts of tubers, leaves, vegetables and fruits.

### Fruits Galore

Homegrown papayas, pineapples, mangoes and avocados have a devout following in Fiji. There's also a good choice of imported (and pricey) fruits.

Navala village (p60)

# PEOPLE OF THE LAND

Fiji is home to a population of happy and friendly people, and it's no surprise that human interactions form a strong pillar of tourism in the country. Smiles and vigorous *bula* greetings are freely available here, as are effusive *talanoa* (group discussion) sessions where strangers become friends over kava and conversations.

## Village Protocol

Carry a *sevusevu* (gift) to present to the village chief, and wear a sulu cloth to cover your legs during your time within a village.

## Homestays

Some villages have homestay facilities (with basic accommodation and home-cooked food) for guests keen on sampling a slice of rustic Fijian life.

**⑤ ③④ ②**
**①**

### BEST VILLAGE EXPERIENCES

Stay the night in **Nabutautau** village during a highland hike, to enjoy a kava session and yummy dinner with friendly village folk.
**①** (p86)

Be pampered by the village community in **Takalana Bay** near Moon Reef and enjoy delicious vegetarian and seafood dishes.
**②** (p85)

Experience **Abaca** village's community tourism project, and enjoy warm hospitality and home-cooked meals during your visit.
**③** (p59)

Go shutter-happy in the unbelievably pretty village of **Navala**, and snap picturesque photos along its *bure*-lined thoroughfare.
**④** (p60)

Be welcomed by the hospitable families in **Wayasewa** into their homes for a sampling of laid-back island life in the Yasawas.
**⑤** (p109)

23

# REGIONS & CITIES

Find the places that tick all your boxes.

Mamanuca &
Yasawa
p94

Nadi, Suva
& Viti Levu
p47

SUVA

## Mamanuca & Yasawa

### FIJI'S MOST POPULAR TOURIST TRAIL

Mamanuca's islands are the poster child of high-end island tourism, featuring a selection of Fiji's best hotels and resorts located on the edge of tranquil waters. North of Mamanuca, the Yasawa islands promise exciting in-water encounters with sharks, manta rays, colourful fish and invertebrates.

**p94**

## Nadi, Suva & Viti Levu

### FIJI'S 'MAINLAND' ISLAND

Centrally located Viti Levu is the largest of Fiji's 330-plus islands. While it fosters untouched rainforests, lofty mountains, roaring mountain rivers and gorgeous coastal scenery, the island is also home to Nadi, Fiji's main tourist entry point, and Suva, its vibrantly cosmopolitan national capital.

p47

## Vanua Levu & Taveuni

### EMERALD FORESTS
### AND SAPPHIRE OCEANS

Fiji's northern islands are a hotbed of diverse interactions and excursions suited to visitors of all ages, interests and inclinations. Botanical gardens, chocolate farms, pearl farms, a volley of scuba sites, free-diving lessons, gushing waterfalls and rugged volcanic scenery – these islands have it all.

**p140**

**Vanua Levu
& Taveuni**
p140

**Ovalau &
Lomaiviti**
p121

Kadavu & Lau

### FIJI'S FAR-FLUNG FRONTIERS

These two remote island groups are an amphitheatre for raw adventure, promising unforgettable scuba diving, surfing and kayaking experiences in relatively unexplored waters. Facilities are sparse in these hinterlands, but intrepid travellers will be rewarded with some of the wildest coastal landscapes ever known to humans.

p167

**Kadavu & Lau**
p167

## Ovalau & Lomaiviti

### CRUCIBLE OF FIJIAN HISTORY

The less visited Lomaiviti group is defined by Ovalau island, where European merchants and seafarers arrived in the 19th century and settled in Levuka, the atmospheric former Fijian capital. Nearby, the coral-fringed islands of Leleuvia and Toberua promise some top-notch snorkelling, diving and waterside relaxation.

**p121**

MARTINA KATZ/GETTY IMAGES ©

Malolo (p102)

## ITINERARIES

# Classic Fiji

This is the classic rite of passage for most tourists, and comes as an antipasti platter of Fiji's best experiences. Along the way, you will stay, wine and dine in Mamanuca's lavish resorts, surf on legendary reef breaks, and meet sharks and manta rays in Yasawa's marine reserves.

**Allow:** 7 days

**①**
### NADI ⏱ 1 DAY

Fly into **Nadi** (p52) to start your Fijian holiday. Recover from jetlag with a soothing mudbath and dip at Sabeto hot springs, then visit the fabulous Garden of the Sleeping Giant to familiarise yourself with hundreds of orchid species. In the evening, go for a modern dance performance at Vou Hub, and finish off with a gourmet dinner at Kanu Gastropub.

🚤 *Take a water taxi from Port Denarau to Malolo*

**②**
### MALOLO ⏱ 1 DAY

**Malolo** (p102) is Mamanuca's iconic resort island. Spend the day lazing on sandy beaches and swimming, snorkelling and kayaking in dazzling waters. You can stay the night, or simply make a day trip to get a feel of stylish island living.

🐾 *Detour: Spend the late afternoon partying at Cloud 9 (p102), a fun mid-sea club and bar. ⏱ 2 hours*

🚆 *Board the Yasawa Flyer from Port Denarau to Kuata.*

NADEZDA ZAVITAEVA/SHUTTERSTOCK ©, JIHUN SIM/SHUTTERSTOCK ©

**③**
### KUATA ⏱ 1 DAY

**Kuata** (p106) is in the Yasawas. Go diving with bull sharks or snorkel with reef sharks in the marine-protected area. In the afternoon, snorkel in the house reef and kayak through the narrow ocean channel between Kuata and Wayasewa, and enjoy sunset from atop the island.

🐾 *Detour: The Vatuvula summit hike (p110) on Wayasewa island is great for hiking buffs. ⏱ 4 hours*

🚤 *Hop on and off the Yasawa Flyer to get from Kuata to Drawaqa.*

SARA PETERSSON/SHUTTERSTOCK ©

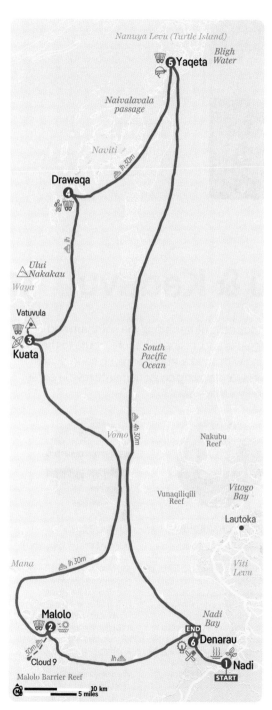

**④**
## DRAWAQA ⏱ 1 DAY

In **Drawaqa** (p111) you can lie in wait for a group of manta rays to swim into the nearby ocean passage, then go snorkelling with these elegant, curious creatures. End the day with a hike to Drawaqa's twin viewpoints. Rise early next morning for a memorable session of snorkelling at daybreak.

**⑤**
## YAQETA ⏱ 2 DAYS

Spend your first day in **Yaqeta** (p115) snorkelling above the seagrass shallows and coral bommies of Blue Lagoon, followed by kayaking in the ocean channel between Yageta and Matacawalevu. Stargaze through the rest of the evening against a clear night sky. Next day, go on a motorboat ride to explore the solitary limestone caves of Sawa-i-Lau.
🚊 *Return to Denarau (p54) aboard the Yasawa Flyer.*

**⑥**
## DENARAU ⏱ 1 DAY

Back at **Denarau** (p54) spend your last day topping up on the good life. Shop, drink and dine at Port Denarau, let the young ones have a field day riding and sliding in Big Bula Waterpark, enjoy a spot of golf or tennis at Denarau Golf & Racquet Club, and spend the night in a swish upscale resort.

VIKTOR HEJNA/SHUTTERSTOCK ©

Sand dunes, Sigatoka (p65)

## ITINERARIES

# Viti Levu & Kadavu

**Allow:** 10 days

This itinerary combines stock adventures along the southern and eastern coasts of Fiji's largest island, taking the scenic route to the far south. If you fancy diving with sharks, clambering up sand dunes, rafting down mountain rivers, and spying on giant manta rays in coral expanses, this trip could be your oyster.

**① NATADOLA** ⏱ 1 DAY

Head from Nadi to **Natadola** (p61), home to the best beach in Viti Levu and a fabulous place for a surfing lesson on nearby breaks or a snorkelling session on a reef near the beach. Natadola has only two beach resorts, allowing guests almost exclusive access to the crescent stretch of sand.

⇢ *Detour: Climbing the **sand dunes** (p65) near Sigatoka makes for a fabulous excursion.* ⏱ *3 hours*

**② PACIFIC HARBOUR** ⏱ 1 DAY

The main reason to schedule time in **Pacific Harbour** (p69) is to go diving with bull sharks and tiger sharks in the protected waters of Beqa Lagoon. It's one of the many definitive experiences in Fiji. Next morning, make your way up to the knife-gash canyons of the Navua River's upper valley, then hurtle down the whitewater course in an inflatable raft.

**③ SUVA** ⏱ 3 DAYS

While in **Suva** (p75), bond with the local population over rugby and football in Albert Park or embark on a guided walking tour through the vibrant, historical downtown area. Visit Fiji Museum and be lost amid its brilliantly curated display of memorabilia and rarities. Grab a coffee at Grand Pacific Hotel and feel classy 19th-century vibes while lounging in its central hall.

NINA JANESIKOVA/SHUTTERSTOCK ©, AQUARIUS TRAVELLER/SHUTTERSTOCK ©, CRE8 DESIGN/SHUTTERSTOCK ©

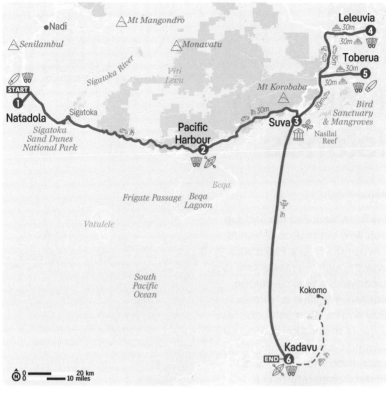

### ❹ LELEUVIA ⏱ 1 DAY

An easy escape from Suva, **Leleuvia** (p133) promises summer-camp-style fun, where the modesty of basic lodgements is compensated by the unbridled thrill of exploring the island's magnificent house reef. Snorkelling here is suited to people of all proficiencies, and you can also go diving in the adjacent ocean passage. Save the evening to stargaze from the southern sandbank of the island.

### ❺ TOBERUA ⏱ 1 DAY

Tiny **Toberua** (p139) is a delightful resort island (comprising a clutch of excellent eco-chic *bures*) known for its high bar of hospitality and cuisine. The island is really close to some of the best coral gardens in the Lomaiviti group. Apart from diving in fish-rich coral reefs, you can also join scheduled snorkelling trips conducted by the resort boat and staff.

### ❻ KADAVU ⏱ 3 DAYS

Return to Suva and catch the weekly flight to **Kadavu** (p167). The Great Astrolabe Reef is within shouting distance from Matava. Go scuba diving, kayaking and surfing along the world's fourth-largest barrier reef, with a third day in Oneta - snorkelling with manta rays, before flying back to Nadi.

🐾 *Detour: Schedule a night at **Kokomo** (p176) private island for luxury in the outback. ⏱ 1 day*

## ITINERARIES

# Northern Islands

**Allow:** 10 days

Fly from Nadi into the antique volcanic landscape of Vanua Levu and Taveuni. Make your way through the rainforests to discover Savusavu's serene ocean bays, dive in Natewa Bay and kayak in Salt Lake, explore the natural splendour around Somosomo and the uncharted shores beyond Matei, before returning to Nadi's nightlife.

### ❶ SAVUSAVU ⏱ 3 DAYS

Heavy on activities, the bayside town of **Savusavu** (p146) warrants at least three days. Dive and snorkel in Savusavu Bay, sign up for a free-diving lesson, take a guided tour of chocolate and pearl farms, explore a botanical garden of tropical palms, and witness thermal geysers pumping scalding hot water from the earth's innards.

🐾 *Detour: Go for a special scuba-diving experience to* **Namena Marine Reserve** *(p153).* ⏱ *5 hours*

### ❷ SALT LAKE ⏱ 1 DAY

Learn about coral conservation over a few educational scuba dives in Natewa Bay, the largest oceanic bay in Fiji. Familiarise yourself with an astounding array of hard corals, and pick up the basics of coral regeneration while touring coral nurseries. On your way out, stop for the night at **Salt Lake** (p154) and enjoy kayaking on the slow-moving waters of a tidal creek.

Divers swimming
with green sea turtle,
Suvasuva (p146)

BRETT MONROE GARNER/GETTY IMAGES ©

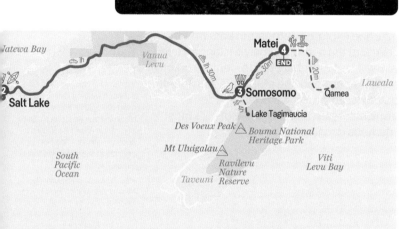

## ❸ SOMOSOMO ⏱ 3 DAYS

Sleepy **Somosomo** (p156) is Taveuni's main town, and a jump-off point for touring the blowhole at South Cape and the Wairiki Catholic Mission, with a birdwatching stop at Nabogiono Farms. It's also the place to embark on dive trips to Rainbow Reef, the world capital of soft corals and a treasure trove of marine life.

🚶 *Detour:* Hike up to **Lake Tagimaucia** (p158) to see Fiji's rare national flower. ⏱ 8 hours

## ❹ MATEI ⏱ 3 DAYS

Venture into Taveuni's northeastern wilderness from the hub of **Matei** (p163). Swim at Tavoro Waterfalls during a hike through Bouma National Park, and follow the long and lonely Lavena Coastal Walk all the way to a waterfall veiled in enchanted forests. Tour a pearl farm, and snorkel in the stunning reef nearby.

🚶 *Detour:* Take a motorboat ride to the nearby island of **Qamea** (p164). ⏱ 3 hours

# ITINERARIES

# Off the Beaten Track

**Allow:** 7 days

This route strays far from the usual tourist trail, and explores outposts in eastern Viti Levu and the nearby Lomaiviti islands. Here you will visit mothballed 19th-century colonial settlements, sparkling atoll reefs with playful dolphins, gorgeous waterfalls hidden in tropical forests, and the grave of Fiji's most infamous cannibal.

**❶ SUVA** ⏱ 2 DAYS

Fly into **Suva** (p75) from Nadi. Visit the Fiji Museum, and take a guided walking tour through downtown Suva. Enjoy a walk along the sea wall, join a game of rugby in Albert Park, then cool off with a chilled beer or cocktail at the waterside bar of Grand Pacific Hotel.

*🛬 Detour: Zip down to **Pacific Harbour** (p70) for a morning dive with bull sharks.* ⏱ *4 hours*

**❷ LEVUKA** ⏱ 2 DAYS

Take a morning ferry to the historic town of **Levuka** (p126) on Ovalau island, and walk along the heritage-building-lined streets of this former economic boomtown. On the following day, hike to Lovoni village (p131), nestled in a lofty volcanic crater, and learn about an intriguing episode of Fijian history.

*🛬 Detour: Go on a drive around Ovalau, stopping at scenic **Rukuruku** village (p131).* ⏱ *2 hours*

ANDREW BAIN/ALAMY STOCK PHOTO ©

**Hiking, Mt. Tomanivi (p93)**

SHEPPS/SHUTTERSTOCK ©, MALOFF/SHUTTERSTOCK ©,

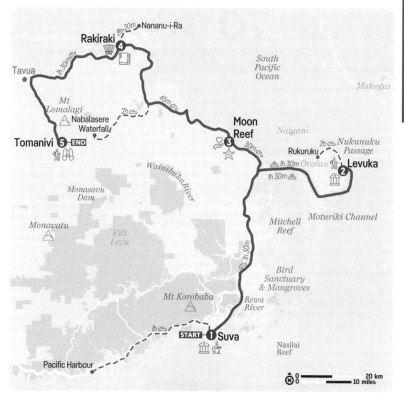

**③**
## MOON REEF ⏱ 1 DAY

Takalana Bay is home to **Moon Reef** (p85), where pods of spinner dolphins collect during the day to feed, and play with the humans who come to meet them in their natural habitat. A couple of community managed ecotourism lodges in the bay area offer warm hospitality.

🐬 *Detour:* Drive up to **Nabalasere Waterfall** (p85) for a swim and a splash. ⏱ 3 hours

**④**
## RAKIRAKI ⏱ 1 DAY

The northern settlement of **Rakiraki** (p89) has some quirky attractions for eclectic travellers. Visit the tomb of Udre Udre, arguably Fiji's most infamous cannibal, tune into the basics of apiculture at a bee farm, and scuba dive on pristine coral reefs in the Vatu-i-Ra marine conservation area.

🐬 *Detour:* Go windsurfing in the breezy ocean passages off **Nananu-i-Ra** (p92). ⏱ 4 hours

**⑤**
## TOMANIVI ⏱ 1 DAY

Tackle the slopes of **Tomanivi** (p93), Fiji's tallest mountain, and attempt a summit push for mind-blowing 360-degree views of Viti Levu from its topmost point. The trailhead for this hike is at Navai village, a couple of hours by road from Rakiraki. After a daylong excursion, simply follow Kings Rd and return to Nadi via the towns of Ba and Lautoka.

# WHEN **TO GO**

Feel free to visit Fiji anytime through the year, but the months from May to August are best for most outdoor experiences.

Fiji's location in the middle of the Pacific means it is far out for most people around the world to visit over a short holiday. Thankfully, the best season for visiting the country coincides with summer breaks in the northern hemisphere, allowing families to plan a holiday that justifies the long flights to get here. The months between April and November are also optimal for nautical tourists to visit Fiji, thanks to prevailing winds that blow across the Pacific. However, this is not to say that Fiji remains devoid of tourists for the rest of the year. With travellers from nearby Australia and New Zealand turning up for extended weekends, Nadi's hotels are perpetually in short supply of rooms. Fiji also sees a fair number of domestic tourists during Easter, Diwali and Christmas holidays.

## New Year Rush

Book your accommodation way in advance for a year-end visit to Fiji. Between mid-December and early January, the country is filled to the brim with tourists. Room rates shoot up exponentially, and some establishments warrant that you commit to staying a minimum number of nights in order to secure a booking.

**Vonu Point, Turtle Island (p116)**

SHEPPS/SHUTTERSTOCK ©

### ⊛ I LIVE HERE

**SUMMER ROAD TRIP**

**Miguel Londoño, a Colombian expatriate in Suva, works with Global Green Growth Institute to combat climate change in the Pacific Islands.**

"The schools close during Christmas in Fiji, so it's a great idea to hit Kings Rd around Viti Levu on a southern summer road trip. We make our first stop in Moon Reef, for one of the most thrilling experiences with the dolphins. Dozens, if not hundreds, come to the boat to dance, jump and play – it's an absolute thrill, especially for the children."

**WET, WET, WET**

Fiji enjoys a temperate climate through the year, without extreme heat or cold. However, it receives abundant rainfall. Isolated pockets in the southeastern highlands can have up to 6000mm of rainfall annually. The northwestern rain shadow areas receive about 2000mm of rain a year.

## Weather Through the Year

|  **JANUARY** |  **FEBRUARY** |  **MARCH** |  **APRIL** |  **MAY** | **JUNE** |
|---|---|---|---|---|---|
| Avg daytime max: **30°C** | Avg daytime max: **31°C** | Avg daytime max: **30°C** | Avg daytime max: **29°C** | Avg daytime max: **28°C** | Avg daytime max: **27°C** |
| Days of rainfall: **16** (Suva) | Days of rainfall: **16** (Suva) | Days of rainfall: **17** (Suva) | Days of rainfall: **8** (Nadi) | Days of rainfall: **4** (Nadi) | Days of rainfall: **3** (Nadi) |

## NATURE'S FURY

The warm season between November and April is dubbed cyclone season in Fiji. This is when tropical depressions brew over the Pacific, resulting in gale-force whirlwinds with squalls. Occasionally, a storm evolves into a destructive cyclone, leading to evacuations and widespread damage of property.

## A Tale of Three Festivals

A venerable trio of celebrations stand out among Fiji's festive dates. The first of these in the calendar year is **Holi**, the Hindu festival of colours, when Indo-Fijians joyfully throw coloured powder at each other while singing, dancing and generally making merry. 🌤 **March**

The other major Indo-Fijian celebration is **Diwali**, the Hindu festival of lights, when families decorate their homes with candles and coloured filigree, distribute sweetmeats and burst firecrackers through the evening. Over time, Diwali has gained popularity among the iTaukei population, and is celebrated as a pan-Fijian festival. ☁ **October or November**

Fiji's biggest nationwide festival is **Christmas**, when effusive church choirs sing harmonic carols in every town and village, families come together over feasts and joyous celebrations, and the country virtually shuts down for a few days. 🌦 **December**

### ISLAND GETAWAY

**Miles is a lawyer who returned home to Fiji after 20 years and makes the most of everything Fiji has to offer, especially the ocean.**

"A year-round favourite spot for my family is Nananu-i-Ra. The island is off the top of Viti Levu, not on the main tourist route – perfect for an idyllic, quiet getaway. The accommodation is basic but comfortable, and there are no big resorts. The short boat ride from the mainland is good fun for the kids (and the adults). Peaceful is how I would describe our stays on the island."

## Local Galas & Carnivals

The ultra-popular **Marist 7s** rugby competition is a nationwide playoff meant to promote rugby among Fiji's youth. It features up to 64 regional teams, and culminates in an action-packed three-day tournament in Suva's HFC Stadium. 🌤 **March**

Organsed in Nadi, the annual **Bula Festival** is a weeklong party that features rides, marching bands, pageant shows, food fiestas and the crowning of Miss Bula. 🌞 **July**

The annual **Fiji Regatta Week** lures avid yachties, maritime enthusiasts and party people from around the world to its venue at Musket Cove Marina in Mamanuca. 🌤 **September**

Edible sea worms called *balolo* rise at midnight about a week after November's full moon. Many island communities across Fiji celebrate the annual **balolo rising harvest** with song, dance and feasting. ☁ November.

### OCEAN CONDITIONS

Sea temperatures hover around 27°C to 29°C during the warm season (November to April) and drop to around 24°C to 26°C between May and September. Cooler waters have better visibility due to less suspended particulate matter and plankton, which makes diving and snorkelling more enjoyable.

| JULY | AUGUST | SEPTEMBER | OCTOBER | NOVEMBER | DECEMBER |
|------|--------|-----------|---------|----------|----------|
|  |  |  |  |  |  |
| Avg daytime max: **26°C** | Avg daytime max: **25°C** | Avg daytime max: **27°C** | Avg daytime max: **28°C** | Avg daytime max: **29°C** | Avg daytime max: **30°C** |
| Days of rainfall: **2** (Nadi) | Days of rainfall: **3** (Nadi) | Days of rainfall: **4** (Nadi) | Days of rainfall: **12** (Suva) | Days of rainfall: **13** (Suva) | Days of rainfall: **16** (Suva) |

KLARA ZAMOURILOVA/SHUTTERSTOCK ©

**Yasawa (p94)**

# GET PREPARED FOR FIJI

Useful things to load in your bag, your ears and your brain

## Clothes

**Activewear:** You will spend much of your time in the outdoors, so bring a good supply of hiking shorts, quick-dry shirts, beach clothes, swimwear and full-sleeve rashguards rated SPF 50+ (a much better alternative to sunscreen, which can impact coral health).

**Weather shields:** It rains in heaps, so pack good-quality rain gear. A waterproof poncho works best when roaming the outdoors in wet weather. Carry a hat and sunglasses for intensely bright days.

**Accessories:** A dry bag is a must for keeping valuables from getting splashed on during boat journeys. Bring a sarong to work as a sulu cloth, with which you must cover your legs during village visits.

### Manners

**Seek permission before entering a village.**
The protocol is to approach a headman who will take you to the village chief. You will then have to present a *sevusevu* (gift) to receive permission – a bundle of kava works well.

**Be patient with delays and deferrals.**
Things move slowly in Fiji, and people adjust their expectations accordingly. A smile and a joke often helps speed things up.

**Shoes:** Bring sturdy hiking shoes and river-crossing sandals for treks, plus reef shoes to protect your feet from cuts and scrapes during watersports.

# 📖 READ

**Worlds Apart:
A History of the
Pacific Islands**
(Ian C Campbell; 2003)
Excellent guide to
Fiji's place in the
Pacific region.

**Broken Waves: A
History of the Fiji
Islands in the 20th
Century**
(Brij V Lal; 1992)
Thorough account of
Fiji's colonial and
postcolonial history.

**Sevens Heaven: The
Beautiful Chaos of
Fiji's Olympic Dream**
(Ben Ryan; 2018)
Incredible story of
Fiji's journey to its first
Olympic rugby gold.

**Kava in the Blood:
A Personal &
Political Memoir from
the Heart of Fiji**
(Peter Thomson; 2008)
Engaging look at
Fiji's cultures.

## Words

**Bula** (mboo-lah) is a catch-all greeting that ranges in meaning from 'hello' and 'what's up' to 'pleased to meet you' and 'excuse me'. You will hear this word a lot, and it's polite to offer *bula* back. For a more sincere greeting, such as meeting an immigration officer at passport control rather than waving at a passing boat, try *ni sa bula* (ni-sa-mboo-lah).

**Yadra** (yan-dra) translates as 'good morning' or 'good day'. You could also say *ni sa yadra* (ni-sa-yan-dra).

**Vinaka** (vi-na-ka) is Fijian for 'thank you'. It's shortened to *naka* in a quick manner of speaking, and extended to *vinaka vakalevu* to express a more heartfelt thanks.

**Moce** (mo-the) is used to say 'goodbye' to someone you may not see again (or for a good while).

**Vosoti au** (vo-sotee-ow) is used to either excuse yourself or apologise for something. However, in most situations, a simple 'sorry' works just as well.

**Io/Sega** (ee-yo/sen-ga) is 'yes' and 'no' respectively.

**Haa/Nahi** is Fiji Hindi for 'yes' and 'no' respectively.

**Shukriya** means 'thank you' in Fiji Hindi. *Maaf karna* is used to excuse yourself or apologise.

**Set** is a word with special status in Fiji, used by everyone all the time. Its scope of meaning is wide – from 'okay', 'alright' and 'makes sense' to 'all good', 'no worries' and 'awesome'.

# 📺 WATCH

AJ PICS/ALAMY STOCK PHOTO ©

**Cast Away** (Robert Zemeckis; 2000) Tom Hanks (above) survives an air crash and gets washed up on a deserted island. Filmed in Fiji.

**World's Toughest Race: Eco Challenge Fiji** (Amazon Prime; 2020) An expedition race through Fiji's wilds. Hosted by Bear Grylls.

**The Land Has Eyes** (Vilsoni Hereniko; 2004) Fijian film about a young woman's struggle against stifling culture.

**The Blue Lagoon** (Randal Kleiser; 1980) Two children grow up on their own after being marooned on an island. Filmed in Fiji.

# 🎧 LISTEN

**Voices of Nature**
(Rosiloa; 2000) This
debut album by the
band Rosiloa (formerly
Black Rose) features the
hit single 'Raude'.

**Old Old Tree**
(Knox; 2010) This
breakthrough album
by singer-songwriter-guitarist Knox has a
mix of English and
iTaukei tracks.

**Isa Lei**
(Sunia Soko Loga;
2022) A rendition of the
popular Fijian farewell
song by Seoul-based
Fijian singer Sunia
Soko Loga.

**Meri Deewangi**
(Sumeet Tappoo;
2010) A contemporary
album of Hindi songs
by Indo-Fijian pop
and devotional singer
Sumeet Tappoo.

CHAMELEONSEYE/SHUTTERSTOCK ©

**Kokoda (raw fish salad)**

# THE FOOD SCENE

Fijian cuisine is a vibrant melange combining cooking traditions of people from diverse cultures who call the country home.

Starchy carbohydrates play a big part in the traditional Fijian diet. Staples include generous servings of *cassava* and *dalo* (taro) roots with every major meal. Breadfruit is also widely taken, either as part of a meal or a standalone snack. Other staples include rice – key to Indo-Fijian and Chinese culinary traditions – and *roti*, originally introduced by Indo-Fijians.

A wide range of vegetables are commonly available and consumed, though the majority (including tomatoes, onions and potatoes) is imported. Seafood is plentiful in the local diet, and popular fish species include tuna, *walu* (Spanish mackerel), *wahu*, *mahi-mahi*, snapper, *paca paca*, grouper, and *nuqa* (rabbitfish). Sustainable fishing is widely practised in Fiji;

this means that village communities impose a temporary ban on fishing in nearby waters through certain months of the year, allowing fish populations to recover and regenerate. Meat – mostly fried or braised – constitutes an important component of Fijian food, though some of the demand is met with imports from Australia or New Zealand.

## Markets & Supermarkets

Every large town in Fiji has a fresh fruit-and-vegetable market and at least one supermarket for stocking up on basic groceries. Those like the Municipal Market in Suva are visitor attractions in themselves, featuring stalls piled high with fresh produce, and areas reserved for heaping

| Best Fijian Dishes | KOKODA | DALO | ROUROU |
| --- | --- | --- | --- |
| | Tuna or mackerel cubes with lime juice, coconut milk, chilli and coriander. | Taro plant root boiled or fried, as an accompaniment to meals. | Taro plant leaves boiled and served as an accompaniment to meals. |

bundles of *yaqona* (kava) roots, aromatic spices, *dalo* roots and *rourou* leaves. Most villages have a small grocery shop; since village residents grow their own fresh produce, stock is often limited to items such as tinned fish, corned beef, instant noodles, bags of peanuts, breakfast crackers etc.

## Restaurants

There are plenty of cheap restaurants serving a mix of Indian and Chinese cuisine, although European fast food and takeaway baked goods, such as puffs and pies, are ragingly popular. Only in Suva, Nadi and Denarau (and resort restaurants) will you generally find great variety in types of cuisines being offered, from Italian to Japanese to contemporary fusion dishes. Food courts (a big-town feature) buzz with activity during office lunches and over weekends, and offer a mixed bag of preparations, ranging from fish and chips and noodle soups to fried chicken and Indian platters.

## Drinks

Fiji Gold and Fiji Bitter are the country's two leading beers. Despite the latter's name, both are lagers, as is the premium Vonu brand (which also markets a low-carb variety of lager). Local rum is quite popular, and was originally

produced as a byproduct from the country's sugar industry. Refreshing coconut water is widely available, as is the tangy juice of kumquat, a mini cousin of the orange, served by the glass or the jug in restaurants alongside meals. Finally, no traditional Fijian assembly kicks off without a ceremonial round of kava (also called grog), a natural relaxant that loosens people up to socialise over copious laughs.

Lovo cooking

FROMACK/GETTY IMAGES ©

### FIJIAN FLAVOURS

**Indian** Indo-Fijian dishes are usually spicy, and a typical meal comprises rice, dhal (lentil soup), roti (flatbread), various curried or fried vegetables, with a serving of fish or meat (chicken or goat).

**Chinese** Strong Cantonese notes dominate Chinese food in Fiji. Common dishes include stir-fries, fried rice, chow mien, noodle soups, and mains featuring chicken, fish, pork, prawn and beef.

**European** Fiji's colonial era introduced European cooking traditions. Steaks, burgers, barbecues, grills, and fish and chips are widely served throughout the country.

**Lovo** In this traditional Fijian banquet, whole chickens, legs of pork, whole fish, *dalo*, onions and other vegetables are wrapped in banana leaf and/or aluminium foil, then cooked for several hours in an underground hot-stone oven.

PEACEFOOD/GETTY IMAGES ©

Nadi produce market

| OTA | NAMA | ROTI | KAVA | BREADFRUIT |
|---|---|---|---|---|
| Fiddlehead fern shoots and coconut milk cold soup palate-cleanser. | Sea algae from shallow lagoons. Served raw (or lightly dressed in lime juice) in salads. | The ubiquitous Indo-Fijian flatbread. Served with meals, or as on-the-go wraps. | The social cement that unites Fijians after sundown. A yaqona root beverage | Carb-rich fruit accompaniment to meals, or a deep-fried chip snack. |

E A GIVEN/SHUTTERSTOCK ©

**Hiking, Suva area (p83)**

# THE OUTDOORS

The heart of Fiji lies in its wilderness, and embarking on a Fijian
holiday means plunging headfirst into its endless natural wonders.

## Diving

Fiji has legendary status as a global diving destination. Its waters are warm, clear and teeming with marine life, from microscopic molluscs to megafauna such as turtles, dolphins, sharks and rays. Best of all are the surreal undersea landscapes that divers can explore, ranging from expansive fields of hard corals along barrier reefs to vertigo-inducing walls plunging into the blue abyss festooned with exquisite soft corals, like flower gardens in riotous bloom.

Fiji is dive-able year-round, but the best season is from April to October. This is when water temperatures range between 24°C and 26°C, and the visibility is stunning, sometimes shooting up to 40m. November to March has more rainfall, which obscures visibility off bigger islands with runoff. However, an increase in suspended food particles in water attracts more megafauna, thus increasing chances of sightings.

For those who are not able – or not inclined – to dive, snorkelling can be just as fun. Fiji is one of the few places in the world where it's possible to snor-

**Other Adventures**

**FISHING**
Go after big game, such as tuna and trevally in the bay area around **Savusavu (p147).**

**HORSE RIDING**
Trot down the gorgeous beach in **Natadola (p63)** on horseback while admiring the sunset.

**SEA KAYAKING**
Row, row, row your tiny boat gently out to sea – on a sea-kayaking safari in **Kadavu (p176).**

## FAMILY ADVENTURES

Sign up for a luxury joyride on **Captain Cook Cruises** (p101) that takes you around Fiji's outer islands for up to 11 days.

**Leap from treetops on giant swings** and enjoy numerous other rides at **Kila World** (p74), Viti Levu's showcase

adventure park.

**A unique e-bicycle excursion** through virgin coastal scenery, **Ecotrax** (p66) is so popular that it can be booked out months in advance.

**Bond during a wilderness camp turned family adventure** on pristine sands

(and in ultramarine shallows) at **Leleuvia** (p138) in the Lomaiviti islands.

The gentle breaks along the gorgeous beach of **Natadola** (p63) give everyone in the family a fair chance at **mastering the basics of surfing.**

kel with reef sharks and manta rays.

## Hiking

Arguably the best hiking in Fiji can be found on Taveuni, where a huge section of the island has been designated a national park. Walking here is a wild experience, featuring lonesome forest trails that meander along deserted shorelines and shoot up through dense rainforests. Fiji's other islands of tourist interest also have a few hikes to put on the table. The islands of Wayasewa, Waya, Drawaqa and Nacula in the Yasawa group have a bunch of interesting

summit hikes and island crossings. Ovalau has one of the country's signature hikes leading into an extinct volcanic crater. Viti Levu, on the other hand, gives hikers multiple options – from day hikes to multiday traverses – that lead them to quaint villages situated in the interior highlands.

## Surfing

Most surf pitches over outer reefs and in ocean passages, and is meant for intermediate to advanced surfers only. For these reefs you need boats and guides. Southerly swells are consistent from May to October, but there is surf year-round. The trade winds are southeast and offshore at the famous breaks. Northerlies, from November to April, blow offshore over Viti Levu and the Coral Coast. Most surfing activities are concentrated in Mamanuca, where the big and bold breaks are located. The Coral Coast on Viti Levu and the southern coast of Kadavu also see a good amount of surfing action – the former has a few gentle breaks suited to novice surfers. Nananu-i-Ra, a tiny island off the northern coast of Viti Levu, has a few fantastic windsurfing spots.

**BEST SPOTS**

For the best outdoor spots and routes, see map on page 42.

JUSTIN LEWIS/GETTY IMAGES ©

**Surfing, Cloudbreak (p105)**

| BIRDWATCHING | RIVER RAFTING | STARGAZING | DOLPHIN-WATCHING |
|---|---|---|---|
| **Taveuni (p157)** promises encounters with some colourful and rare avian species. | The **Navua River (p73)** flows through a spectacular canyon featuring a 24km rafting course. | The sky in **Leleuvia (p136)** is a fabulous canvas for counting stars and planets through the night. | A matchless meeting with spinner dolphins awaits you in the calm waters of **Moon Reef (p85).** |

# ACTION AREAS

Where to find Fiji's best
outdoor activities.

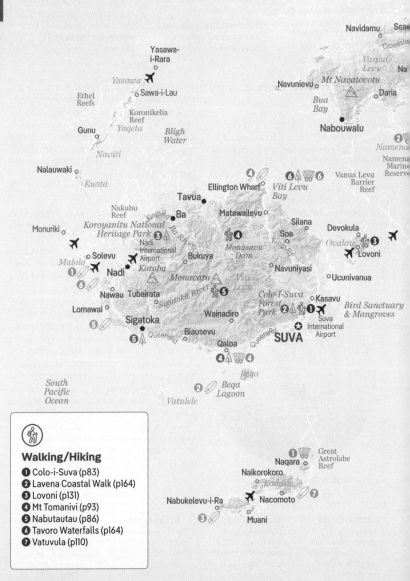

Navidamu · Sea

*Vanua*
*Levu* · Na

Navunievu · *Mt Navatovotu* △ · Daria

*Bua*
*Bay*

**Nabouwalu**

Yasawa-
i-Rara ○

*Yasawa* ✈

○ Sawa-i-Lau

Ethel
Reefs

Koronikelia
Reef

*Yaqeta*

Gunu ○

*Bligh*
*Water*

❷ *Namena*

Namena
Marine
Reserve

*Naviti*

Nalauwaki ○

*Kuata*

❹ ▷

Ellington Wharf ○

❻ △ 🏸 ❻

*Viti Levu*
*Bay*

Vanua Levu
Barrier
Reef

**Tavua**

*Monuriki* ○

Nakubu
Reef

*Koroyanitu National*
*Heritage Park* ❸

○ Ba

Matawailevu

Silana

Devokula

*King's Rd*

Nadi
International
Airport

Bukuya ○

*Monasavu*
*Dam*

Soa ○

*Kings Rd*

Ovalau ❸ ✈
Lovoni

*Malolo*

○ Solevu

❶ ✈

**Nadi** ✈

*Koroba*

Monavatu △

Navuniyasi ○

○ Ucunivanua

❻ ▷

Nawau ○
Tubairata

*Sigatoka River*

🧍❺

*Viti*
*Levu*

*Colo-I-Suva*
*Forest*
*Park* ❷ 🧍❶ ✈

Kasavu ○

*Bird Sanctuary*
*& Mangroves*

Lomawai ○

❺ ▷

**Sigatoka**

Wainadiro ○

Biausevu

Suva
International
Airport

**SUVA**

❺ △

*Queens Rd*

Qaloa ○

*Queens Rd*

❹ △ 🏸 ❹

*Beqa*

❷ ▷

*Beqa*
*Lagoon*

*South*
*Pacific*
*Ocean*

*Vatulele*

*Great*
*Astrolabe*
*Reef*

❶ ▷
Naqara

Naikorokoro

*Kadavu* ❼ ▷

Nabukelevu-i-Ra ○

❸ ▷

Nacomoto ○

○ Muani

## Walking/Hiking

❶ Colo-i-Suva (p83)
❷ Lavena Coastal Walk (p164)
❸ Lovoni (p131)
❹ Mt Tomanivi (p93)
❺ Nabutautau (p86)
❻ Tavoro Waterfalls (p164)
❼ Vatuvula (p110)

Ⓝ 0     60 km
0     30 miles

Great
Sea Reef

au
• Labasa
Nakelikoso
Wainigadru

Napuka
o  *Rabi*

*Delaikoro*
*Natewa
Bay*

Waivunia  Bagasu  Matei o ✈
Naweni  *Bouma National
Heritage Park*
Rainbow
Reef  △
*Des Voeux Peak*
*Tavenui*  oKanacea

*namaki*
*Koro*
✈
*de*

*ro Sea*

*rai*
oTovulalai

❼
*Malawai
iau*
*Vadravadra*

South
Pacific
Ocean

*Vanua Balavu*
oMavana
*Kanacea*  ✈ oSawana

*Yacata*

*Mago*

*Tuvuca* oTuvuca

✈
Mabula  *Cicia*

Liku o *Nayau*

*Lakeba*
✈
Tubou

*Vanua
Vatu*

*Oneata*
Waiqori o

*Moce*

*Moala*  ✈
Vadra o

Natokalau
o

*Matuku*

## National Parks
❶ Bouma National Park (p164)
❷ Colo-i-Suva Forest Reserve (p83)
❸ Sigatoka Sand Dunes National Park (p65)
❹ Koroyanitu Natural Heritage Park (p59)
❺ Shark Reef Marine Reserve (p70)
❻ Vatu-i-Ra Conservation Area (p92)

## Surfing
❶ Cloudbreak (p105)
❷ Restaurants (p105)
❸ Natadola (p63)
❹ Frigates (p63)
❺ Vesi Passage (p175)
❻ King Kong Left (p175)
❼ Nananu-i-Ra (p92)

## Diving
❶ Great Astrolabe Reef (p173)
❷ Namena Marine Reserve (p153)
❸ Natewa Bay (p154)
❹ Pacific Harbour (p70)
❺ Rainbow Reef (p160)
❻ Vatu-i-Ra (p92)

# THE GUIDE

Vanua Levu
& Taveuni
p140

Mamanuca &
Yasawa
p94

Ovalau &
Lomaiviti
p121

Nadi, Suva
& Viti Levu
p47

● SUVA

Kadavu & Lau
p167

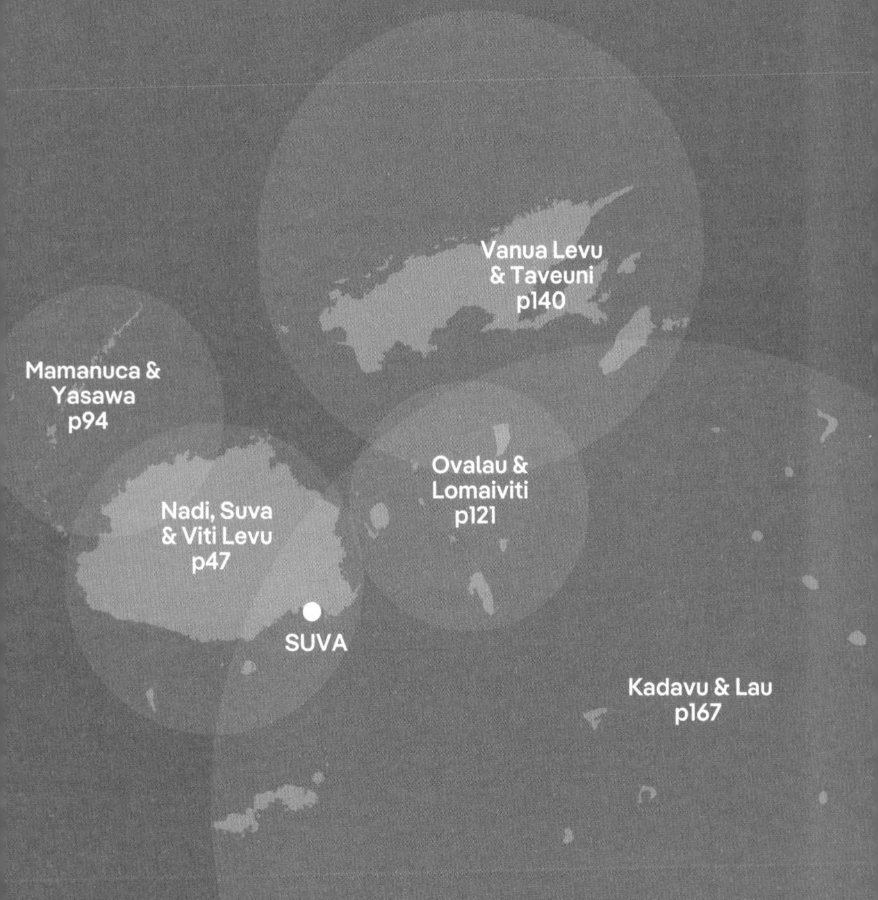

Chapters in this section are organised by hubs and their surrounding areas. We see the hub as your base in the destination, where you'll find unique experiences, local insights, insider tips and expert recommendations. It's also your gateway to the surrounding area, where you'll see what and how much you can do from there.

**Koroyanitu National Heritage Park, Viti Levu (p59)**

**Above: Korotogo Coast, Viti Levu (p68) Right: Sri Siva Subramaniya Temple, Nadi (p53)**

# NADI, SUVA & VITI LEVU

Suva

## FIJI'S 'MAINLAND' ISLAND

With a fabulous mix of metropolitan comforts and natural splendour, Viti Levu offers several reasons for travellers to linger longer.

Such is Viti Levu's mass and spread in Fiji's cartographic centre that it's is often referred to as the country's 'mainland'. The international airport in Nadi – and its much smaller counterpart near Suva – ensures that everyone flying into Fiji must effectively pass through the island. Many visitors capitalise on this mandatory transit to explore Viti Levu for a few days before slipping away to a palm-fringed island of their choice.

The largest of Fiji's islands, Viti Levu houses about three-quarters of the country's population, featuring a mix of communities and ethnicities that are either native to Fiji or have migrated here over time, such as Indo-Fijians, Europeans, Chinese and other Pacific Islanders. This makes Viti Levu one of the most cosmopolitan places in all of the South Pacific, and a melting pot for the diverse ingredients of Fijian society. Add to that a mix of undiluted outdoor experiences – shark diving, river rafting, dolphin safaris and highland hiking, to name a few – and you have a fine place to spend a good part of your trip.

Nadi and Suva, Fiji's biggest urban centres, are as different as chalk and cheese, yet contain enough between them to keep travellers occupied for a few days. These are also pretty much the only places in the country where you can indulge in that obligatory bout of shopping to round off your holiday.

SARA PETERSSON/SHUTTERSTOCK ©

### THE MAIN AREAS

| NADI | NATADOLA | PACIFIC HARBOUR | SUVA | SUNCOAST |
|------|----------|-----------------|------|----------|
| Eat, drink, lounge, shop, repeat. p52 | Viti Levu's best beach for families. p61 | Home of the famed shark dives. p69 | Colonial buildings and quaint locales. p75 | Viti Levu's unexplored northern shores. p88 |

# Find Your Way

A circular road (called Queens Rd between Nadi and Suva, and Kings Rd for the rest of its length) runs along the periphery of Viti Levu, serving as the principal road corridor on the island.

*South Pacific Ocean*

*Bligh Water*

*Wayasewa*

*Vomo*

Nakubu Reef

Nailaga

Ba

*Ba River*

Vunaqiliqili Reef

Vitogo

**Lautoka**

Lauwaki

*Koroyanitu National Heritage Park*

Toge

Viseisei

*Nadi Bay*

Namaka

Bukuya

*Malolo*
Malolo Barrier Reef

**Nadi**

*Nadi River*

*Senilambuli*

Yako

Yavuna

Koroba

Keiyasi

Navula Reef

Nawau

Vunimoli

*Tuvutau (Mt Gordon?*

Lomawai

Tubairata

Tilivalevu

Naduri

*Natadola Beach*

Sanasana

Cuvu

**Sigatoka**

Vatukarasa

Natawarau Reef

Namatakula

## Nadi, p52
Fiji's main hub for transport, tourism and commerce also has a good inventory of restaurants, cafes, watering holes and shopping centres.

## Natadola, p61
A spectacular curving beach in a deserted bay, featuring two pleasant resorts and a variety of activities for everyone in the family.

### CAR
A self-drive rental car may be the best transport option for Viti Levu in terms of flexibility, and is quite economical if you share the cost within your group. Typical rentals range between $100 and $150 a day. Note that Fiji drives on the left of the road.

### AIR
Fiji Airways operates several flights a day between Nadi and Nausori Airport near Suva. This allows quick shuttling between the east and west of Viti Levu, especially to return to Nadi after completing your explorations out east.

### TAXI
Metered taxis are readily available in Nadi and Suva. Taxis in Viti Levu are radio cabs, and report to their respective control bases on the move. You can call a base to request a pickup around the clock.

## Suncoast, p88

This forlorn stretch of golden sands and azure bays makes a bold statement, trumpeting its undiscovered natural attractions to global visitors.

*Vanua Levu*

Namena Marine Reserve

Cakau Vatu Laca Reef

Naivalavala passage

Togowere ○

○ Rakiraki

○ Vatukacevaceva

●Tavua

Naseyani ○

○ Matawailevu

Suva ○

*Makogai*

*Mt Lomalagi* △

Iladarivatu ○

Vanuakula ○

○ Nalalawa

Dawasuma ○

Rukuruku ○

Vuma ○

*Viti Levu*

*Monasavu Dam*

○ Wairuarua

○ Nagai

Lodoni ○

*Ovalau*

Balavu Reef

*Moturiki* ✈ ○ Nacobo

*Batiki*

*Sautaka River*

○ Nabutautau

Natokalau

*Kings Rd*

Matacaucau ○

○ Niubasaga

*Monavatu* △

Naitauvoli ○

○ Vunidawa

*Moturiki Channel*

○ Savu

Bird Sanctuary & Mangroves

Nausori ✈

○ Waivaka

*Colo-I-Suva Forest Park*

○ Lokia

○ Nasilai

*Namosi Highlands* △

Lami ●

*Nasilai Reef*

Ilabukelevu ○

*Navua River*

*Queens Rd*

*Fiji Museum* 🏛 ●SUVA

○ Korovisilou

Pacific ●Navua Harbour

hark Reef ☆ Marine Reserve

*Beqa*

*South Pacific Ocean*

rigate Passage

## Suva, p75

Fiji's capital is also the biggest city in the South Pacific, and packs a bunch of experiences to acquaint visitors with Fijian culture and colonial history.

## Pacific Harbour, p69

The main draw of this picturesque settlement is a thrilling scuba-diving experience in shark-infested waters of the adjacent Beqa Lagoon.

🅝 0 ⎯⎯ 20 km
0 ⎯⎯ 10 miles

# Plan Your Time

Many tourists experience Viti Levu in the course of a short transit immediately after arriving in Fiji, or just before flying back home. However, the island only reveals its innermost wonders to those who have more time to spare.

Scuba diver and pufferfish, Beqa Island (p70)

## If You Only Have Two Days

● Focus on **Nadi** (p52), and nothing more. Start your first day with a shot of adrenaline and go **skydiving** (p54), or make a splash on dirt trails riding a **quad bike** (p54).

● In the afternoon, drive out of town to see the spectacular orchid collection in the **Garden of the Sleeping Giant** (p58), then go for a dip in the healing mud pools of **Sabeto hot springs** (p58).

● The next day, zip down to the tourism hub of **Denarau** (p54), for shrill-emanating water rides at **Big Bula Waterpark** (p56), followed by eating and shopping at **Port Denarau** (p55)

## Seasonal Highlights

Eastern Viti Levu receives more rain through the year compared with the western side, which is drier and perceptibly warmer. The winter months between May and July are the best time to explore the island.

**JANUARY**
The Navua River is in spate, thanks to heavy rains, and this is the best time to go **whitewater rafting**.

**APRIL**
The **Easter holidays** weekend sees a surge in domestic tourism in all the activity zones around Viti Levu.

**MAY**
Winter brings clear skies and glorious weather for diving, surfing and other water sports.

JOEBELANGER/SHUTTERSTOCK ©, MARTIN PROCHAZKACZ/SHUTTERSTOCK ©, RADEK BOROVKA/SHUTTERSTOCK ©

DANITA DELIMONT/SHUTTERSTOCK ©

# One Week to Travel Around

● A week allows you to explore the stretch of shoreline between Nadi and Suva.

● Visit the **sand dunes** (p65) of Sigatoka, followed by a fun-filled **rail-cart ride** (p65) on abandoned rail lines through a quaint landscape, then stay at a plush resort on the scenic **Coral Coast** (p65).

● The following day, sign up for a **glassblowing session** (p68) and learn about sustainable farming on a **coffee-plantation tour** (p67).

● Next, saunter down to Pacific Harbour and plunge into the waters of Beqa Lagoon for a thrilling **shark dive** (p70), or go **whitewater rafting** (p73) through the ravines of the Navua River.

# Ten Days or More

● Start your second week with a couple of days in **Suva** (p75).

● Visit the brilliant **Fiji Museum** (p76), admire diverse botanical species in **Thurston Gardens** (p78) and pursue colourful photo-ops in the crowded lanes of the **Municipal Market** (p79).

● Join Suva's residents for an afternoon game of rugby in **Albert Park** (p78), or admire gorgeous coastal vistas on a walk along the sands of **Laucala Bay** (p81).

● Finally, venture north to explore the isolated **Suncoast** (p88), stopping en route to see the waterfall at **Nabalasere** (p85), and spy dolphins in the calm atolls of **Moon Reef** (p85)

**JULY**
Dry conditions make it easier to explore the **highlands**, where the savannas assume a brilliant golden hue.

**SEPTEMBER**
This is a good month for **diving** the northern reefs off Suncoast. The water visibility is usually stunning.

**OCTOBER**
**Diwali**, the Hindu festival of lights, unites all communities across the island over a few days of joyful celebrations.

**DECEMBER**
Hotels book out weeks in advance, as people unplug and unwind between **Christmas** and New Year.

# NADI

Nadi

★ Suva

Most travellers pass through Nadi twice: its brazenly hot and humid air slaps you in the face when you first step off the plane upon arrival in Fiji, then sends you packing as you board the flight home at the end of your stay. For some, this is twice too often, and many people ensure that their Nadi exposure remains as brief as possible. Its ramshackle urban chaos — as well as its solitary beach at Wailoaloa — is hardly worth writing home about, yet it's a good place to stock up on supplies, plan trip logistics and avail yourself of facilities that may be lacking elsewhere in Fiji. On the bright side, there are a few excursions and activities to add some excitement to your stay here, and the satellite hub of Denarau has a good supply of high-end resorts, fine restaurants and shopping outlets to keep you in touch with the good life.

## TOP TIP

Nadi is perpetually in short supply of hotel rooms, so book your accommodation well in advance. There's a good selection of hotels in the vicinity of the airport. You can also stay in Denarau, as it takes no more than 30 minutes to access the airport from its resorts.

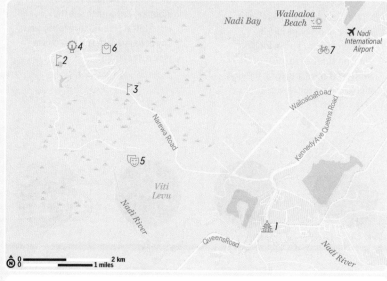

## HIGHLIGHTS
1 Sri Siva Subramaniya Swami Temple

## ACTIVITIES, COURSES & TOURS
2 Denarau Golf & Racquet Club
3 Skydive Fiji

## ENTERTAINMENT
4 Big Bula Waterpark
5 Vou Hub

## SHOPPING
6 Port Denarau

## TRANSPORT
7 Go Dirty Tours

MARIA LETIZIA COLACCHIA/EYEEM/GETTY IMAGES ©

Nadi

## NADI'S FESTIVALS

The Sri Siva Subramaniya Swami Temple is an important venue for several Hindu festivals throughout the year, when devotees from across the Pacific region are drawn to its premise.

Notable ceremonies occur during **Karthingai Deepam** (November), **Panguni Uthiram** (April) and **Thaipusam** (January or February). Visitors circle the temple while offering bananas, smashing coconuts to mark auspicious beginnings, burning camphor and other incenses, and receiving the priest's blessing. Nadi also hosts the **Bula Festival** each July – this weeklong carnival celebrates the Fijian spirit with rides, stalls galore, the occasional appearance of a Bollywood star from India, and the crowning of 'Miss Bula'.

# Visit the Sri Siva Subramaniya Swami Temple

COLOURFUL HINDU SHRINE

This riotously bright Hindu temple – the biggest of its kind in the South Pacific – is one of the few places outside India where you can see traditional Dravidian architecture prevalent among temples in South India. The wooden carvings of deities enshrined here travelled all the way from India, as did the artists who dressed the edifice in its colourful coat and impressive ceiling frescoes. Dress modestly (no shorts or sleeveless shirts) and remove your shoes at the temple entrance. Photographing the exterior is permitted, but not within the shrine. The inner sanctum is reserved for devotees who bring offerings with their prayers. If you are keen on interpreting the stories and myths embellished in the murals and frescoes, the on-site temple custodians can help you make sense of it all. The temple is best visited in the late afternoon, when the colourful *gopurams* (temple spires) are lit up dramatically by the falling sun.

 **WHERE TO STAY IN NADI**

**Fiji Gateway Hotel**
Busy hotel opposite the airport with a mix of single, double and family rooms, plus a popular poolside restaurant. **$$**

**Tanoa International**
This Nadi branch of a Fijian hotel chain is a good choice for families and business folk alike; it's near the airport. **$$**

**Mercure Nadi**
Located in the centre of town and within easy reach of several standalone restaurants and a shopping centre. **$**

# Aerial Adventure over Denarau

GO SKYDIVING

You may have gone skydiving elsewhere in the world, but it's quite a different experience to leap out of a plane and see the spectacular earthly canvas of Fiji's western reefs, lagoons and beaches spread out below you in a dumbfounding palette of luminescent blues, greens and golds. Shout out to the gorgeous scenery below as you tandem-jump with experienced instructors from a height of 4km. Free-falling at a dizzying speed of 200km/h, your instructor deploys the parachute at about 2.5km, and then lets you enjoy the ethereal experience as he glides you down safely to the ground on Denarau Island. **Skydive Fiji** is a trusted operation for the sport here. For a special experience of skydiving over the nearby Mamanuca islands, enquire at the time of booking your jump.

# Quad-Bike Tours

GET DOWN AND DIRTY

Leave your Sunday best behind for these grandly grubby rides through nearby Sabeto Valley. The aptly named **Go Dirty Tours** leads guided scrambles that allow guests to zoom through the bush on bouncy 500cc two-seater quad bikes. Apart from being the ultimate cathartic experience that lets you wallow gleefully in the muddy mess, these tours often combine a visit to outlying points of interest such as the Garden of the Sleeping Giant (p58) and the Sabeto hot springs (p58). Trips are conducted twice daily, usually at 9am and 1pm, but you will need to report 30 minutes earlier to complete the mandatory safety briefing process. The rides are brilliant fun any time of the year, but best enjoyed in the wet season when the landscape in the valley turns soupy with slush.

# Attend a Dance Recital

ANCIENT STORIES ON STAGE

After the sun goes down over Nadi, a lonely circus tent pitched in the dark void of its wide open outskirts buzzes to life with a group of energetic dancers, who enact intriguing stories from Fiji's past to the sheer delight of a mesmerised audience. **Vou Hub** is a dance collective that has toured 35 countries with its dance productions, including an appearance at the UK's prestigious Glastonbury Festival, and strives to support performance arts and artistes in Fiji. Using modern and

**I LIVE HERE: BEST NIGHTLIFE SPOTS IN NADI**

**Tarani Kamoe,** geoscience alumnus at USA's Georgia State University and tennis coach based in Nadi, recommends her favourite bars and nightclubs in town.

**The Hive**
This is easily the most popular nightclub among Nadi's partygoers. It has neon interiors, a relaxed and cheerful vibe and a great selection of drinks.

**Wailoaloa Beach Club**
People love the awesome location of this seaside shack on Wailoaloa Beach. The cocktails are delicious, the nibbles are tasty, and the music is groovy.

**The Lab Fiji**
This happening nightclub has themed evenings for music and dance, such as Bollywood fusion nights, all-night happy hours and ladies' nights.

## WHERE TO EAT IN NADI

**Kanu Gastropub**
The brainchild of one of Fiji's premier chefs, with imaginative dishes fusing Fijian and global cuisine. $$

**Bulaccino**
Busy hangout famous for its aromatic coffee, and popular for savoury puffs and pies, plus scrumptious cakes and desserts. $

**Daikoku**
Table-side chefs slice, dice, flip and serve delicious teppan-yaki at this ever-busy Japanese restaurant. Daily lunchtime specials. $$

NIGELSPIERS/SHUTTERSTOCK ©

**Port Denarau**

innovative dance techniques, the outfit has signature shows titled *Fiji Untold* (Thursdays and Fridays), *Sacred Flame* (Wednesdays and Saturdays) and the somewhat eerie *Cannibal Chase* (Fridays), each focusing on a unique tale or tradition from Fijian history. The dance quality is top-notch, the out-of-town atmosphere is absolutely magical, and there's even a popcorn vending machine on site to supply you with a bucket of munchies for the show. Complimentary pickups and drop-offs are offered to guests residing in Nadi's hotels, and you can buy tickets for the shows at the front desk.

## Downtime at Port Denarau

MARINA AND SHOPPING COMPLEX

**Port Denarau** is as swish as things get around Fiji. A riviera-like annexe to Denarau (an island developed as a resort project contiguous to Nadi), this stylish marina-turned-shopping-complex buzzes with tourists throughout the day, and is somewhat of an activity central for Fiji's western region. People come here for three main reasons. The marina is the main gateway to the Mamanuca and Yasawa islands, as well as a docking point for hulking cruise ships that roam the Pacific on tourist voyages. It is also where most of the ferry lines and adventure operators maintain their booking offices, making it the best spot to plan and book journeys and activities. Finally, the complex has a string of lively bars, fine restaurants and popular shopping outlets to keep visitors busy for hours on end. Late afternoons come with bonus sunset views, reflected dramatically over the rippling waters.

### BEST LUXURY RESORTS IN DENARAU

**Hilton Fiji Beach Resort & Spa**
A resort located on the northern tip of Denarau Island, with a fabulous seafront location, featuring grassy lawns and a long pristine beach. $$$

**Sheraton Fiji Golf & Beach Resort**
Stately rooms and infinity pools are the standard at this beachside property, along with easy access to Denarau Golf & Racquet Club across the road. $$$

**Sofitel Fiji Resort & Spa**
One of Fiji's plushest resorts, known for its pampering five-star facilities, children-friendly atmosphere and super-amiable service team. $$$

 **WHERE TO SHOP IN NADI**

| **Jack's** | **Prouds** | **Tappoo** |
|---|---|---|
| Clothing store with local designer wear, casual wear and sportswear; a wide choice of colourful floral prints changes seasonally. | Upscale departmental store and the place to go for premium Fijian cosmetics, jewellery, perfumes and other fine accessories. | One of Fiji's most recognised department stores, with a large inventory of clothes, accessories, gadgets and souvenirs. |

## Golf & Tennis Action

18-HOLE PUTTING EXPERIENCE

If you're itching for some golfing action on your holiday, the **Denarau Golf & Racquet Club** has a beautiful 18-hole course sprawled across the breadth of Denarau Island. The club is open to nonmembers who can walk in between 7am and 4pm for a round of putting, but you will have to book a slot in advance. If you are a guest at the Sheraton Fiji Golf & Beach Resort located across the road, you will get a discount on your day's playing charges ($130 for 18 holes and $110 for nine holes, plus $75 for equipment hire). The club also has a number of excellently maintained tennis courts, which come in a mix of grass and hardcourt surfaces.

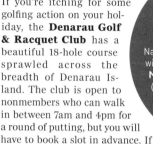

**ISLAND DAY TRIPS**

Nadi makes a fantastic base for those wishing to embark on day trips to the **Mamanuca** (p100) and **Yasawa** (p94) islands, while staying on Viti Levu, given its wider choice of accommodation and amenities.

### BEST RESTAURANTS IN DENARAU

**Cantina Grill & Bar**
Located in the Port Denarau complex, this popular place serves tasty and wholesome Tex Mex platters and nibbles, and has chilled beer on tap. $$

**Byblos**
This beachside bistro is the go-to place for yummy Lebanese dishes, especially the vegetarian fare. It's located within the Radisson Blu Resort. $$

**Koro**
The in-house restaurant at Hilton Fiji is sited on a superb headland surrounded by the lagoon on three sides, and is a good option for romantic diners. $$$

## Rides & Slides

FUN FOR FAMILIES

Themed on a variety of aquatic rides, rolls and tumbles, the thoroughly enjoyable **Big Bula Waterpark** promises a few hours of screaming fun for children and adults alike. Claiming to be the world's largest inflatable waterpark, the complex has everything from gravity defying water slides and mega surfing waves to head-spinning water chutes and colourful inflatable rides intended especially for kids. A number of slides and chutes pass through the toothy jaws of massive inflated shark heads, which presumably adds some uncanny sense of excitement to the rides. You will need to dress in proper swimwear for the action, and children under 12 must be supervised by adult members of the family. You must also remove loose accessories, such as jewellery or sunglasses, as sharp objects may be hazardous both for the riders and the inflatables.

**GETTING AROUND**

Apart from self-drive cars, you can always hire a tourist cab – with a dedicated driver – to show you around Viti Levu. Pehicle Tours has a fleet of well-maintained cars in Nadi (as well as Suva), which can be booked for sightseeing trips across the island, either as day tours or multiday excursions. For Nadi and its surrounds, you can simply hail a metered taxi on the road and have it whisk you away to your destination.

# Beyond Nadi

Garden of the Sleeping Giant · Abaca · Navala · Sabeto Hot Springs · Nadi

Day trips into the valleys north of Nadi reveal lush highland forests, natural geysers and traditional Fijian villages.

The undulating countryside north of Nadi, all the way to the town of Lautoka, is a lovely area to explore by day. It's hard to believe that this peaceful scenery dotted with farms and villages is less than 30 minutes away from the din of Nadi. Much of this region is covered in sugarcane plantations, one of Fiji's chief agricultural economies. Driving along the road you will see narrow-gauge rail tracks intersect the tarmac from time to time; these are lines used for transporting harvested sugarcane to sugar-processing factories between May and September. A similar – and equally beautiful – hilly terrain extends south of Nadi up to Natadola, before spilling onto the Coral Coast.

## TOP TIP

If you're driving, note that interior roads in the area are not well marked, but villagers are always eager to give directions.

STEPHANIE KINDERMANN/SHUTTERSTOCK ©

Natadola, Nadi

## FIJI'S OLDEST VILLAGE

About 12km north of Nadi, **Viseisei** is reputedly the oldest settlement in Fiji. One of the *mataqali* (extended community) in the village are descendants of the first ocean-going Melanesians who landed about a kilometre north of here around 1500. Fiji's first Methodist missionaries also landed here in 1835.

The village's Centennial Memorial is the focal point for annual celebrations, and the ceremonial *bure* (traditional thatch dwelling) opposite has received dignitaries such as Queen Elizabeth II. To look around, you may have to pay a small donation to the people who run the craft market (remember to remove your hat and cover your shoulders and knees). Beyond the village is picturesque **Vuda Marina**, attracting yachties with a great cafe, a restaurant and other facilities.

# Explore the Garden of the Sleeping Giant

ORCHID COLLECTION AND TROPICAL GREENERY

A sprawling private garden abloom with more than 200 varieties of orchids, plus indigenous flora and other tropical beauties, this 20-hectare plantation laid out along a hill slope in Sabeto Valley is a gorgeous getaway for botany enthusiasts. Peak orchid flowering seasons are June to July and November through December, though a fairly brilliant display of epiphytes can be expected year-round. Tours of the garden are included in the entrance fee, but you can also go on a meandering trip along boardwalk trails through the forest on your own. En route, you will pass a number of pretty landscaping features, such as a lily pond, a wedding deck and a picnic spot for families. For all the wonderful sights, there is one tiny downside: the exhaustive botanical collection lacks identification plates or information related to their origin, so you are left to your own devices to make sense of the flora.

To get here, follow Kings Rd north out of Nadi and turn on a gravelled road branching right just after the bridge over Lutunakuve Creek. Drive along this track for about 10 minutes to get to the main gate. The entire drive takes about 20 minutes.

# Relax in Sabeto Hot Springs

THERAPEUTIC THERMAL GEYSERS

Driving about 10 minutes further along the gravelled track past the Garden of the Sleeping Giant, you will arrive at a grassy complex shaded with clumps of trees on the right of the road, where geothermal pools have been spouting hot sulphurous water from the earth's recesses for millennia. Never mind the pricey resort spas of Denarau; a relaxing session in the hot springs of Sabeto Valley will leave you feeling like a million bucks, even if it is from all the stress-busting giggling and mud-sliding you'll be doing. The drill here is to first dress down in the on-site changing rooms, before proceeding to the mud pool in the far end of the complex. Here you will slop around for some time to cover yourself in brown mud enriched with minerals, before plunging in the thermal pool nearby and letting the water work magic on your knotty sinews for as long as you like. If all the mud-glooping and pool-dipping proves too much of an exertion, you can stop by at the massage pavilions, where local villagers offer soothing massages.

 **WHERE TO STAY BEYOND NADI**

**Viseisei**
A number of families offer simple rooms and meals to visitors interested in spending a night or two in the village. **$**

**Vuda Marina**
The marina complex has a collection of cottages which can be booked in advance by yachties as well as tourists. **$$**

**Abaca**
Two simple dorm-style lodges are available for overnighting in Abaca village, with meals provided by local families. **$**

# Excursion to Abaca

UNTOUCHED FORESTS AND RUSTIC LIFE

The flagship village in Koroyanitu's community based tourism project, Abaca provides access into the national park, and calls out to trekkers who are interested in hiking through the pristine mountain landscape. You can't go alone, as trails are overgrown and require an experienced guide to navigate. Once the village has fixed you up with a local guide, it's possible to hike to the summit of **Mt Batilamu**, which is a strenuous three-hour hike up followed by a knee-wobbling couple of hours down. Alternatively, you could go for a walk to a nearby waterfall, which also takes a couple of hours to complete. Walking through the forest, you may come across some rare bird species, such as the green swamphen or the purple-breasted musk parrot.

For an additional taste of rustic life, consider spending a night in Abaca, in one of its two dorm-style lodges. You are free to carry your own rations and use the cooking facilities on site, or ask the locals of Abaca to stir up inexpensive but tasty local platters for dinner and breakfast.

To get to Abaca, drive north from Nadi to Lautoka (25km north along Kings Rd), then take a village road leading southeast out of town into Koroyanitu National Heritage Park. Feel free to ask locals for directions along the way.

### COMMUNITY-BASED TOURISM IN KOROYANITU

Despite being just a half-hour drive from Nadi's airport, the sylvan biosphere of **Koroyanitu National Heritage Park** seems like a journey deep into Viti Levu's forested interior. Within the park are six small and largely self-sufficient villages that cooperate as part of a community based conservation project to protect Fiji's only unlogged tropical montane forest. The villages are fairly remote, and record low visitor numbers through the year. However, guided walks in the forest area can be arranged if you reach out to the people of Abaca village through your hotel's front desk. The park is open every day of the week.

MAXIMILIAN WEINZIERL/ALAMY STOCK PHOTO ©

**Abaca**

---

## WHERE TO EAT BEYOND NADI

**Boatshed Restaurant & Sunset Bar**
A popular place in Vuda Marina that whips out pizzas, curries, seafood and an assortment of grills and roasts. **$$**

**Boatyard Cafe**
Vuda Marina's casual boardwalk cafe is a great hangout, with ambience, good views, aromatic coffee and tasty sandwiches. **$**

**Viseisei**
Given advance notice, host families in the village will cook home-style vegetarian and nonvegetarian meals for their guests. **$**

NADI, SUVA & VITI LEVU

## I LIVE HERE: TREE-SPOTTING IN VITI LEVU'S FORESTS

**Jake Taoi**, botanist and conservation officer with NGO NatureFiji-MareqetiViti, points out unique trees to spot in Viti Levu's wilderness:

### Ma/Yanita
This critically endangered tree can grow up to 40m tall, and produces clusters of bell-shaped red flowers. Less than 250 mature trees are believed to remain in Fiji, most of them in western Viti Levu.

### Dakua
A pine cousin that often grows higher than 30m, produces baseball-sized spherical seeds, and is found in forests all over Viti Levu. Its highly flammable sap is used by villagers to light fires.

### African tulip
This invasive species introduced during colonial times has spread like wildfire through Viti Levu's forests over time. Its highly visible vermilion blossoms can be spotted during treks or drives.

MARY DIMITROPOULOU/SHUTTERSTOCK ©

**Bures, Navala**

## Go Shutter-Happy in Navala

PICTURESQUE TRADITIONAL VILLAGE

Nestled in rugged grassy mountains, Navala is arguably Fiji's prettiest village, and features the largest agglomeration of traditional Fijian *bures* (thatch dwellings) seen anywhere in the country. Strict building rules enforced by the village committee ensure that the *bures* are all laid out in neat avenues, with a central promenade sloping down to the banks of the Ba River. All the houses are built with local construction materials, with the odd concrete structure or corrugated-iron sheet visible in public buildings like the school house, church and radio shed. Navala is a photographer's delight, but you will need to get permission from the village chief to enter. It helps to have a local guide, who can take care of the entrance protocol and advise you on visitor etiquette.

The easiest way to get to Navala is to drive from Nadi to Ba via Lautoka, then head inland along the road branching right. The drive can easily take up to two hours each way, meaning you may have to schedule an entire day to visit the village.

**GETTING AROUND**

The inland gravelled roads in Sabeto Valley and Koroyanitu National Heritage Park can be a slush-fest during the wet season, if you're planning a trip to Abaca or Navala between November and March.

60

# NATADOLA

Natadola
Suva

Gorgeous Natadola is home to one of Viti Levu's best stretches of sands, as well as a host of activities – ranging from surfing, snorkelling and even horse riding – that makes it an incredibly popular destination for families. Needless to say, it is perpetually occupied with domestic tourists who routinely drive here from Nadi and Suva. In spite of its popularity, however, this quiet seaside outpost somehow manages to retain its atmosphere of tranquillity and make people believe that they have exclusive access to its peaceful environs.

Natadola has two upscale resorts along the sands – the grass-fronted Yatule Beach Resort and the exclusive Intercontinental Fiji – where you could potentially spend a few nights. There are no budget hotels or standalone restaurants here, but the two resorts welcome guests to walk freely between the properties and enjoy meals in their on-site restaurants.

## TOP TIP

If you wish to surf in Natadola, especially by yourself, it helps to carry your own gear, as resorts may not always have boards to rent out. However, if you sign up for a surfing lesson you will have equipment supplied to you as part of the course.

61

# Unwind at Natadola Beach

PERFECT FOR RELAXATION

Hugging the shoreline for a couple of kilometres on Viti Levu's southwestern corner, **Natadola Beach** is a curving strip of white sand sliding into a cobalt-blue sea. It offers fantastic swimming, but strong longshore currents have resulted in a steep drop in the seafloor along the beach. Therefore, Natadola's waters may be rough at times – sometimes choppy enough to bodysurf along with the breakers – and there could be some undertow with every receding wave.

The southern end of the beach is busier, as the **Intercontinental Fiji** is situated there. A few hundred metres north stands **Yatule Beach Resort**. The two resorts share an informal boundary, allowing guests to move freely between them. Midway between the resorts, a few shacks are strung out on the beach where locals offer rejuvenating foot and back massages.

The section of beach fronting Yatule is flanked by a grassy lawn with large trees. The shaded areas have sunbeds laid out for guests to lounge on. North of Yatule, the beach is deserted for the rest of its length, and sees few people through the day, except for the odd jogger, ambler or horse rider. While this forlorn stretch seems more inviting for a swim, there are no lifeguards here, and the nearest group of fellow swimmers may be much farther in the southern part of the beach.

## GUNS OF MOMI

A pleasant daytime drive along pristine back roads takes you to **Momi Bay**, about 40km north of Natadola. Travelling through barren hills, pine plantations and sugar-cane fields, the tar-sealed road is mostly in good condition, though in the final stretch to Momi Bay's headland it breaks down to an alternation of tarmac and dirt sections.

Dominating the headland at Momi Bay is the **Momi Battery Historical Park**, a bunkered military lookout dating back to WWII, where heavy artillery guns were installed by the New Zealand 30th battalion in 1941 to protect Fiji against a possible Japanese invasion from the sea.

DAVID WALL/SHUTTERSTOCK ©

**Natadola Beach**

## WHERE TO EAT IN NATADOLA

**Toba Bar & Grill**
Poolside diner at the Intercontinental with a great selection of wood-fired pizzas, fresh salads, burgers and grills. **$$**

**Navo**
The Intercontinental's fine-dining restaurant serves ocean-inspired modern cuisine and has a fine selection of wines. **$$$**

**Na Ua**
The restaurant at Yatule scores with delicious Asian dishes, hearty Indian meal platters and generous seafood servings. **$$**

# Surfing Natadola's Breaks

GENTLE WAVES FOR BEGINNERS

Natadola is a great place for first-timers to acquire a taste for surfing. One of the gentlest waves in the bay, less than a metre high, breaks about 50m out from the Intercontinental on a shallow reef. This is where children are taught to catch a wave by experienced instructors on weekends. There's also the **Natadola Inside** break some distance away (but well within the reef) that is good for novices. The more daunting **Natadola Outside** break, at the entrance of the channel, is for experienced surfers only. The waves are surfable year-round but tend to be more prominent when the southwesterly winds blow in. **Fiji Surf Co** offers lessons for beginners in Natadola, and you can book a session directly with them or through your resort.

Not far from Natadola, the mouth of the **Sigatoka River** has a few small breaks ideal for beginners. Further out, more than 20km from the coast, a mid-sea surf break named **Frigates** produces a powerful and consistent barrelling left up to 150m long, suitable only for advanced surfers.

# Go Horse Riding at Natadola

TROT ALONG THE BEACH

At the common car park between the resort premises of the Intercontinental and Yatule, local villagers tie up their horses under trees and pounce on tourists as soon as they arrive. They are fairly persistent, and if you relent, an enthusiastic local will promptly take you out for a ride on the pristine sands of Natadola's beach. If you are proficient, you can simply take the animal around on your own, while novices or untrained riders will have their horses handled by the handler walking alongside throughout the ride. Once you have completed your ride, you will be accosted by a flock of coconut sellers with same high-pressure sales tactics as the horse owners.

**Above: Natadola Beach**

## OVERWATER PARADISE

Midway along the drive from Natadola to Momi Bay, at the end of a feeder road that leads through the wilderness to a secluded coastline, stands the unbelievably luxurious **Marriott Momi Bay**.

Sprawled over an artificial lagoon stretching almost a kilometre along its outer edge, and hemmed by several acres of tropical gardens and forests, this grand resort is home to a showcase collection of stylish overwater *bures* (bungalows) located on the lagoons, as well as a mix of deluxe rooms and villas (more than 200 of them) scattered across its premises. There's a whole rush of activities to keep guests busy (surfing, tennis, swimming pools), three themed fine-dining restaurants, plus a top-notch spa for guests to get pampered in.

## GETTING AROUND

The narrow one-lane forest road dipping down to Natadola from the back road branching off Queens Rd is not entirely tar-sealed, and has a few steep ascents and descents. Taxis are used to plying this route, but self-drivers should be careful of oncoming cars that can suddenly emerge around a bend ahead.

# Beyond Natadola

An exciting mix of land- and water-based activities line the scenic stretch of Queens Rd leading to eastern Viti Levu.

Natadola
Ecotrax
Sigatoka Sand Dunes
National Park
Bula Coffee
Hot Glass Fiji

Past the Natadola intersection, Queens Rd takes a hard left turn to align itself with the southern shoreline of Viti Levu, and opens on to a spectacular terrain, with the coast on the right and jade-green mountains to the left. Featuring white-water reef breaks, blue-green lagoons and golden beaches that wash up almost to road level, Viti Levu's famed Coral Coast gives the phrase 'scenic route' a whole new meaning. Extending for nearly 100km, the panoramic coastline is home to luxury resorts and fun activities that keep travellers occupied on their way towards the eastern side of the island. Many of these experiences are thrown around the sleepy town of Sigatoka, a convenient midway stop with petrol stations and supermarkets.

### TOP TIP

East of Sigatoka, the beachfront road at Korotogo called Sunset Strip has a few boutique resorts and is a relatively quiet place to break your journey.

STEPHANIE KINDERMANN/SHUTTERSTOCK ©

BENEDEK/GETTY IMAGES ©

**Sigatoka Sand Dunes National Park**

## COASTAL BEACH GUIDE

Despite being one of the most beautiful shorelines, the Coral Coast is noticeably short on good-quality beaches. Before it plunges dramatically into the deep blue ocean, the fringing reef here skirts the coast to form a shallow lagoon that is several hundred metres wide in places. Given strong tidal fluctuations, large swathes of the lagoon remain exposed for long periods of time, forcing swimmers to either confine themselves to the pools within their resorts, or wait for the high tide to go swimming or snorkelling in the sea.

One of the few good natural swimming spots along the coast is **Sovi Bay**, about 2.5km east of Korotogo, but one must be wary of strong channel currents.

# Hike the Sigatoka Sand Dunes

EXCURSION IN NATURAL HISTORY

One of Fiji's best natural history sites, the impressive **Sigatoka Sand Dunes National Park** is a ripple of peppery monoliths skirting the shoreline near the mouth of the Sigatoka River. Windblown and rugged, the sand dunes stand around 5km long and up to 1km wide, and reach a maximum height of about 60m on their western end. Bearing resemblance to beachside dunes in other parts of the world, Sigatoka's dunes were formed over millions of years as sediments brought down by the nearby river, washed ashore by the surf and blown into dunes by prevailing winds. The sand here is mostly of a grey-brown colour, featuring a coating of slate-coloured grains with which the wind paints constantly shifting patterns on the surface of the dunes.

There are two ways in which you can get to the dunes. Coming from Natadola along Queens Rd, you will see the main **park office** to your right, about 5km before you reach Sigatoka. From here, signposted trails will lead you through a section of tropical forest and grassland all the way to

 **WHERE TO STAY ALONG THE CORAL COAST**

| **Naviti Resort** | **Matanivusi Beach Eco Resort** | **Fiji Beachouse** |
|---|---|---|
| Upscale Naviti combines 200-plus rooms with four restaurants, five bars, a swim-up bar, a putting green and a health spa. **$$$** | An elegant resort featuring graceful seafront *bures*, fine in-house dining, and some fabulous surfing opportunities. **$$** | Aimed at budget travellers, this popular dig combines simple living and heady social activities into a winning formula. **$** |

THE GUIDE

NADI, SUVA & VITI LEVU

## YANUCA ISLAND ESCAPE

A tiny offshore island located in the sheltered Cuvu Bay, **Yanuca** is connected to Viti Levu by a short causeway. The private island is home to the impressive **Shangri-La Resort**, one of Coral Coast's premier and biggest holidaying hot spots. It's a destination in itself for many local families who come here on weekends.

If armies of squealing children don't daunt you, you can enjoy the swimming pools, fantastic restaurants and tennis courts, while also stepping into the sea for some snorkelling or surfing. If you are looking for a less expensive option to break your drive at Yanuca, consider staying at the pleasant **Gecko's Resort**, located on the main island just opposite the causeway turnoff to Yanuca.

the dunes. This hike can take up to two hours. Alternatively, you can pass the visitors centre and take the first unmarked village road branching right. Follow this meandering road for a couple of kilometres until you reach **Kulukulu** village. Helpful locals here will point you toward the mud trail that branches right, and leads past a few hutments straight to the foot of the dunes.

To climb the dunes, simply scramble up the sand slope. It's a tricky ascent, and you can create mini avalanches if you step on loose sand. Make sure you wear proper trail shoes, and don't attempt the climb in flip-flops or sneakers.

Once on top, hike across the tabletop summit of the dunes to treat yourself to sweeping views of the Coral Coast stretched out in front of you. You can amble as far and wide as you wish, but make a note of your bearings and your trail markings, as it's easy to lose your orientation (and your way) amidst the patterned landscape of the dunes. The tin-roof patch of Kulukulu village, prominently visible down the eastern edge of the dunes, is a good reference to orient yourself at all times. It also helps to carry a stash of water and snacks.

Since the coastal margin of the dunes is largely unstable, human bones and early pottery fragments can sometimes be revealed by strong winds blowing over the sands. Archaeological excavations here have uncovered **antique pottery** more than 2600 years old, along with a **human burial site**, both of which can be traced back to the ancient Lapita people who settled in Fiji on their eastward migratory journey through the Pacific. The site of the dunes marks what was possibly one of the largest Lapita occupations in Fiji.

## POTTERY EXHIBITS

Some of the better samples of Lapita pottery, exhumed from sites around the sand dunes, are on display at the **Fiji Museum (p76)** in Suva. A few pieces are reconstructed to their nearest original shape, and are presumably more than 2000 years old.

## Ride the Sugar Train

JOURNEY ON OLD RAILS

Who would have guessed an out-of-commission railway track could rise from its ashes to become one of Fiji's most exciting joyrides? **Ecotrax**, an adventure operator with a knack for innovations, has done exactly that. A 14km section of defunct railway line near Sigatoka – part of a narrow-gauge

 **WHERE TO STAY ON SUNSET STRIP**

**Outrigger Fiji**
This stylish resort on Korotogo's hillside offers spacious rooms with sweeping sea views and diverse cultural experiences. **$$**

**Crow's Nest**
A resort with front-row access to the promenade, featuring different categories of villas in a grassy compound. **$$**

**Seafront Apartment**
These modern serviced apartments at the start of Sunset Strip are great for families and couples alike. **$$**

66

network used by diesel-powered trains to transport harvested sugarcane to the sugar mills at Lautoka – has now received a second lease of life as a circuit for modified electric-bicycle carriages known as velocipedes. Instead of hauling cane, these newfangled buggies carry enthralled tourists through the beautiful local scenery comprising of mangrove forests, river crossings, rocky passes and wide open coastlines.

The entire experience takes up to three hours, and tours are offered twice daily (at 8.45am and 1.45pm). Riders have the choice of pedalling or simply sitting back to enjoy the journey, as the carriage powers itself through the landscape. There are a few scheduled stops along the way, when travellers can take photos, have a sip of coconut water and learn more about the terrain and its people from informed guides. The final stop is at scenic **Vunabua Beach**, where everyone can cool off with a session of snorkelling in the lagoon.

Given its high entertainment quotient and popularity, the ride usually gets booked out several weeks in advance, especially through holiday weeks. Reserve your spot a couple of months earlier if you can.

## Bula Coffee Tour & Tasting

SUSTAINABLE FARMING AND COFFEE TASTING

On the eastern outskirts of Sigatoka, an informative tour takes visitors on an educational journey through the sustainable farming process for **Bula Coffee**, one of Fiji's homegrown coffee brands. The immersive 'cherry to cup' tour explains how the wholesale aggregator promotes sustainable agronomy by sourcing wild harvest coffee directly from villagers in

JOMEL BARTOLOME/EYEEM/GETTY IMAGES ©

### GOURMET CUPPA

Coffee-lovers journeying east from Sigatoka, take note. About 200m short of the traffic roundabout at Korotogo, hidden within the foliage of a manicured garden, is the modest establishment of **Cafe Planet**.

Somewhat legendary among Fiji's caffeine connoisseurs, this gourmet roaster produces small batches of coffee from grains sourced around the world (Brazil, Nicaragua, Uganda and Ethiopia, to name a few), which are then roasted and blended according to its signature in-house specifications.

You can stop here to sample some of its creations (grab a side order of hot and crunchy samosas to go with your brew), then buy a few packets to take home.

**WHERE TO EAT ALONG THE CORAL COAST & SUNSET STRIP**

| Wicked Walu | Sitar | Crab Shack |
|---|---|---|
| Warwick's speciality seafood restaurant, on a fabulous outcrop in the lagoon, serves immaculately made marine delights. $$ | A popular restaurant in the Seafront Apartment complex that does Indian curries and grills, including vegetarian options. $ | This speciality restaurant at the far end of Sunset Strip has delicious platters of marine delights, including jumbo crabs. $$ |

## KOROTOGO'S SUNSET STRIP

From the traffic roundabout at Korotogo, a short service road extends east along the sea face, providing access to homes and tourist establishments located within the village. Over time, the road has gained the moniker **Sunset Strip**, thanks to the stunning end-of-day views it affords along its palm-lined promenade. Many people come here simply to enjoy the ambience – the grassy lawns along the seafront are quite inviting if shooting the breeze features prominently on your day's agenda. The strip also has a few decent restaurants and resorts (some are located one street over within the village) that call out to travellers with a preference for solitude.

CORLEVE/ALAMY STOCK PHOTO ©

**Korotogo**

Fiji's highlands, and how nearly 5000 coffee harvesters are supported through the initiative. The 90-minute interaction features a complimentary coffee-tasting session and a small bag of coffee to take away as a souvenir. Tours run hourly between 8am and 11am, and it is advisable to book a spot in advance, as sessions can often get booked out by big tour groups.

If your trip schedule is too tight to accommodate this coffee tour, you can still purchase a few packs of Bula Coffee to take back home at any of the leading supermarkets in Nadi or Suva. Fijian highland coffee is full-bodied, aromatic and mild, making it delightful to drink as an espresso or a long black straight out of the brewer.

## Blow Your Own Glass in Korotogo

MAKE YOUR OWN GLASS SCULPTURES

Founded by an expatriate British artist who made Fiji her home years ago, **Hot Glass Fiji** is an interactive blown-glass studio (the only one of its kind in Fiji) set amid stepped lawns on Korotogo's Sunset Strip. You can drop in here on weekdays to purchase the owner's spectacular creations – look out for the unique lampshades cast in coconut shells. If you make a prior appointment, you can even sign up for a quick-and-slick glassblowing session, which can be great fun for children above seven. Blow your own unique souvenir, or sand-cast your own creation with molten glass, and have the memento collected (or shipped to you) the following day.

### GETTING AROUND

Given the frequency in connections between Nadi and Suva, Coral Coast is one of the few places in Fiji where you could consider commuting by public transport.
Buses and minivans will happily drop you at a resort of your choice, or pick you up from any point along the road, and it will only cost you a few dollars. However, be aware that timings are a moveable feast, and there's virtually no public transport plying the route on Sundays and public holidays.

# PACIFIC HARBOUR

Pacific Harbour ● ★ Suva

About 50km short of reaching Suva, Queens Rd suddenly leaps up from the flat Coral Coast terrain to meander through a few steep mountain passes, before spilling onto a scenic foreshore drive where the Qaraniqio River flows out to sea. Thrown around the river's estuary is the tiny commune of Pacific Harbour, a self-billed adventure capital of sorts, thanks to the legendary shark dives that take place in nearby Beqa Lagoon (although the sleepy settlement looks anything but adventurous). Founded in the 1970s as a canal development project, Pacific Harbour evolved into a place for wealthy people to have their holiday homes. This resulted in the creation of a manicured landscape with cul-de-sac driveways and riverside housings that mix American suburb aesthetics with bayou country feel. The main hub of activity here is a multi-facility tourist complex called Arts Village, as well as the main market area by the river-mouth.

## TOP TIP

Pacific Harbour has a good choice of hotels, from lavish resorts with private beaches to smart hotels with riverfront views. It makes a good base for a couple of days to experience the region's signature activities, such as shark diving, river rafting and hiking in the forests.

JOE ELDRIDGE/ALAMY STOCK PHOTO ©

**Bure Kalau (spirit house), Pacific Harbour Arts Village**

## BEST SHARK DIVE OPERATORS

**Aqua-Trek**
The pioneers of shark diving in Pacific Harbour, this dive shop is located within The Pearl, and does its dives at a site called 'the bistro'.

**Beqa Adventure Divers**
This operator uses a feeding site called 'the arena' at a relatively deep 30m. The dives have shorter bottom times but attract more sharks.

**Coral Coast Divers**
This dive shop works in close association with the local village community. Shark feeding is done at 'the colosseum', located at a depth of 19m.

# PACIFIC HARBOUR

# Dive with Bull Sharks

HAIR-RAISING UNDERWATER ADVENTURE

A daring dip in **Beqa Lagoon** with resident sharks for company is an obligatory rite of passage for scuba divers passing through the South Pacific. Indeed, many divers come to Fiji simply to travel to Pacific Harbour and sign up for a shark dive or two, only to come back a couple of years later to relive the experience. Most numerous among return visitors are underwater photographers who can't get enough of snapping up-and-close shark portraits from within a couple of feet of these graceful beasts circling in the water. And these aren't wimpy reef sharks that we're talking about. Designated in 2004 as a marine-protected area for shark conservation – the **Shark Reef Marine Reserve** – Beqa Lagoon is one of the few places in the world where it's possible to dive in open water with massive, barrel-chested bull sharks, as well as seven other species of sharks. All dives that visit the reef include a fee that goes towards the reef community fund.

Several dive shops in Pacific Harbour offer shark dives as a half-day, two-tank excursion (which sets you back by about $350, including gear rental). Each dive shop maintains its own underwater viewing arena in different parts of the lagoon,

 **WHERE TO STAY IN PACIFIC HARBOUR**

**Nanuku Resort**
Stretched along a private beach almost 2km long, many of the luxury *bures* have private pools and kitchenettes. **$$$**

**Pearl**
One of the most popular midrange options, located by the boat pier on the river-mouth lined by thick mangrove forests. **$$**

**Uprising Beach Resort**
Ecofriendly yet sophisticated, this resort attracts budget travellers and families, and has great beachside vibes. **$**

where a small amount of chum — comprising tuna heads and entrails — is used to attract sharks every morning.

As divers drop down to take their positions behind a stone corral, hefty bull sharks — as well as nurse sharks and lemon sharks — hungrily swirl in the viewing arena, waiting for the food to be distributed. If you are lucky (and have the guts to match), you might even see a hulking 4m tiger shark pay you a visit from the blue beyond.

The buildup to the feeding spectacle, which extends for about 30 minutes, is the best part of the dive, when you can watch and photograph these fearsome yet beautiful creatures swim by within a couple of feet of the stone corral. The actual feeding is over within a few minutes, following which dive guides slowly escort divers back to the surface. On the way up, you might catch a glimpse of smaller blacktip and white-tip reef sharks swimming at lesser depths.

Hairy as it is, shark diving is a harmless activity as long as proper safety protocol is followed during the dives.

Ironically, there is less threat here from sharks than there may be from an individual's own lack of situational awareness. Bear in mind that these dives require you to stay at depths between 18m and 25m for extended periods of time, significantly shortening your bottom time and inching you closer to your no-decompression limit.

It's possible to lose track of time in all the adrenalin-laced excitement, but keep a close eye on your dive computer at all times. Begin ascending early, and remember to perform a three-minute safety stop on the mooring line at 5m on your way out of the water. It is also recommended that you have an advanced open-water certification, as some of the feeding sites are located deeper than the open-water certification limit of 18m.

**SHARK DIVES IN YASAWA**

Apart from Pacific Harbour, you can also dive with sharks at **Kuata Island** (p107) in the Yasawa group. However, bull shark (as well as tiger shark) sightings are more common in Pacific Harbour, even in the mating season between November and February.

**WHAT TO DO WHEN SHARK DIVING**

Stay behind the coral
Don't stick your arm out to take photos from a closer distance. Sharks may mistake a solitary limb protruding from the wall for food.

Dress inconspicuously
Avoid wearing brightly coloured dive gear or shiny jewellery. These may either annoy the sharks or make them curious to approach you.

No electric signals
Turn off Wi-Fi and bluetooth connections on your camera. Sharks are sensitive to electric signals. The less interference you create, the better.

**GETTING AROUND**

Pacific Harbour is about 90 minutes by road from Sigatoka, and is serviced by public transport plying between Nadi and Suva. Resorts will readily arrange for a taxi if you are headed back to Nadi to catch a flight, or are continuing further to Suva, which is an hour's drive eastward along Queens Rd.

THE GUIDE

NADI, SUVA & VITI LEVU

# Beyond
# Pacific Harbour

Explore the Navua River valley and its
contiguous highlands by embarking on
thrilling river rides or forest jaunts.

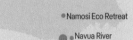

The mountain landscape north of Pacific Harbour
is carved out by a network of deep ravines through
which the Navua River flows down to meet the sea.
The adjacent Namosi Highlands – a steamy patch of
tropical greenery – is home to some of Fiji's most spectacular highland scenery, including dense rainforests, craggy
ranges and tall waterfalls. Most forays into this untamed interior are best organised from Pacific Harbour, and the proximity means you can comfortably schedule these outings as
day trips. These journeys will involve plenty of driving along
dirt tracks and logging roads, so make sure you hire a 4WD
to explore the formidable terrain.

## TOP TIP

Rainproof clothing and
waterproof bags are a
must for any trip into
the Navua Valley or the
Namosi Highlands.

EA GIVEN/SHUTTERSTOCK ©

**Hiking, Navua River**

**Navua River**

# Rafting the Navua River

ROLLING ON THE RIVER

The upper valley of the Navua River is an impossibly beautiful terrain of interconnected gorges that slice through the highlands like deep knife gashes. For about 24km of its upper course, the river meanders through narrow ravines that are canopied under rainforests resplendent with birdcall, alternating in form and force from quiet stretches of gently flowing water to gut-churning rapids rumbling through stony gullies.

**Rivers Fiji**, an adventure operator based in Pacific Harbour, organises exciting rafting safaris along the Navua's upper course, allowing you to experience the brute force of the river as it runs through the virgin landscape. The starting point is high up in the mountains, accessible via a logging road, and takes about an hour to reach from Pacific Harbour. Rowing down from here, you will pass through canyons barely wide enough for your inflatable rubber raft to pass, then tumble down rushing whitewater rapids (up to class III) to land in eddies of gently swirling water.

## RIVER TUBING

Looking for an activity that's easier on your muscles – but no less fun – than river rafting? **River Tubing Fiji** has a fleet of inflatable rubber tubes, called 'donuts', that can easily navigate the Navua's lower reaches, where the river loses its force and exuberance to become a gentle and wide tract of flowing water, with the occasional gurgling rapid thrown in for thrills. You start by going upstream in a slim open-top motorboat, which can be great fun every time the vessel makes its way up a rapid, like a jumpy salmon. From the starting point, you then float downstream on your donut, essentially retracing your boat journey, with watchful guides tracking your moves in the water at all times.

 **RAFTING TERMINOLOGY**

**Rapid**
A short course of the river squeezing through a narrow, shallow and rocky part of the riverbed, producing a vigorous gush of frothy water.

**Eddy**
A pool-like area in a river's course that usually forms downstream of a rapid to a side, with water flowing in reverse direction to the river.

**Left & right**
Used to tell the two riverbanks from each other, while looking downstream of the river (if you're headed upstream, the sides reverse).

Occasionally, and thrillingly, you will power your way through the course of a cascading waterfall pouring into the river from the cliffs above. Gradually, the river channel will broaden as you descend, eventually spilling onto a wide lower valley, where you will bring your raft to shore on the banks of a tiny village. Midway along your journey, you will be served a picnic-style lunch of sandwiches, fresh fruits, crisps, crackers, juice, tea and coffee on a sandbank wedged between the river and one of its tributaries.

No prior training or experience is required for this expedition, as long as you are reasonably fit and comply with your guide's safety briefing and instructions along the course. The excursion includes pickups and drops at Pacific Harbour.

# A Taste of the Namosi Highlands

HEARTLAND COMMUNITY LIFE

Branching off Queens Rd near the settlement of Navua, a gravelled road darts up the mountains of Namosi. Here you can get a taste of Viti Levu's quaint highland life, which has continued pretty much unchanged for centuries. A one-hour drive through forested areas will bring you to the fantastic **Namosi Eco Retreat**, a village-style ecofriendly complex that welcomes day-trippers as well as overnight guests to experience the charms of rustic Fijian living. Activities-wise, you can go on jungle hikes, birdwatching tours and guided walks through nearby **Navunikabi** village, or learn to navigate a *bilibili* (indigenous bamboo raft) on the river. Upon prior notice, you can also arrange a waterfall trip with a *lovo* (pit roast) lunch thrown in. Lodging is provided in basic *bures* built with sustainable material sourced from the wilds, and meals are included in the stay package.

Apart from outdoor activities, Namosi also offers a range of fabulous interactions with the local community. You could dabble in farmwork, learning the daily agricultural drill by helping with a day's work in the fields. Or you could go for a crash course preparing some of the signature dishes of Fijian cuisine – using fresh produce harvested from the fields – and then rate your skills by tasting your own handiwork. Finally, you could drink copious amounts of grog with newfound friends, and learn about Fijian culture and legend through stories narrated by the community elders.

## TREETOP ADVENTURES

Aimed at entertaining the whole family, and located not far from the turnoff to Namosi, **Kila World** is an eco-adventure park filled with exciting ropewalks, zip lines, abseiling courses, and what it self-bills as Fiji's biggest swing.

Unsurprisingly named the Giant Swing, this bungee-like ride lets you jump off a platform 12m high and oscillate like a shrieking pendulum amid treetops, all the while being secured by cables fastened to your seating harness. You can also go on a walk through the wilderness, stopping at picnic spots along the way and cooling off at the waterfalls.

The park is an easy half-hour drive from Pacific Harbour.

### GETTING AROUND

Rafting and tubing operators offer complimentary transport from Pacific Harbour to the start and end points of the river courses.

For bigger groups, they can even arrange transfers from resorts along the Coral Coast. For Namosi, it is best to have your own transport.

# SUVA

Suva

Suva is the cosmopolitan heart of Fiji, home to half of the country's urban population and the biggest metropolis in all of the South Pacific. It's a lush, green city sited on a hilly peninsula close to Viti Levu's southeastern corner, which gets more than its share of rain and is home to a large community of expatriates (and, therefore, a vibrant multicultural scene).

Downtown Suva is the most diverse part of town, with a jigsaw of colonial buildings, modern shopping plazas, abundant restaurants and a busy esplanade overlooking the placid waters of Suva Harbour. Small passages are lined with Indian curry houses and Chinese food stalls, fashion houses peddle tinselled saris as well as edgy attire, fish markets stare at multistorey shopping malls from across the road, while Bollywood and Hollywood square off at the local cinema – all of this within a mere square kilometre of each other.

## TOP TIP

Despite buzzing with activity through office hours, downtown Suva empties out by 6pm and is virtually deserted, except for a few scattered nightlife spots. Schedule your sightseeing and shopping well within daylight hours. The city also goes on the blink on Sundays and public holidays.

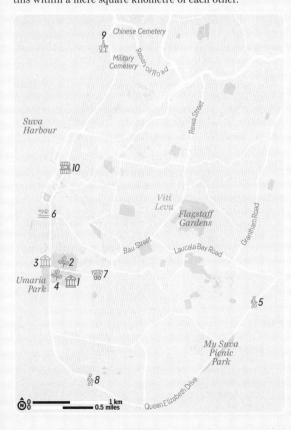

**HIGHLIGHTS**
1 Fiji Museum

**SIGHTS**
2 Albert Park
3 Grand Pacific Hotel
4 Thurston Garden

**ACTIVITIES, COURSES & TOURS**
5 Laucala Bay
6 Olympic Swimming Pool
7 Suva Scuba
8 Suva Sea Wall

**DRINKING & NIGHTLIFE**
9 Royal Suva Yacht Club

**SHOPPING**
10 Suva Municipal Market

### BREADFRUIT & THE BOUNTY

Walking around Suva, you will see plenty of breadfruit trees laden with delicious round fruits. However, few people make the connection between breadfruit and the HMS *Bounty,* famously commandeered by Mel Gibson in the 1984 film *The Bounty.*

This merchant ship acquired by the Royal Navy in 1787 was sent to the South Pacific to collect breadfruit saplings that could be planted in the West Indies. I
n 1789, a series of standoffs resulted in rebellious crew members forcing captain William Bligh off the ship before rerouting it to Pitcairn Island, where it was burned down. Bligh and a few loyalists travelled across open ocean in a rowboat to reach Timor, and returned to England in 1790.

IAN TROWER/ALAMY STOCK PHOTO ©

**Fiji Museum**

## Touring the Fiji Museum

FABULOUS COLLECTION OF ARTEFACTS

A must-visit in Suva, this renovated and excellently curated museum offers a great journey into Fiji's historical and cultural evolution. To enjoy the exhibits in a chronological manner, start with the displays immediately behind the ticket counter and work your way around clockwise. Themed on the subject of voyages, the gallery documents the arrival of various seafaring peoples to Fiji, all of whom contributed to shaping its society and culture over centuries.

The centerpiece in the main hall is the majestic **Ratu Finau**, Fiji's last remaining vintage *drua* (a double-hulled seaworthy canoe of unique design) that was restored in 1914 and made its final voyage sometime in the 1920s. Other attractions include mastheads; war clubs, objects of daily use from neighbouring nations such as Kiribati and Solomon Islands; and the severely weathered wooden rudder of the infamous HMS *Bounty*, an 18th-century merchant ship associated with the most legendary mutiny in Pacific waters. You will also see panels devoted to **Lapita pottery** exhumed from the sand dunes near Sigatoka, dresses and shoes worn by early Chinese settlers in Fiji, stunning necklaces and protective shields made from whale ivory, protective headgear made from the shells of porcupine fish, and fine specimens of *tabua* — the rare teeth of sperm whales exchanged as highly coveted ritualistic offerings in Fijian culture. On the far end of the hall, a door leads into an annexe with displays related to Fiji's **Girmit history**, which began with the arrival of Indian indentured labourers to Fiji in the 1880s, and notes

 **WHERE TO STAY IN SUVA**

**Holiday Inn**
This Suva outpost of the global chain has pleasant 1st-floor rooms and a seaside deck featuring a pool and dining area. **$$**

**Grand Pacific Hotel**
The rooms in the heritage block pack tons of old-world charm; the new wing's stylish rooms have fabulous sea views. **$$**

**Tanoa Plaza**
The city branch of Fiji's Tanoa hotel group, on a central thoroughfare, is popular with businesspeople and holidayers alike. **$$**

important contributions made to Fijian society and culture by their descendants.

The growing influence of European cultures in Fiji is well documented in the museum's historical gallery, a part of which is devoted to Fiji's past **cannibalistic era**. Fijians accept their history of cannibalism prosaically, with neither glory nor shame. Housed here is the well-chewed shoe of Thomas Baker, a Christian missionary eaten for his indiscretions on a journey through Viti Levu's highlands in 1867. Lending credence to the incident (mentioned in the historical annals as the last recorded act of cannibalism in Fiji) is a four-pronged wooden cannibal fork believed to have been used by a village chief to eat some of Baker's flesh. Held in high regard as representatives of ancestral deities, chiefs were neither allowed to handle human flesh nor let it touch their lips while eating, thereby warranting the use of this unique tool during ceremonial cannibal feasts. Replicas of wooden cannibal forks are available as mementos from the museum gift shop.

Flanking the exit past the gift shop is **Ginger Kitchen**, the laid-back museum cafe where you can lounge for a while and reflect on the newly imbibed information over a smoothie or a cappuccino. The museum is open daily, but remains shut on public holidays.

## SUVA'S ORIGINS

Suva was something of a backwater until the rise of local chief Cakobau, who declared himself Fiji's sovereign ruler after gaining massive sway over eastern Fiji in the mid-19th century. In an attempt to clear mounting debts while forming his government, Cakobau leased the land around Suva to the Australian Polynesia Company in the 1860s. The Australians cleared the land and drained its swamps in an unsuccessful attempt to grow cotton and sugarcane. In the 1880s, after Fiji had been ceded to the British and the capital Levuka proved too tight for expansion, two Melbourne merchants encouraged the colonial government to make Suva Fiji's capital. By the 1920s, Suva had become a flourishing colonial centre.

DAVID SUTHERLAND/ALAMY STOCK PHOTO ©

**Sailing display, Fiji Museum**

 **WHERE TO STAY IN SUVA**

**Five Princes**
The charming heritage hotel in the suburb of Tamavua is immaculately maintained and hidden amidst beautiful gardens. **$**

**Quest Suva**
Excellent business hotel with comfortable rooms, suites and serviced apartments in the heart of Suva's downtown. **$$**

**Novotel**
Luxury hotel on a gorgeous plot by a mangrove-lined bay in the western suburb of Lami. Incredible harbour views. **$$**

# Trees of Thurston Gardens

PUBLIC PARK AND BOTANICAL HUB

WESTEND61/GETTY IMAGES ©

## SUVA WALKING TOURS

For a unique journey through Suva's evolution as a cosmopolitan hub of cultures, communities and cuisines, book a two-hour excursion on foot with **Guided Walking Tours Suva**. Starting from the main bus stand and winding its way through Suva's downtown all the way to Fiji Museum, this brilliant tour familiarises you with the history of diverse peoples who migrated to Fiji and contributed to its multicultural fabric, from Polynesians in ancient times to more recent European, Chinese and Indian immigrants. The tour is conducted on Mondays, Wednesdays and Fridays twice daily, and stops at 14 landmarks along the way.

Reach out to the organisers via their Facebook page, or write to them at guidedwalksfiji@gmail.com to join a walk.

Founded in 1881 by John Thurston, governor of colonial Fiji, this botanical park marks the spot where Suva's original village stood before the surrounding peninsula was built up as Fiji's capital in the late 1880s. A rich diversity of flora, including various tropical flowering trees, palms, ferns and water plants flourish within the gardens, and visitors can walk along shaded trails to acquaint themselves with the species, many of which are clearly signposted. Don't miss the ficus tree in the garden's centre, with a pleasant seating area beneath its giant canopy. Notable architectural monuments in the park include a stone water fountain installed for public use in 1914, and a bandstand and clock tower erected in 1918 to commemorate GJ Marks, the first mayor of Suva. The gardens are next to the Suva Museum; in fact, the latter technically occupies the garden's eastern grounds. Thurston Gardens is free to visit and open all day.

# Fun & Games at Albert Park

SUVA'S CENTRAL PUBLIC GROUND

This fabulous patch of open greens (named in honour of Prince Albert, consort of Queen Victoria) was originally cleared to house a cricket field in the 1880s. It also gained the reputation of serving as an airfield when Australian aviator Charles Kingsford Smith scheduled a landing in Suva during his epic 1928 flight from the US to Australia. Over the years, Albert Park has evolved into Suva's foremost public playground, and residents turn up in droves every evening to play rugby or football on the sprawling grounds – visitors are welcome to join in. The clubhouse on the southern edge hosts power-training sessions open to walk-ins for a small fee, while two excellently maintained tennis courts in an adjacent plot can be booked through the on-site Paradiso restaurant for hourly use. You can also simply join hundreds of joggers and walkers on the 1.5km walkway around the greens, and admire the dramatic sunset as you notch up your day's step count.

**Above: Clock Tower, Thurston Gardens**

## WHERE TO EAT IN SUVA

**Bar Belle**
Popular lunchtime canteen in the HFC Stadium complex; amazing Fijian platters for meat and fish eaters and vegetarians. **$$**

**Kanu**
Fabulous preparations of seafood and meat in Fijian and international flavours; it's housed in an atmospheric heritage bungalow. **$$**

**Fong Lee**
Unassuming restaurant with an excellent selection of Cantonese fare, spanning rice, noodles, meat, fish and vegetarian dishes. **$**

# Welcome to the Grand Pacific Hotel

ICONIC ARCHITECTURAL JEWEL

This stately colonial hotel – affectionately called 'GPH' by Suva's residents – was commissioned in 1914 to house wealthy travellers and traders along transpacific maritime routes passing through Fiji. It simultaneously gained popularity with visiting officials and dignitaries of Fiji's colonial government, who stayed in the lofty suites of its ivory-white porticoed heritage building and enjoyed the hotel's fine facilities for a princely sum of 15 shillings. After hosting a train of 20th-century celebrities – King Edward VIII, Queen Elizabeth II, cricketer Don Bradman, and actors Burt Lancaster and Joan Rice, to name a few – the hotel's fortunes dwindled and it was eventually shut in 1992. It was only in 2011 that a renovation drive saw the building rise from its ashes to once again become one of the Pacific's iconic grand old hotels.

Over time, the main heritage building (which curiously served as a military barracks through its years of disuse) has undergone extensive renovation, while most rooms are now in a sensitively designed new annexe at the rear. But you don't need to check in as a guest to enjoy its neo-nostalgic ambience. The sea-facing bar and restaurant to the rear, the coffee shop and bakery out front, as well as the gym and spa are all open to day guests, so you can drop in for a few hours whenever you wish.

# Explore the Suva Municipal Market

BRIGHT COLOURS AND FRESH PRODUCE

This buzzing market is the beating heart of Suva, and a great place to spend an hour or two poking around with a camera. Rows of vegetable and fruit stalls extend over several open-air blocks, each stall sheltered under its own polythene canopy and heaped with the day's supply of products straight from the farmlands around Suva. There's also a two-storey market building next to the main bus stand housing permanent occupants. Look out for bitter gourds, breadfruit, bundles of taro and cassava, various greens such as fiddlehead ferns and spinach, and fruits such as papaya, pineapple and the orange-like kumquat. On the upper level of the market building, you can buy conical packages of yaqona (kava) roots, handy if your onward journey involves performing *sevusevu* (gift) ceremonies in villages. You can also buy kava in its powdered form in small packets, but these don't make for a worthy *sevusevu* presentation, so buy a pack only if you're planning

## SUNDAY AT THE MARKET

On the third Sunday of every month, a street looping around a downtown block on Queen Elizabeth Dr transforms into a daylong fete attracting Suva's residents in droves. The fair, which goes by the name **ROC Market**, is an initiative to promote the city's small enterprises, which set up stalls along the street for the day to sell their wares to attendees.

If your visit coincides with the month's market date, drop in for a few hours to buy handmade artisanal products, cosmetics made from natural ingredients, stylish clothing and other diverse arts and crafts. In between, you can stop at the many food-and-drink stalls to hydrate with a chilled glass of fruit juice or bite into a tasty hotdog.

## WHERE TO EAT IN SUVA

**Daikoku**
Japanese diner serving quick and light daily lunch platters; dinners are a more elaborate teppanyaki exercise for families. $$

**Maya Dhaba**
Delicious Indian vegetarian and non-vegetarian staples, including curries, kebabs, dhal and a variety of breads and rice. $

**Swagat**
Indian restaurant matching the best of curry houses in Delhi; a well-stocked bar complements its spicy and aromatic dishes. $$

to consume it by yourself. Around the market area are some grocery stores selling condiments and ingredients dedicated to specific cuisines like Chinese or Indian.

Mornings are the best time to visit the market, when buyers and sellers trade vigorously, resulting in some excellent photo-ops. On Saturday morning, an adjacent lane on the banks of a canal to the south of the market turns into a weekly **fish market**, featuring a wide array of fresh fish and other marine edibles.

## BEST SHOPPING COMPLEXES IN SUVA

**Tappoo City**
Four floors of contemporary shopping, including fashion wear, accessories, kitchenware and gadgets, topped with a busy multi-cuisine food court.

**MHCC**
A one-stop, multistorey maze of shops and kiosks within one of Suva's original downtown shopping malls, trading in endless products and services.

**Damodar City**
Suva's biggest shopping complex in the city's eastern district, with several commercial blocks housing shops, restaurants, bars and cinemas.

# Toast the Sunset at the Royal Suva Yacht Club
DRINKING AND HARBOUR VIEWS

This colonial-era establishment is a popular watering hole for yachties and locals alike. It has great sunset views looking out to Suva Harbour, augmented by the mountains of the Namosi Highlands to the right, and the distant silhouette of Beqa Island looming in front. Even without a yacht, visitors are welcome to absorb the convivial atmosphere at the bar – where everyone has a story to tell – and tuck into massive platters of food at the restaurant.

The reef fringing Suva Harbour has an interesting undersea topography, where giants waves breaking on the barriers over countless centuries have carved an intriguing maze of caverns, passages and ravines in the shallow areas down to about 20m. These ragged-edge canyons are excellent to explore on guided scuba dives, and the Yacht Club (five minutes away) is unsurprisingly the best access point for dive boats to get to the reef. **Suva Scuba** is a popular outfit that schedules fun dive trips out of the Yacht Club. Contact them via their Facebook page or suvascuba@gmail.com to book your dives.

# Seaside Strolls
WATERFRONT PROMENADE WALK

The **sea wall** is a concrete barrier that hems the Suva peninsula for its entire length along Suva Harbour, guarding the town from erosion and surges during storms. A popular place for residents to go for walks, the promenade along the sea wall can be accessed in two sections. The first stretch, about a kilometre long, begins south of Suva's port docks near the Municipal Market, then runs parallel to Queen Elizabeth Dr all the way to the contiguous premises of Holiday Inn and Grand Pacific Hotel, across the road from Albert Park.

 **WHERE TO EAT IN SUVA**

**Paradiso**
Alfresco restaurant next to Albert Park serving wood-fired pizzas, grilled seafood dishes and barbecue platters. Live music in the evenings. **$**

**Seoul Restaurant**
This restaurant at the Southern Cross Hotel does mouthwatering Korean food, and has barbecue evenings on weekends. **$**

**Eden**
This fine-dining, multi-cuisine restaurant in the suburb of Tamavua has fantastic meat, seafood and vegetarian dishes. **$$**

## FISH DIRECTORY

Get a lowdown on the most common edible fish species, as well as staple vegetables and fruits popularly used in Fijian cuisine, in **The Food Scene** (p38).

Past the two hotels, the walkways is once again accessible from the public volleyball courts, and runs for nearly 2km until merging with a stretch of mangroves off the neighbourhood of Nasese. On rainless evenings, you can watch million-dollar sunsets from the promenade.

# Chilling Out in Laucala Bay

POPULAR    SEASIDE HANGOUT

Serene **Laucala Bay** flanks the eastern side of Suva peninsula, and is hemmed to its north by the mangrove delta of the Rewa River. The best place to access these calm waters is the seawall off the Laucala Bay campus of the University of South Pacific, and a short stretch of contiguous sands that just about passes as Suva's only 'beach'. Residents turn up at both these promenades in the evenings or on weekends to have impromptu picnics, walk their dogs and shoot the breeze while Bluetooth speakers belt out the latest Fijian hits. Both places are also great for a refreshing dip in the ocean, especially at high tide when the bay fills up to the brim.

# A Splash in the Olympic Swimming Pool

SUVA'S MAIN AQUATIC HUB

Given the stark lack of beaches and public swimming spots in Suva (most of the peninsula being lined by seawalls), the only decent place to go for a swim in the city is the **Olympic Swimming Pool**. Located in the heart of town on Queen Elizabeth Dr, this 50m pool attracts large groups of kids taking swimming lessons, fitness enthusiasts of all ages pulling endless laps along the lanes, and entire families splashing about in the shallows and having a whale of a time. The pool is open to walk-in guests, from as early as 8am on weekends. The downside is that it shuts by 6pm, which rules out that refreshing evening swim after a long day of exploring the town.

## MANTAS OF THE BAY

Scientific studies conclusively proved in 2022 that Laucala Bay is home to a small population of giant oceanic manta rays. Growing to an unbelievable wingspan of up to 7m, these graceful creatures presumably roost in the lagoon to feed on large volumes of plankton pumped in by the Rewa River, which empties its catchment of highland water in the neighbouring delta.

This theory is seconded by earlier studies that have confirmed the high density of phytoplankton and zooplankton in parts of the bay. Oceanic manta rays are somersault feeders, and do stunning backflips on the water's surface as they come up for food. Occasionally, a ray might even breach the water in a spectacular leap.

### GETTING AROUND

Suva has more taxis than it has commuters. You can readily flag down a metered taxi anywhere in town, and get transported to your destination in a flash for a few dollars. Buses and minivans from Suva's main bus stand connect the city to its suburbs, such as Nausori, where the airport is located. You can also take a bus to get to Nadi; the journey takes four hours. Drivers will dish out a complimentary serving of eardrum-defying music on these rides, so carry earplugs if you're not in a mood to jive along.

# Beyond Suva

Nabalasere Waterfall

Moon Reef

Wailotua

Colo-i-Suva    Nasilai

Suva

The eastern expanse of Viti Levu is
a scantly visited area that treasures
some incredible outdoor experiences
and cultural interactions.

Unexplored by most travellers visiting Fiji, the hinterlands
thrown around Suva are a goldmine of uncharted adventures.
In these remote areas, pods of dolphins patrol tranquil ocean lagoons, quaint villages nestled in the highlands preserve crucial
stories from Fiji's history, astounding waterfalls thunder down
slate-black cliffs, and hiking trails lead up vertigo-inducing rock
outcrops. Access through the region is provided chiefly by Kings
Rd, but you will have to drive off the main carriageway every
time you wish to visit a point of interest, and follow village roads
or gravelled tracks snaking through the countryside. Along the
way, you will pass beautiful rural scenery and meet villagers
ever willing to provide you with assistance should you need it.

## TOP TIP

Stock up on essential
field supplies such as
food supplements, ready-
to-make beverages,
toiletries and medicines
before leaving Suva.

MARINA_KU/SHUTTERSTOCK ©

# A Day Out at Colo-i-Suva

RAINFOREST OASIS WITH WATERFALLS

A fabulous swathe of rainforest in the hills north of Suva, **Colo-i-Suva** is a rich repository of tropical flora and melodic avian life. At an altitude of 120m to 180m, it's a cool and peaceful respite from Suva's urban hubbub. The mahogany and pines here were planted after a period of aggressive logging in the 1940s and 1950s, in order to stabilise the topsoil without encroaching on native vegetation. Among the resident wildlife are 14 species of birds, including scarlet robins, spotted fantails, Fiji goshawks, sulphur-breasted musk parrots, Fiji warblers, golden doves and barking pigeons.

A 6.5km walking trail – featuring a few steep descents and ascents – cuts through the forest, navigating past clear natural pools and gorgeous vistas. Slipping and sliding through the forest over waterworn rocks is the **Waisila Creek**, which makes its way down to Waimanu River and forms the swimming ponds along the way. The recommended route through the park heads first along Kalabu Rd, turning up Pool Rd leading to the car park. From here, you can take the **Nature Trail to the Lower Pools** for swimming, and find a quiet spot to sit and enjoy your packed lunch. It's then a sweaty uphill walk back to the main road via the **Falls Trail**. The loop takes about two hours to complete, not counting stops.

The park is open seven days a week, between 8am and 4pm. Taxis take less than 30 minutes to get here from Suva's centre, and will wait a couple of hours to take you back.

# Excursion to Nasilai

TRADITIONAL CRAFT AND CHRISTIANITY

The lush delta of the Rewa River, Fiji's largest inland waterway, is a patchwork of mangrove forests held together by a network of canals and river channels defining the entire southwestern bulge of Viti Levu. Tucked away in these riverine wetlands are a few interesting villages that can be explored on day trips from Suva. The most popular among these is **Nasilai**, a settlement well-known for its pottery. The craft is a major source of income for the village and, when large orders are placed, everyone participates in the making process, helping to collect and prepare the clay and make the pots. Close to the village is the **Naililili Catholic Mission**, built by French missionaries at the turn of the 20th century, featuring stained-glass windows imported from Europe but incorporating Fijian writing and imagery.

## JOSKE'S THUMB

Located about 15km west of Suva, this craggy pinnacle shoots into the sky in the shape of a giant thumb, dominating the volcanic mountains bordering Namosi Highlands. Named after an Australian businessperson who started the first sugar mill in Fiji, the outcrop is about 440m high and fosters a rich biosphere of tropical plants and bird species.

Climbing the summit is not for everyone; legend has it that even Sir Edmund Hillary was defeated in his first attempt to climb Joske's Thumb.

Hikes in the area can be arranged via **Fiji Rucksack Club**, a Facebook community that organises regular excursions from Suva. Some of these outings are combined with cultural interactions, meals and kava sessions in local villages.

 **SCENIC DRIVES BEYOND SUVA**

**Nausori to Natovi**
This stretch of Kings Rd passes through almost 40km of lush rainforests, interspersed with small villages and drive-through towns.

**Silana to Volivoli**
Some drivers continue from Takalana Bay to Volivoli in northern Viti Levu along the gravelled foreshore road going past Silana village.

**Burenitu to Nabalasere**
This fantastic off-road journey winds through beautiful highland terrain and passes tiny hamlets en route to Nabalasere waterfall.

## THE TRANSPORT HUB OF NAUSORI

The township of Nausori, on the eastern banks of the Rewa River, is home to the country's second-largest airport servicing Suva. It's a busy service centre and transport hub for agricultural and manufacturing workers shuttling between their Suva workplaces and village residences every day.

Nausori was built around a sugar mill that operated here for eight decades, until the 1950s when Fiji's sugar industry shifted to western Viti Levu.

However, the town's strategic location as a transit point retained its civic relevance, and spurred the growth of satellite neighbourhoods that now line most of the 20km stretch between Nausori and Suva. Even if you don't have a flight to catch, a stroll through town offers an interesting perspective into Fijian suburbia.

Dolphins, Takalana Bay

# Descend into Snake God Cave

SHRINE OF INTRIGUING RITES

This magnificent cave system – one of Fiji's largest – is located in **Wailotua** village, about 75km from Suva along Kings Rd. The name Snake God Cave is derived from six glittering stalactites in the shape of snakes' heads. During times of tribal war, the village would pack up en masse and seek shelter in the cave's pitch-black labyrinth. Certain places within the caverns were used for human sacrifice, while a partner's fidelity was put to test in other spots (the two are not related). The cavern culminates in a huge chamber inhabited by a colony of rare blossom bats.

There are no formal arrangements to visit the caves, but you can always approach residents of Wailotua to arrange a guide for you. Most guides are surprisingly good storytellers, and provide detailed commentaries on the cave and its associated legends as they show you around. Don't forget to bring a sulu cloth to cover your legs, as well as a torch to illuminate the dark recesses of the cave.

 **SCENIC DRIVES BEYOND SUVA**

**Suva to Colo-i-Suva**
Passing Suva's northern suburb of Tamavua, this drive ascends through sections of rainforest with views of Suva Harbour in the distance.

**Sawani to Naga**
This beautiful off-road adventure passes emerald forests featuring scarlet African tulip blossoms, with views of distant valleys and ranges.

**Nabutautau to Sigatoka**
Unpaved logging trails join up with a hill road, which bears with the Sigatoka River while descending from the highlands to the Coral Coast.

# Moon Reef Dolphin Safari

SOCIALISE WITH SPINNERS

One of eastern Viti Levu's most underexplored yet exciting outdoor activities plays out every morning in the placid waters of Takalana Bay, two hours by road from Suva. In a shallow atoll called **Moon Reef**, pods of spinner dolphins spend the daylight hours foraging for food, and it's possible to see them on a leisurely motorboat safari. Attracted by the sound of overboard engines, the dolphins race playfully with the boats, entertaining watchers on board by repeatedly breaching the water and then diving back into the water, where they briefly assemble in circular formation before surfacing again. The waters of Takalana Bay are exceptionally clear, and you will hardly lose sight of the animals, whether on the surface or at depth. Local regulations prohibit visitors from jumping into the water when the dolphins are around. But safari boats will usually take you in between sighting sessions to snorkel at the channel that serves as the passage into the atoll. Here you can hover peacefully over brilliant coral bommies and walls – remember to bring your snorkelling gear along.

It's easy to do the dolphin safari on a day trip out of Suva. Drive along Kings Rd to Korovou, 50km north of the capital, then turn right from the roundabout and go another 35km. Once you cross Natovi Landing, the final 12km of this arterial road is on a gravelled surface. For a very special overnighting experience out in the countryside, consider spending a night at **Natalei** village, from where the boats depart every morning. Follow Takalana Bay's community tourism project via their **Dolphin Watching Fiji** Facebook page. Alternatively, email them at takalana@gmail com for overnight reservations and safari bookings.

# Visit Nabalasere Waterfall

WATERFALL HIKE AND SWIMMING

Located deep in Viti Levu's forested heartland, Nabalasere (also known as Savulelele) might just be Fiji's most spectacular waterfall. Walking through the forest, you will hear the thunderous roar of water long before you reach the waterfall. But the most dramatic moment comes when the jungle suddenly parts to reveal a smooth, deep swimming hole scalloped out of the rocks by the falling water. As you climb

---

## LOMAIVITI JUMPOFFS

A string of boat landings along Viti Levu's eastern coast provide quick and easy access to the islands of the **Lomaiviti** group (p121). The main piers are located at Natovi (for Ovalau), Bau (for Leleuvia) and Nakelo (for Toberua).

## BEST PLACES TO STAY NEAR MOON REEF

**Takalana Bay Retreat**
High on a lookout near Silana village is this two-room community-run homestay, with wide-open views of Takalana Bay. $

**Natalei Eco Lodge**
Featuring cute eco-huts lining Takalana Bay's black-sand beach, this resort is the starting point for Moon Reef boat safaris. $

**Tailevu Hotel**
Located in Korovou, this unfussy hotel works as a convenient night stop if you're continuing towards northern Viti Levu. $

---

### PACKING ESSENTIALS FOR NABUTAUTAU

**Hiking shoes**
Sturdy footwear is needed to walk along rough and slippery pony trails, negotiate steep terrain and cross rivers that are knee-deep in places.

**Sun & rain gear**
The weather can change from hot, sweaty and blindingly sunny to damp, cold and rainy within a few minutes – and without any notice.

**Medicine kit**
Carry all prescription medicines, as well as some basic over-the-counter pills and creams for aches, fever, diarrhoea, allergies etc.

## WHY I LOVE VITI LEVU

**Anirban Mahapatra**, writer

As a resident of Suva, within shouting distance of Viti Levu's exciting activities, I never pass up an opportunity to embark on my next adventure across the island.

My three top outdoor jams here are the invigorating highland hike to Nabutautau, the spine-chilling shark dives at Pacific Harbour, and rafting down the Navua River's upper valley.

My best three recreational experiences, on the other hand, would be a multiday scenic drive around the perimeter of Queens Rd and Kings Rd, resort-hopping along the gorgeous Coral Coast, and feasting on gourmet food and boozy liquid delights in the joyous restaurants and bars of Nadi and Denarau.

higher, the massive falls are slowly revealed, dropping nearly 70m into the huge pool. It's an extraordinary spot for a swim, so feel free to jump in. If you're feeling brave, walk around the bottom of the cliff to stand in a recess behind the falling curtain of water.

Getting here involves a long day trip out of Suva, or you can weave it in as a stopover on your journey to northern Viti Levu. Journeying along Kings Rd, turn left at Burenitu village, about an hour's drive from Korovou. From here, the gravelled road (navigable by sturdy non-4WD vehicles) meanders inland for about 30 minutes, crossing the healthcare centre at Nasavu before turning right towards Nabalasere. The access to the waterfall is via a 1km forest walk on the other side of the village from the parking area. You will need to arrange for permission to enter the village – Suva-based **Talanoa Treks** can help you with the formalities, and even arrange a car with guide out of Suva if you wish to simply sit back and enjoy the outing. Remember to carry lunch and water, as there's no restaurant in these remote parts.

# Trek to Nabutautau

HIGHLAND HIKE AND HISTORY

High up in the forested mountains of interior Viti Levu is **Nabutautau**, a quaint village with a unique place in Fiji's history. It was here that a British missionary named Thomas Baker was killed and eaten by the local population in 1867, marking the last recorded incident of cannibalism in Fiji. Today, the village is part of a successful community tourism project operating in close association with Suva-based **Talanoa Treks**, which runs a highly popular trek into the intriguing heartland of Fiji's landscape and culture.

The trekking itinerary stretches over three days, and departs on set dates (usually once a month) between May and October. Driving out of Suva in 4WD vehicles, trekkers make a three-hour journey to the village of **Naga**, where they are graciously hosted by the village community for the night. Early next morning, guests begin an intense seven-hour trek that passes through 11km of challenging but breathtakingly beautiful undulating terrain, spanning undulating savannas, bouldery mountain streams and mossy forest trails. The first scheduled stop en route is at a river crossing by the site of an ancient village, not far from the sharing stone, a large slab of rock where it is possible to learn graphic details of Baker's fate at the ceremonial feast. The second stop is under a shaded grove on the banks of a lazy stream, ideal for lunch followed by a refreshing swim.

 **BEST NATURE PHOTO-OPS IN EASTERN VITI LEVU**

**Highland savanna**
Golden grasslands extend over the hills in the first part of the Naga to Nabutautau trek, before dropping down to an emerald river valley.

**Moon Reef**
The technicolour atolls of Moon Reef sparkle beneath the crystal-clear waters of Takalana Bay, perfect for dazzling GoPro snapshots.

**Nabalasere**
To convey a sense of the waterfall's scale, have a friend pose like a tiny dot on a rock platform as you take a photo from a distance.

**Nabutautau**

## HIGHLAND FOOD & LODGING

During overnight stays on your hike, you will be served wholesome and delicious dinners and breakfasts by the host communities of Naga and Nabutautau villages. Elaborate as these spreads may be, the menu mainly revolves around locally harvested vegetables, given the remoteness of these settlements from urban centres.

It's not uncommon to have a few different takes on the humble pumpkin or *rourou* (taro) leaves served during a meal – the monotony perhaps broken with a sprinkling of canned tuna on one of the variations. Other dishes usually include roti, dhal and vegetables such as potato or eggplant.

Mattresses and pillows are provided in the village community hall; bring your own sleeping bag or liner to add a layer of comfort.

The final part of the hike involves a treacherous 200m ascent along a near-vertical hillside, which finally spills into a valley and leads into Nabutautau. After catching their breath over snacks and tea, guests are shown around key sites in the village, including the ceremonial *bure* as well as the stone memorial raised in memory of Baker (in 2003, believing they had suffered a spell of bad luck as a result of their ancestors' karma, the people of Nabutautau held a ceremony to apologise to the descendants of the missionary).

The rest of the evening is spent over a kava session, where village residents recount the story of Baker's death and the dramatic circumstances that led to his demise. At some point during the storytelling session, the original axe that was used to kill the missionary is brought out and passed around for closer inspection.

On the third day, guests embark on a gruelling yet thoroughly enjoyable circuit hike through the forests and hills around Nabutautau. The trail drops more than 300m down the valley of a river, passing a delightful natural water slide along the way where you can enjoy the juvenile thrill of sliding down a stony waterfall and plunge into a deep pool of clean mountain water. Post lunch, it's a steep climb back to the village, where guests hop into 4WD vehicles and make their way out of the wilderness via a network of logging trails and village roads, eventually joining with Queens Rd near Sigatoka.

### GETTING AROUND

For explorations into the highlands, tour organisers will always provide you with complimentary transport from and to Suva. For road trips along the coast or inland areas, it is best to self-drive (as that allows you to travel at your own pace) or hire taxis from Suva.

Using public transport, such as buses and minivans, can be a compelling but time-consuming adventure, given that connections are not always frequent and timetables are flexible, to say the least.

# SUNCOAST

The northern coast of Viti Levu remains largely unexplored, but local tourism entrepreneurs have recently made efforts to attract visitors to this secluded part of the island. To contend with Coral Coast, its southern counterpart, the shoreline now goes by the moniker of Suncoast. Geographically, this new branding covers the section of coastline from the vicinity of Viti Levu Bay, near the settlement of Rakiraki, to the mining town of Tavua further east. Along the way are a few tertiary roads that lead into the highlands of the Nakauvadra Range. According to local legend, the mountains are home to the snake god Degei, creator of all the islands. The closing and opening of his eyes prompt night and day, and thunder is said to be Degei turning in his sleep. The weather along Suncoast is similar to western Viti Levu – dry and suited to growing sugar cane, but far windier.

## TOP TIP

If you are heading offshore or into the mountains, it is a good idea to stock up on provisions in Rakiraki. Amenities in town include taxi stands, ATMs accepting international cards, supermarkets, a market for fresh produce and fast-food restaurants that can pack a takeaway lunch for road trips.

LOUIELEA/SHUTTERSTOCK ©

**Rakiraki, Viti Levu**

THE LEGEND OF UDREUDRE

Barely a kilometre west of Rakiraki, just off Kings Rd, is the underwhelming but intriguing tomb of Udreudre, a chief who went down in history as Fiji's most infamous cannibal. According to popular lore, the 19th-century chief had a fondness for devouring prisoners of war.

While the numbers vary between accounts, it is estimated that he ate anywhere between 99 and 999 people in his lifetime. A midway figure of 872 is widely presumed accurate, going by a row of stones discovered near Udreudre's former home, where he supposedly placed a stone for every person he ate.

So compelling was his legend that even the *Guinness Book of World Records* listed Udreudre as the world's hungriest cannibal.

# St Francis Xavier Catholic Mission

CHURCH OF THE BLACK CHRIST

About 25km southeast of Rakiraki, along Kings Rd en route from Korovou, stands a stocky church that looks like it was airlifted straight out of western Europe. Overlooking the waters of Viti Levu Bay, this 1917 Catholic mission is famous for a mural behind the altar (painted by French artist Jean Charlot in 1962) that features the image of a black Christ. Painted as a triptych inspired by biblical scenes, the mural depicts Christ on the cross, draped in a printed *masi* cloth made of bark, with a *tanoa* (ceremonial kava bowl) positioned at his feet. Indigenous Fijians are shown offering mats and *tabua* (whale's tooth) to the saviour, while Indo-Fijians are shown presenting flowers and oxen. St Francis Xavier, after whom the mission is named, also finds a place in the mural, as does an altar boy.

# Visit a Bee Farm

APIARY TOUR IN RAKIRAKI

On the outskirts of Rakiraki, a few hundred metres past Udreudre's tomb, stands **Waitika Bee Farm**. Noted as one

## WHERE TO STAY IN RAKIRAKI

**Tanoa Rakiraki Hotel**
The Rakiraki branch of this Fijian chain of business hotels has smart rooms and a refreshing swimming pool to relax in. **$$**

**Volivoli Beach Resort**
This beachfront property has premium villas, and the in-house Ra Divers is one of Viti Levu's leading scuba operations. **$$**

**Dua Dua Beach Resort**
Comfortable living, wholesome dining and an in-house beauty and wellness spa are the top draws at this beachside resort. **$$**

of the flag-bearers of Fiji's small-scale apiculture industry, the farm has more than 50 beehives located in the slopes of hills north of the Nakauvadra Range. The farm produces limited batches of premium honey, as well as fine condiments such as honey butter and chilli honey. For tourists exploring the Suncoast, the farm also offers an educational bee tour, a three-hour experience where guests can participate in honey extraction with smokers and study the behaviour and characteristics of bees in their habitat. You can even get a crash course on how to roll your own beeswax candles. Contact the proprietors via their Facebook page, or through waitika@live.com to book a tour.

Apiculture is a relatively modern discipline in Fiji. After all, bees are not native to the country, and were likely introduced to the islands by beekeepers from Australia in the 1870s. It was only in the first two decades of the 21st century that beekeeping took off as an organised small-scale industry. Honey produced in Fiji is poly-floral (sourced by bees from different flowers), and is unique in terms of taste and content due to the country's unique climate and soil constituents, which have an influence on the quality and composition of the nectar. Beehives used by Fiji's beekeepers are of the Langstroth design, where bees build honeycombs within frames that can be easily removed for extraction. Most apiaries are concentrated in northern and western Viti Levu, as well as in Vanua Levu and Taveuni.

# Ocean Views at Volivoli

VISTAS AND ADVENTURES

The northernmost cape of Viti Levu – referred to as **Volivoli** for all touristic purposes – is where most of Rakiraki's accommodation options are concentrated. Driving into Rakiraki along Kings Rd, about 5km east of town, you will see the well-signposted turnoff to Ellington Wharf, Volivoli's main pier, branching right. This is where resorts collect their guests for a 15-minute boat ride across to Nananu-i-Ra island (p92), and dive shops pick up the day's divers heading to the Vatu-i-Ra marine conservation area (p92). Apart from being a vantage point for embarking on aquatic adventures, Volivoli woos visitors with gorgeous ocean views that open northward towards Nananu-i-Ra, and extend both to the left and right.

## GETTING AROUND

Public buses plying Kings Rd connect Rakiraki to Suva via Korovou, and to Nadi via Ba and Lautoka. However, connections can be infrequent, with long delays.

Taxis can be hired out of Rakiraki to move around the Suncoast, and explore all points of tourist interest along the main thoroughfares.

# Beyond Suncoast

Venture beyond Rakiraki's urban patch to climb lofty mountain peaks or dive into pristine ocean waters.

Suncoast ● Nananu-i-Ra
Nadarivatu
Navai ● ● Mt Tomanivi

The northern highlands of Viti Levu flank the Suncoast to the south, and are defined by the mountains of the Nakauvadra Range. They contain vast swathes of high-altitude montane forest that comprise important biospheres for highland flora and fauna. The island's biggest rivers – Sigatoka, Navua, Rewa and Ba – all originate in these highlands, before winding their way down to the sea in different directions.

To the north of the Suncoast is an ocean channel named Bligh Waters (through which HMS *Bounty* captain William Bligh canoed his way to safety). Over 100 sq km of these waters – home to unspoiled coral reefs and lagoons – are designated as the Vatu-i-Ra conservation park, managed by local coastal communities.

## TOP TIP

Accommodation is scarce on Nananu-i-Ra. The hike to Mt Tomanivi can be done as a day trip from Volivoli.

J.S. LAMY/SHUTTERSTOCK ©

**THE PROTECTED WATERS OF VATU-I-RA**

The Vatu-i-Ra conservation park covers about 110 sq km of ocean channel within Bligh Waters, extending around Vatu-i-Ra island. Since being designated as a park in 2012, almost 80% of these waters have become a no-take zone.

The communities who have historically depended on the waters for their subsistence now oversee and manage the park, and have access to designated fisheries on its fringes. Vatu-i-Ra provides fabulous diving opportunities amidst its coral reefs and pinnacles. You can easily visit the park from Nananu-i-Ra or Volivoli – a nominal $15 fee covers visits for a whole year. This revenue goes directly into incentivising the park-monitoring activities by the local communities, apart from funding tertiary education for local children.

Nananu-i-Ra island

## Nananu-i-Ra Island Escape
WINDSURFING AND KITESURFING

This pocket-sized, hilly island in the northernmost tip of Viti Levu (a 15-minute boat ride from Volivoli) is surrounded by scalloped bays, white-sand beaches and mangroves. There are no roads or villages here, and accommodation is simple and scant. The original inhabitants were wiped out by disease and tribal war, and their land was sold by surviving heirs, mostly to Fijians of European descent. Cattle grazing in the past cleared much of the dense vegetation, resulting in rolling hills of grass.

Apart from providing access to the dive sites of Vatu-i-Ra, Nananu-i-Ra is renowned for its offshore reefs, windsurfing and kiteboarding. It can get very windy on the island's eastern side from June through August – when southeasterly trade winds blow at 15 to 20 knots – and from late October to December at the start of the cyclone season. The narrow strip of land separating the west (**Front Beach**) from the east (**Back Beach**) is only 200m wide, and whichever way

 **WHERE TO STAY & DIVE IN NANANU-I-RA**

**Macdonalds Beach Cottages**
A smart and cosy collection of villas and rooms, with numerous activities, including kiteboarding and scuba diving. $

**Dolphin Island**
Located on a private island off Volivoli, this five-star resort offers easy access for aquatic activities in the nearby waters. $$$

**Kai Viti Divers**
The on-site dive shop at Macdonalds beach cottages can arrange dives in Bligh Waters and the Vatu-i-Ra conservation park. $

NADI, SUVA & VITI LEVU

THE GUIDE

92

the wind blows, it's only a short walk to the calmer side.

Walking tracks across the hills offer a good chance to stretch your legs. Hiking to the top provides wonderful views of Viti Levu. A common sight from the island's southern side is billowing white clouds swallowing the Nakauvadra mountain range. The grassy hilltops also provide bird's-eye views of the surrounding reefs. If you time it right with the tides, you can walk around the island in about four to five hours (passing the mangroves at low tide). Parts of this hike are rocky, so sturdy hiking shoes (and reef shoes for in-water wading) are recommended.

## Jaunts in the Hills

TACKLE FIJI'S HIGHEST PEAK

In the dry season, you can head up from Rakiraki to the forestry settlement of **Nadarivatu** (30km southeast of the mining town of Tavua, branching left off Kings Rd). From here, you can hike to the top of Fiji's highest mountain, the 1323m **Mt Tomanivi** (formerly called Mt Victoria) or to nearby **Mt Lomalagi** ('sky' or 'heaven' in Fijian). The Lomalagi hike takes about three hours return and has great views. You can also access Tomanivi from the village of **Navai**, which stands 8km further southeast of Nadarivatu. This is a longer hike, and can take up to five hours return. The last half of the climb is practically a lesson in rock climbing and can be very slippery, so don't just attempt this section on a whim.

Guides for the hikes can be hired informally in both villages. However, it is recommended that you come here with a tour guide, who can arrange a *sevusevu* (gift) ceremony for you and sort out logistics in case you want to spend the night in a village homestay.

The Wainibuka and Wainimala Rivers (eventually merging to form the Rewa River) originate around these scenic highlands, as does the Sigatoka River. Past Navai, the road going southeast eventually crosses the placid reservoir of Monasavu Dam before connecting with the inland road that leads all the way to Suva. With your own 4WD vehicle and guide, this can turn out to be a compelling off-road adventure, but you might need to schedule an overnight stop at Navai.

### A FULL-CIRCLE ROAD TRIP

Driving westward for about 45km from Rakiraki along Kings Rd, you reach the quaint mining town of **Tavua**, the site of Fiji's only gold mine. About 25km past Tavua lies the sugar-producing town of **Ba**. Southwest of Ba, some 35km away, is **Lautoka**, from where Nadi is 25km further south.

This route constitutes the northwestern arc of a 460km road circuit around Viti Levu – the other two sections being the 180km stretch between Nadi and Suva, and the 150km section from Suva to Rakiraki. With your own vehicle, this can be a delightful road trip, taking in all the sights and activities along the island's periphery. Allow a minimum of five days for the drive, scheduling stops in Natadola, Pacific Harbour, Suva and Rakiraki.

### GETTING AROUND

Journeys into the Nakauvadra Range and the highlands to the south of the Suncoast will require you to hire a 4WD. The dirt roads leading up into mountain terrain are difficult to access with sedans, hatchbacks and other 2WD vehicles.

# MAMANUCA & YASAWA

## FIJI'S MOST POPULAR TOURIST TRAIL

Pretty as a picture postcard, these islands attract the lion's share of inbound travellers and remain busy throughout the year.

⚓ Suva

Replete with tropical beauty, Mamanuca and Yasawa constitute a slender archipelago of about 50 islands marking Fiji's western boundary. Easy access from Nadi's international airport, and a generous supply of rustling green palms, sparkling white sands and blinding blue waters, mean these two subgroups attract disproportionately large volumes of tourists compared to the country's other regions.

There are several other reasons for this raging popularity. Mamanuca, to the south of the archipelago, has some of the most luxurious resorts in Fiji, ideal for families looking to spend a fun-filled holiday while splurging on creature comforts. The 20-odd coral atolls – scattered across a large lagoon formed between the Malolo Barrier Reef and Viti Levu – promise impressive surf breaks and vast numbers of colourful fish in snorkelling sites. Yasawa, further north, amps up the essence of raw adventure in the marine wilderness that surrounds its islands. Here you can snorkel and dive with sharks, swim with manta rays and discover hauntingly beautiful limestone caves hiding turquoise pools within.

Mamanuca and Yasawa are an eden open to all, and for many tourists a Fijian holiday often simply translates to a week of island hopping here. You will always find accommodation (with matchless sea views) to fit your budget, and an itinerary to suit the time you have. And the overall enjoyment, it goes without saying, will be priceless.

DON MAMMOSER/SHUTTERSTOCK ©

Above: Snorkelling, Mamanuca; right: Malolo, Mamanuca

**THE MAIN AREAS**

| **MAMANUCA** | **KUATA** | **DRAWAQA** | **YAQETA** |
|---|---|---|---|
| Luxury resorts scattered in azure waters. | Dive and snorkel with sharks. | Snorkel with manta rays in winter. | Quaint villages and placid lagoons. |
| p100 | p106 | p111 | p115 |

95

# Find Your Way

Travelling in Mamanuca and Yasawa is largely dependent on ferry lines operating out of Port Denarau from Viti Levu. Ferry schedules are meticulously planned to drop and pick up guests at fixed island stops along the run.

**Drawaqa, p111**
Bob lazily in the drifting current of a shallow ocean channel while curious manta rays ascend to the surface to take a good look at you.

**Kuata, p106**
Sharks, sharks and more sharks: the waters here are home to several species of the toothy sea predator swimming at various depths.

Gunu
Naviti
Manta Rays
Naukacuvu
Viwa

Nalauwaki
Waya
Waya Levu
Natawa
Yamata
Wayasewa (Wayalailai)

Navadra
Kadomo

Tokoriki
Tavua
Monuriki
Mana
Castaway Island
Malolo Islar
Solevu
Malolo Barrier Reef
Malolola (Plantatic Island)
San Re
Treasu Islar (Elevu
Tavaru
Navula Reef

**Mamanuca, p100**
Laze in style in a lavish resort, tuck into delicious international cuisine and enjoy a variety of water sports and beach activities.

## YASAWA FLYER

The lifeline of these islands, especially the Yasawa group, this brilliantly managed catamaran service departs Port Denarau at 8.45am daily, stopping at 11 mooring points along its shuttle to the far north of Yasawa. It returns to Denarau around 6pm. The journey takes four to five hours each way.

## AIR CHARTERS

If you are pressed for time (or lack the patience to match the Flyer's schedule), sea planes and helicopters provide quick but costly access across the islands. Ask your resort to arrange a charter in advance, as they may not be available immediately.

## WATER TAXIS

A few smaller water-taxi services depart Port Denarau at fixed hours through the day, carrying passengers around dedicated island circuits within the Mamanuca group. These services have quicker turnaround times compared to the *Yasawa Flyer.*

Yasawa-i-Rara

Bukama

*Vawa*

*Yasawa*

Nabukeru

Sawa-i-Lau

Nacula

*Nacula*

Enadala

qeta

### Yaqeta, p115

Snorkel in the clear waters of spectacular shallow lagoons, exploring a variety of seascapes such as seagrass beds and coral bommies.

*South Pacific Ocean*

*Malake*

Rakiraki

Vitawa

Togowere

Tavua

Rabula

Korovou

Naseyani

*Bligh Water*

Nailaga

Vatukoula

Burelevu

Nakubu Reef

Ba

Covuli Reef

Nadarivatu

Vanuakula

unaqiliqili Reef

Vitogo

Vakabuli

*Ba River*

Lautoka

*Koroyanitu National Heritage Park*

Toge

Navala

Nagatagata

Lauwaki

Viseisei

Navilawa

Nadrau

Koro-ni-O

*Vaturu Dam*

*Monasavu Dam*

Naboutini

Namaka

Natawa

Bukuya

Nabutautau

arewa

Namulomulo

Nadi

Korovuto

0    20 km
0    10 miles

Keiyasi

# Plan Your Time

Always factor extra time into your itinerary to account for ferry journeys. The *Yasawa Flyer* only arrives and departs the islands once daily each way.

Beach, Malolo (p101)

FRITZ16/SHUTTERSTOCK ©

## Only a Weekend

● From Denarau, hop across to one of the **resort islands** (p101) in Mamanuca, such as **Malolo, Mana, Serenity Island** or **Treasure Island.**

● Spend your day kayaking, snorkelling or diving in the waters of the lagoon, while treating yourself to a stylish resort experience.

● On your second day, catch the tall waves at **Cloudbreak** or **Restaurants** (p105) for some top-notch surfing, or go for a relaxed session of kayaking and snorkelling.

● Later in the afternoon, ride a motorboat out to **Cloud 9** (p102), the mid-sea bar and club that promises an unforgettable partying experience surrounded by sparkling blue waters.

**Seasonal Highlights**

Mamanuca and Yasawa are visited all year; there's no low season to travel to these islands. Holidays such as the New Year week see a massive influx of tourists.

**JANUARY**

The days are steamy hot and the evenings are clammy, with a chance of scattered thundershowers across the islands.

**MARCH**

There's a noticeable dip in daytime temperatures, though the occasional storm can still result in choppy seas and transport delays.

**APRIL**

The skies begin to clear as rains depart, ushering in cool days with mellow sunshine. The water temperature drops by a few degrees.

## Three or Four Days to Play

● Checking out of Mamanuca, venture north to **Kuata** (p106), the first island in the Yasawa chain.

● Slip into your wetsuit and get an adrenaline rush snorkelling with curious **reef sharks**, or dive deeper for an encounter with fearsome **bull sharks** and graceful **lemon sharks** (p107).

● In the evening, be informed of the importance of shark conservation by Kuata's marine-science team over drinks.

● On your final day, attempt the vigorous climb to the top of **Vatuvula** (p110) on Wayasewa island, across the narrow ocean channel from Kuata, and reward yourself with astonishing ocean panoramas from the summit of the outcrop.

## If You Have a Week

● With a week up your sleeve, the next stop on your Yasawa itinerary is the island of **Drawaqa** (p111), adjacent to a narrow ocean channel that promises a snorkelling date with **manta rays** through the winter months.

● Venturing further north, the *Yasawa Flyer* will drop you at **Yaqeta** (p115), from where you can embark on snorkelling trips to see pipefish hidden in reef crevices off **Nanuya Levu** or giant sea cucumbers slumbering on grassy sea beds at **Blue Lagoon** (p116).

● Last, head to the limestone caves of **Sawa-i-Lau** (p119) for a swim in its secret ocean pools.

| MAY | JULY | SEPTEMBER | DECEMBER |
|---|---|---|---|
| Water visibility begins to improve for **diving and snorkelling**. The **manta rays** arrive in the passage off Drawaqa island on their annual winter visit. | This is a fabulous time for **stargazing**, thanks to clear skies on cool winter nights and long spells of good weather across the islands. | This is the last window of opportunity to **snorkel with manta rays** off Drawaqa island, before they migrate away until May the following year. | Resorts get packed to the brim with visitors, and the islands (especially in Mamanuca) get busier than ever until January. |

# MAMANUCA

● Mamanuca

✪ Suva

The Mamanuca islands tick every box on the checklist for a holiday in tropical paradise. With romance and relaxation aplenty, and a large number of fantastic resorts on offer, this tiny cluster of islands is one of Fiji's most travelled destinations. In the brochure-blue shallows of the surrounding ocean lagoon, kaleidoscopic corals and masses of marine life await snorkellers and divers. Despite the overall calm at the surface, the waters here are also home to a collection of world-class surf breaks.

Back on their sandy microcosms, the islands have a wide range of facilities, activities and environments to satisfy everyone from families travelling with children to couples looking for privacy and solitude. The tourism industry here has long-standing links with local communities. Two of the biggest resort islands, Malolo and Mana, support villages with revenue generated from tourism, while most other properties lease their land and hire staff from local communities.

## TOP TIP

Mamanuca is a small group of islands and can easily be explored from a single base. Malolo and Mana have the most connections to nearby islands and activity spots, so stay on one of these if you're keen to move around the islands and sample a little bit of everything.

Kadomo

Vomo Island

Tokoriki

Samu Reef

Vunaqiliqili Reef

Tavua Island

Modriki Island

Tivua Island

Mana Island

North Beach

Treasure Island

Beachcomber Island

Bounty Island

Sunset Beach

Mana Island Airstrip ✈

Nukasiga Sand Bar

South Sea Island

Navini Island

Castaway Island

Malolo Island

Solevu

Malamala Island

Nadi Bay

✈ Malolo Lailai Airport

South Pacific Ocean

Malolo Barrier Reef

⛴ Cloud 9

Korovuto

Wilkes Passage

Tavarua Island

Yako

Queens Rd

Ⓝ8    5 miles / 10 km

_FR/TZI6/SHUTTERSTOCK ©_

**Malolo**

# Island Hopping in Mamanuca

SUN, SEA AND SAND UNLIMITED

A stunning celebration of natural beauty, the islands of Mamanuca resemble brilliant blotches of gold and green dabbed onto a sapphire-blue canvas by the impressionistic brush of a celestial painter. The skies here are azure with ivory-white clouds, and the sun shines on the sand and sea to create striking brilliance. Gleaming in the lucid depths below the water's surface are vibrant coral growths and brightly coloured fish.

Most people feel spoilt for choice while picking the ideal island to spend time here. It helps to go by a rough categorisation based on the purpose of your holiday. **Malolo** and **Mana** are the biggest and busiest islands, where you can expect a convivial atmosphere and plenty of long-stay families for company. **South Sea Island**, **Bounty Island**, **Beachcomber Island** and **Treasure Island** are ragingly popular with day-trippers, thanks to their proximity to Denarau. These are also among the first stops made by the _Yasawa Flyer_ catamaran on its daily journey. **Navini** and **Vomo**, on the other hand, cater exclusively to guests who pay premium tariffs to enjoy the serenity and privacy of these retreats in the absence of distracting crowds.

## BEST RESORTS FOR PRIVACY

**Wadigi Island Lodge**
This five-star island occupies an exclusive spot on a tiny outcrop across from Malolo island, and welcomes children as guests. $$$

**Tadrai**
This adults-only luxury resort is located on the secluded northeastern side of Mana island, away from the busy central patch. $$$

**Likuliku Lagoon**
Hidden away in an isolated bay to the northeast of Malolo island, this premium resort features a collection of overwater villas. $$$

### MAMANUCA FROM DENARAU

If you aren't staying on a resort island, you can conveniently explore Mamanuca on day trips from **Port Denarau** (p55). Pick your accommodation from a wider selection of hotels and resorts across Nadi and Denarau.

## ACTIVITIES OPERATORS FOR MAMANUCA

**South Sea Cruises**
This outfit runs tons of tours, trips and cruises from Denarau to islands in the Mamanuca and Yasawa groups.

**Captain Cook Cruises**
Day trips, sunset cruises, overnight stays, and three-night cruises covering Mamanuca and the southern Yasawa islands.

**Whale's Tale**
Intimate seven-hour cruises on a 100ft schooner through the Mamanucas, with Champagne breakfast and free booze.

## EXPLORING MALOLO ISLAND

If you have time to visit only one of Mamanuca's islands (or are just too confused to choose from the many options), set your sights on Malolo. The biggest island in the group, Malolo is home to a bunch of resorts – from busy family-oriented affairs to plush romantic hideaways – that offer a variety of accommodation and luxury. Activities wise, **Malolo Island Resort** is a clear favourite, offering a bouquet of water- and land-based experiences such as snorkelling trips, dolphin-watching safaris, diving, line fishing, walks to the island's hilltop viewpoint, and Fijian cooking lessons. Day-trippers get free access to the swimming pool, as well as complimentary lunch (one beer or cocktail included) at the fabulous terrace restaurant.

# Party at Cloud 9

FLOATING CLUB AND BAR

A two-level pontoon bobbing all by itself on the waters of a sapphire lagoon, **Cloud 9** (cloud9.com. fj) promises guests a thrilling party experience in a spectacular mid-sea location. There's a fantastically stocked bar here, where bartenders shake up tempting cocktails to go with yummy wood-fired pizzas, and the ambience is set by visiting DJs who bring the house to its feet. What's more, this unique fun zone is carbon neutral in its day-to-day operations, relying exclusively on solar power and having stringent waste-disposal protocols in place. Apart from the raucous partying, you can also spend some of your time here doing a **jet-ski** run to nearby islands or buckling up for a session of parasailing (those under the influence, though, would be denied a shot at these sports).

To get to Cloud 9, book a seat on one of its boats departing Denarau at 9am and 1pm. Return trips are at 2pm and 6pm. A $229 package includes return transfers as well as a $60 bar tab. Note that the place shuts at sundown, in order to ferry guests back to the safety of their island homes before nightfall.

### ACTIVITIES DAY TRIPS

Most activities offered across Mamanuca's resort islands can be booked via independent operators in **Port Denarau** (p55). If you're not overnighting in Mamanuca, you can take day trips starting from and returning to Port Denarau.

# Cruises & Charters

PLEASURE TRIPS ON YACHTS

Placid ocean conditions year-round make the Mamanucas a fantastic place for embarking on a yacht charter. From half-day catamaran sightseeing cruises to floating picnics aboard a brigantine and from sunset dinner cruises featuring Champagne and lobster to overnight jaunts on a schooner, you will find a wide permutation of experiences to match your time, interests and budget. Some of the longer (and pricier) cruises include a visit to a private island, where you can snorkel in a pristine lagoon, quaff grog during a kava ceremony and tuck into a barbecue lunch of fresh seafood. Most cruise operators are based in Port Denarau (p55), and offer complimentary transfers to and from the island where you're staying.

 **ACTIVITIES OPERATORS FOR MAMANUCA**

| **Subsurface Fiji** | **Malolo Fisher Sports** | **PJ's Fishing Charters** |
|---|---|---|
| This scuba operation runs dive shops at several island resorts, offering two-tank fun dives and PADI open-water courses. | Half- and full-day fishing charters aboard an air-conditioned boat with cabins, showers, kitchenette and freezer. | Four-hour charters that take anglers on two boats to prime fishing spots within the lagoon and outside the barrier reef. |

# Diving & Snorkelling Sites

PERFECT FOR NOVICE DIVERS

Mamanuca's dive sites teem with schools of vibrant fish running circles around psychedelic coral reefs. The visibility here astounds first-time divers, averaging about 30m throughout the year. On a particularly clear day, you can see up to 40m through the lucid water. The currents here are weak compared to many other places in Fiji, which makes it easier for inexperienced divers to enjoy the undersea world. Notable dive sites include **Bird Rock**, a 40m wall with caves and swim-throughs, **Fish Market** (self explanatory), **Sherwood Forest** with its waving gorgonian fans, **Gotham City** with groups of resident batfish, and the artificial reef at the wreck of the **Salamanda**. Many of Mamanuca's resorts have their own in-house dive operations, but you will also find a few standalone dive shops in Port Denarau.

# Go Fish

ANGLING FOR BIG GAME

Game fishing is a niche but popular sport in Mamanuca, and some dedicated anglers regularly go trolling and casting in its waters for various species of reef or deep-sea fish. A typical half-day tour runs for four hours, during which boats skim the shallow waters within the reef, allowing guests to troll for inshore species such as wahoo, mahi-mahi and Spanish mackerel. Longer full-day tours range between six and eight hours and venture to deeper waters beyond the reef, where you can cast for big game such as trevally and tuna. Charters require a minimum of four guests, and prices (ranging from $350 to $900) include fishing-gear rental as well as complimentary snacks and beverages. Some boats may even allow you to cook your catch on board and enjoy it with a round of cold beers. For more on fishing trips and charters, see gamefishingindenarau.com and pjfishsailfiji.com.

## BEST SMALLER ISLANDS IN MAMANUCA

**Modriki**
The Tom Hanks movie *Cast Away* was filmed on this island, and this claim to fame still draws hordes of visitors to its secluded shores.

**Castaway**
This reef-fringed 70-hectare island is home to a wide tongue of golden sand as well as the Castaway Island Resort, popular with families.

**Tavarua**
A southern island located close to Mamanuca's legendary surf breaks, and thus a favourite place for surfers to camp.

**GETTING AROUND**

The *Yasawa Flyer* is operated by Awesome Adventures Fiji (awesomefiji.com). Tickets must be purchased in advance, either online or at its office in Port Denarau. If you plan to linger for a few days in Mamanuca and Yasawa, consider buying a Bula Pass, which is valid for five to 15 days and allows you to shuttle up and down the island chains as many times as you wish. However, only one return to Port Denarau is allowed.

The Flyer doesn't stop at individual resorts along its route. Instead, it halts at designated mooring points between clusters of islands, where each resort sends out its own feeder boat to exchange the day's incoming and outgoing guests with the mothership.

Mamanuca

●Tavarua Island

# Beyond Mamanuca

Reef breaks at the southern end of Mamanuca offer world-class surfing opportunities for seasoned surfers and serious enthusiasts.

A cluster of small islands at the southern tip of Mamanuca has a reputation for attracting passionate surfers from around the world. The shallow mid-sea reefs in the vicinity produce some of Fiji's biggest waves, created when water is pushed up along steep and lengthy sections of undersea barriers. Over the years, several of these breaks have gained popularity among the global surfing community for the challenges they pose as well as the enthralment they inspire in the minds of surfers. From towering serpent heads straight out of a Hokusai artwork to long barrels of swirling water, Mamanuca's southern reefs have a wave for every surfer worth their salt.

**TOP TIP**

Surf outfits often allow non-surfers to tag along as day trippers and admire the waves from the boat.

TOBIAS/O/GETTY IMAGES ©

Tavarua Island

ANTHONY BRITTEN/SHUTTERSTOCK ©

Surfing, Cloudbreak

# Cloudbreak: A Surfing Legend

THRILLS FOR ADVANCED SURFERS

While it may not offer the towering monster waves of Nazaré or breaks as plentiful as Oahu's, the surf in Mamanuca has a special place in the hearts of avid boarders. The most iconic wave here is **Cloudbreak**, located near Tavarua island in the far south of Mamanuca. Routinely voted one of the top 10 challenging waves in the world, the daunting break is a barrelling left passing over shallow reefs. Between March and July, when the southeasterly winds sweep in, the wave can reach heights of up to 6m. The best swell angle is with the southwesterly winds, which sometimes form tubes up to 250m long. Cloudbreak is best surfed during low-to-mid-tide, but it can be tricky to negotiate given that it becomes faster and more critical in the shallows. Needless to say, you must have a fair bit of surfing experience to tackle this wave.

Beyond Cloudbreak, impressive waves can be found at **Restaurants**, a powerful and fast left-hander over shallow coral almost 200m long; **Namotu Left**, a cruising, longboard-type left-hander nearly 150m in length; **Swimming Pools**, a fun and easy right-hander good for longboards; and **Wilkes Passage**, a long, fast, down-the-line right that's also a swell magnet, and can get as hairy as Cloudbreak on some days.

Surfing in Mamanuca is typically conducted as a half-day trip. Expect to pay $200 to $250 (including surfboard rental, snacks and water) for a spot on a shared boat. If you wish to charter the entire boat for a tailored surfing experience, you're looking at around $1000.

## SURF TRIP ORGANISERS

**Fiji Surf Co.**
Established in 1995 as Fiji's foremost surfing operation, this veteran outfit runs half-day trips from Nadi year-round.

**Dream Surf Fiji**
Based in Momi Bay on Viti Levu; gives special attention to first-timers as well as experienced surfers.

**Tavarua Island Resort**
Staying right next to the breaks means you're out on your board long before other boats turn up from Viti Levu.

## GETTING AROUND

Most standalone surfing operations that cover the Mamanuca breaks are based in or around Nadi on Viti Levu. If you want to go surfing while staying in one of Mamanuca's resort islands, you'll have to charter a boat through your resort to get to the breaks. A four-hour charter will cost upwards of $300 depending on distance.

# KUATA

The southernmost of Yasawa's islands, Kuata is a tiny, anvil-shaped speck of land that promises close encounters with one of the most feared animals in the ocean: the marine protected area to its north is a thriving sanctuary for up to five species of shark. Depending on how much adrenaline you can handle, there are the options of snorkelling with docile reef sharks in shallow waters and diving with massive bull sharks circling deeper waters. Kuata's shark safaris are one of the experiential highlights of the Yasawas. Rein in your fears and take the plunge.

Accommodation on the island is at the eco-minded Barefoot Kuata Resort, which offers full-board packages to go with the option of simple villa-style *bures* or tented dorms (both accommodation categories are excellently maintained). The meals at the communal dining area are a wholesome feast, and there's an overall congenial atmosphere, with travellers socialising over food and drinks.

● Kuata

✪ Suva

## TOP TIP

If you're keen to see bull sharks, bear in mind that the animals take time off during their mating season from November to February. During these months there are fewer bull sharks in the marine protected area, and you may not always see one on a dive.

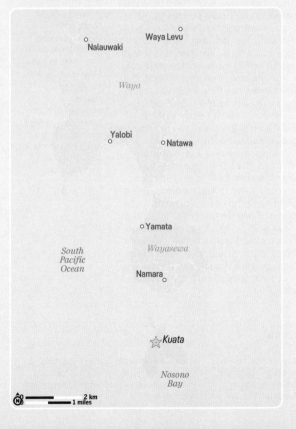

JORG SEIFERT/EYEEM/GETTY IMAGES ©

**Bull Shark, Yasawa**

# Kuata Shark Dives

MEET SAW-TOOTHED PREDATORS

Designed by the resort's in-house marine-science team as a means of raising general awareness and fostering conservation through sustainable tourism, Kuata's 'awakening' shark dives are conducted in a safe environment and divers are escorted by guides with years of experience in conducting these excursions. The dive site is a 15-minute motorboat ride to the northwest of the island in the marine protected area, where divers can drop to a depth of around 18m to a viewing area behind a stone corral. In front of the viewing area is the feeding arena, featuring a feeding platform where dive guides place a box filled with fish heads. For the next 30 minutes or so, divers watch from behind the stone wall as the expert guides hold out the tuna heads at the end of a long pole, releasing them moments before a peckish shark swoops in to make a mid-morning snack of it. Up to five species of shark gather here to feed, and there could be more than a dozen individuals on a given day. The scene stealer, of course, is the massive bull shark, which grows up to 3m long and puts on a robust show of muscle and flair.

At all times during the dive, a team of assistant guides – armed with aluminium prods – keep a close eye on the feeder as well as the spectators, just in case the odd shark strays too close for anyone's comfort. Once the feeding is over, the sharks retreat into deeper waters for the rest of the day and the awestruck divers slowly fin up to the boat before being escorted back to the resort.

## OTHER SHARK SIGHTINGS IN KUATA

**Lemon shark**
Characterised by two dorsal fins of near-equal length and a long, sweeping tail that contributes to its graceful motion through the water.

**Nurse shark**
A demure bottom dweller with long, flappy pectoral fins and equally showy dorsal and pelvic fins cutting a particularly elegant profile.

**Tiger shark**
A blood-curdling hulk that can grow up to 4m long, the tiger shark lives in Kuata's marine park but only makes the odd appearance from time to time.

 **OTHER ACTIVITIES IN KUATA**

**Snorkelling**
The reefs at the southern end of Kuata, extending to the right from the main beach fronting the resort, are rich in hard corals.

**Kayaking**
The channel between Kuata and Wayasewa Island is great for kayaking, a lovely way to spend a calm-water afternoon.

**Sunset Viewpoint**
Kuata has a hilltop lookout just above the resort where you can hike up and enjoy incredible ocean views, especially at sunset.

THE GUIDE

MAMANUCA & YASAWA

## THE FACTS ABOUT SHARK TOURISM

Feeding sharks to draw them closer to human spectators is a practice that generates a fair amount of debate. Detractors say sharks should simply be left alone in their wild habitat and that exposing them to human interactions may lead them to associate humans with prey. Supporters say that, left to their own devices, sharks would simply be hunted to extinction or near-extinction, as they already have been in large numbers. Converting them into long-term revenue-generating assets, however, would deter people from killing them for a one-time income. Some studies have crunched the numbers to suggest that a single reef shark is worth $100,000 of tourism revenue through its life but less than $100 dead.

SEBASTIEN BUREL/SHUTTERSTOCK ©

**Shark diving**

The conservation team at Kuata is of the firm belief that feeding a small number of fish heads to the sharks does not alter their preying instincts or make them dependent on easy food. The large revenue generated by shark tourism (the proceeds go into research and also contribute to the local economy) ensures that the sharks are seen as assets by local communities and therefore safeguarded from poaching. This unique experience costs $350 for a one-tank dive. In addition to having a thrilling experience, divers make a contribution towards this conservation model.

## Snorkelling with Reef Sharks

SAFE AND FUN FOR CHILDREN

A more conservative – but no less exciting – experience than the dives with bull sharks, shark snorkelling simply involves jumping off a motorboat to swim in the company of harmless black-tip and white-tip reef sharks. The snorkelling site is a 15-minute boat ride east of the island. Here the sharks gather around midday to feed in a shallow section of the reef, which is when resort boats take groups of snorkellers to watch them roam the waters. Reef sharks are shy yet curious – if you can float quietly without kicking up too much water they will sometimes swim within a few feet of you to take a closer look before quickly slipping away into the depths. If you're travelling with children, this is undoubtedly the best form of shark spotting you can treat them to.

### GETTING AROUND

Apart from private charters, the *Yasawa Flyer* is the only way to visit Kuata. If you are hopping across multiple islands, plan your arrival and departure according to your activity wish list.

For instance, people who schedule only one night on Kuata but still want to go shark diving usually arrive on the southbound boat in the late afternoon, do the following morning's dive trip and then catch the southbound boat once again on their way out of Yasawa.

# Beyond Kuata

Waya Island
Wayasewa Island
Kuata

The islands of Wayasewa and Waya offer some exciting hiking experiences that familiarise you with the Yasawas' volcanic past.

Wayasewa, also known as Waya Lailai, is located to the north of Kuata, across a narrow ocean channel that provides access to boats making their way from the Mamanucas to the northern Yasawas. This island sees few tourists through the year, especially compared to its popular neighbour. However, if you're craving a good workout on the island's steep slopes, you can challenge yourself to a strenuous half-day hike to the summit of Vatuvula, the island's highest point. North of Wayasewa is the bigger island of Waya, exquisite with its picture-postcard scenery of rugged hills, beautiful lagoons and a coastline that alternates between long, sandy beaches and rocky headlands.

## TOP TIP

Hiking unguided is not recommended. Apart from getting lost in the wilderness, you could could stray onto private land.

**Waya (p110)**

ASIATRAVEL/SHUTTERSTOCK ©

# Climbing Vatuvula

WAYASEWA SUMMIT HIKE

Wayasewa is dominated by a massive volcanic plug known as **Vatuvula**, shaped like a twin-headed summit that towers to 500m and looms dramatically over the waters below. An overgrown trail starts in a village at the base of the island facing Kuata and snakes up steep terrain for about 4.5km. After passing through a forested stretch, it goes around to access the summit via a stony trail from the rear. The outing takes about four hours to complete, and you will have to carry your own snacks and water. Guided Vatuvula tours can be arranged through Barefoot Kuata Resort or from Octopus Resort in Waya.

# Waya Viewpoint Hike

SPECTACULAR YASAWA VIEWS

A summit trek to **Ului Nakauka** leads to a panoramic viewpoint overlooking the oceans all around Waya. It's a three-hour return excursion from the village of Nalauwaki. The track circles around the back of a huge rock outcrop before ascending to the summit. The views south past Wayasewa and north towards Drawaqa are simply gorgeous, and you can enjoy them in the company of herds of headstrong goats.

# Snorkelling in Waya

OFFSHORE SWIMMING SPOTS

A thick rim of hard coral follows Waya's shoreline and provides an especially good snorkelling experience just off the beach in front of the Octopus Resort, in the northwestern corner of the island. In the bay to the south of the island, fronting Yalobi village, yachties drop anchor on one side or the other (depending on the wind) of the sand bridge that has formed between Waya and Wayasewa. The bay's calm, sheltered waters are good for swimming.

## YASAWA DAY TRIPS

Not ready to commit to an extended stay in the Yasawas? No problem: the southern Yasawa islands are easily visited on a day trip from Port Denarau. The *Yasawa Flyer* goes to the Barefoot Kuata Resort and Octopus Resort. This works fantastically well for visitors who want to enjoy a slice of Kuata's midday shark-snorkelling experience, followed by the lavish buffet lunch that's included in the package. Day guests have access to the common areas, bar, restaurant and swimming pool during their time on the island. Note that if you opt for a day trip, your return will be bound to the *Yasawa Flyer's* evening journey: there's no other transport back to Denarau.

## GETTING AROUND

If you wish to move from one island to another during your stay in the Yasawas, enquire with your resort about water-taxi options. Often these are open motorboats with no rain cover or sun shade, and with wooden planks hammered across the hull to serve as seats. Owned by locals, they putter around in various stages of disrepair (and with scant regard for safety equipment). However, the boatmen know the water, reefs and weather like the backs of their hands. Alternatively, you can hitch rides in resort boats ferrying staff to nearby villages at the end of their shifts.

# DRAWAQA

● Drawaqa

✪ Suva

A tiny island hidden away in the mid-lower section of the Yasawa's backbone-like stretch, Drawaqa is a hotbed of activities and attracts huge flocks of tourists especially during the winter months. This is, after all, one of the best places in the world to go snorkelling with manta rays. The island is also known for its coastal coral abundance, which promises amazing snorkelling and diving opportunities. Out of the water, hikers will particularly love the one-hour circuit hike that goes up to two viewpoints located on a western cliff and a central ridge, affording brilliant views of the surrounding archipelago.

Lodging on Drawaqa is available at the Barefoot Manta Resort, although the neighbouring islands of Nanuya Balavu and Naukacuvu also have a couple of nice properties that offer easy access to the manta-ray snorkelling site and dive sites in the vicinity.

## TOP TIP

Staying at Barefoot Manta Resort comes with the unmatched advantage of heading out to the snorkelling site as soon as mantas are sighted for the day. This translates to a better viewing opportunity and more alone time with the animals, before visitors from neighbouring resorts arrive in their boats.

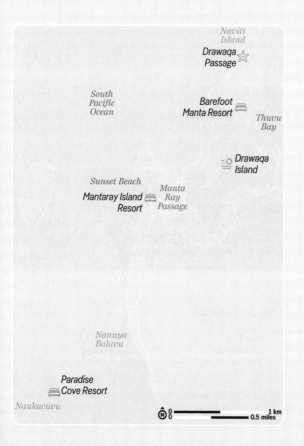

Naviti
Island

Drawaqa ☆
Passage

South
Pacific
Ocean

Barefoot 🛏
Manta Resort

Thuvu
Bay

🌅 Drawaqa
Island

Sunset Beach

Mantaray Island 🛏
Resort

Manta
Ray
Passage

Nanuya
Balavu

Paradise
🛏 Cove Resort

Naukacuvu

Ⓝ 🧭

1 km
0.5 miles

# Snorkel with Manta Rays

WINGED DWELLERS OF THE DEEP

## MORE ABOUT MANTAS

Also known as devil rays due to their horn-like pectoral-fin extensions, manta rays are the largest of all rays and belong to two subspecies. Reef manta rays, characterised by T-shaped markings on their dorsal side, stay closer to reef areas and usually grow to about 4m between wingtips. Most mantas you'll see in the Drawaqa Passage are of this type. If you're very lucky, you might spot a giant oceanic manta ray, a pelagic cousin of the reef manta that can grow to a wingspan of 7m and has Y-shaped markings on its dorsal side. Despite their bulk, manta rays are capable of great speed, but they mostly glide in seemingly synchronised manoeuvres executed in slow motion.

Between May and September, large numbers of manta rays migrate to the **Drawaqa Passage** – a narrow ocean channel between Drawaqa and Naviti Islands. Barely 4m at its deepest, the channel experiences moderate to strong currents during these months, which brings in a rich supply of nutrients for mantas to feed on. It's exhilarating to see one of these dark flying carpets emerge from below and swim up to take a closer look as you float on the surface. Harmless to their core, mantas are incredibly curious, and often retrace their glide path many times to socialise with snorkellers. Approaching or chasing mantas is strictly forbidden, but given the proximity at which sightings routinely happen, you'll hardly be disappointed.

Most mantas in Drawaqa Passage are the subjects of long-term study by the marine-science team at Barefoot Manta Resort. They're usually repeat visitors with names, though the odd newcomer will often turn up in the course of a season. If you happen to snap a photo of a manta clearly showing its ventral (belly-side) markings – unique to each animal like human fingerprints – you can submit them to the team for identification.

Given the consistent water current, snorkelling tours in the passage are conducted with the drift: the boat will drop you at one end of the channel and you'll be carried by the moving water to the other end to be picked up. Scuba diving is prohibited in the passage.

INTERTOURIST/SHUTTERSTOCK ©

**Manta Ray, Yasawa**

 **WHERE TO STAY IN & AROUND DRAWAQA**

**Barefoot Manta Island Resort**
The best among all resorts in terms of its proximity to the manta rays in Drawaqa Passage. Has *bures* (cottages) and tented dorms with bunk beds. **$**

**Mantaray Island Resort**
This happening place on Nanuya Balavu walks the fine line between backpacker party central and high-end escape for sophisticated travellers. **$**

**Paradise Cove Resort**
Beautiful *bures,* villas and suites come in a variety of configurations at this gorgeous resort calling out to families and couples on Naukacuvu Island. **$$**

# Top Island Hike

WESTERN AND SOUTHERN PANORAMAS

Best done in the early morning or late afternoon, this thoroughly enjoyable hike follows a foot trail leading into the wilderness from the southern end of Barefoot Manta Resort. A half-hour walk up the trail – meandering through sparse jungle – brings you to the first viewpoint, perched on a sheer cliff overlooking a western seascape. Below you are forested slopes that crash into the blue waters below, lined by golden sands. You can also see Nanuya Balavu Island to your left. After catching your breath, follow the trail south as it gradually ascends along a ridgeway shaded by scrub trees. A 20-minute walk brings you to the second viewpoint, opening onto a southern vista, with the jagged profile of Waya Island piercing the horizon. From here the descent is through a silent forest of mossy trees, and the trail hops over a precarious section of boulders before leading down to the sands of Drawaqa's southeastern beach. The entire outing takes about 1½ hours, including stops at both viewpoints.

DON MAMMOSER/SHUTTERSTOCK ©

# Dive the Nearby Reefs

BAG OF SCUBA GOODIES

Close to 40 dive sites have been identified in the waters around Drawaqa, although in reality only a dozen or so sites are routinely visited by dive boats. There's a good mix of undersea landscapes here, comprising expansive coral gardens, pinnacles and swim-throughs. For wreck-diving enthusiasts, there are two scuttled longliner fishing boats that were purpose-sunk in 2016 to become artificial reefs. The island's sheltered bays are fabulous places to become certified as an open-water diver over four days of training. Non-divers may also take to the water for a 'discover scuba diving' experience, in which an experienced instructor takes them on a brief outing in the calm shallows.

**Inset:** Drawaqa coastline and Nanuya Balavu

## PACKING ESSENTIALS FOR DRAWAQA

| Rashguards | Sunscreen | Insect Repellent |
| --- | --- | --- |
| You will be spending a lot of time in the water, so bring a rash vest marked SPF50 or above. Better still, wear a wetsuit. | Have a good supply of sunscreen, but avoid brands that are not marked 'reef-safe', as their zinc components can damage coral health. | The interiors of these islands are forested and will invariably have large mosquito populations that invade the resort premises after dark. |

**WHY I LOVE YASAWA**

**Anirban Mahapatra,** writer

The Yasawa Islands have three irresistible attractions that make me want to return over and over again.

**Snorkelling** with reef sharks in Kuata is one of the most relaxed yet exciting activities I have ever enjoyed in the ocean.

**Diving deeper** with hefty bull sharks is an adventure too, tinged with the uncanny anticipation that a gigantic tiger shark might suddenly emerge from the blue. In Drawaqa, I could never tire of **snorkelling with manta rays** (which explains my annual trips there between May and August). Last but not least are the **mysterious caves of Sawa-i-Lau,** where the child in me gets to play out his *Indiana Jones* fantasies.

# Sunrise Snorkelling

ADMIRE CORALS AT DAWN

The bay to the southeast of Drawaqa has some of the most beautiful corals that you can see in one place in Fiji. Most people who spend time on the island go snorkelling here, but the secret is to swim out at sunrise, then watch in awe as the first rays of morning light dart through the still water and reveal the corals in a splendid array of colours. Particularly stunning is the vast field of blue staghorn corals to the left of the sand gully used by resort boats to navigate in and out of the reef. You might also spot a baby reef shark or two weaving their way through the giant boulder or table coral formations to the right of the gully.

**MOST STRIKING CORALS TO LOOK FOR WHEN SNORKELLING**

**Staghorns**
Resembling the branched antlers of a stag, these are one of the most beautiful hard coral varieties, and often grow in the form of large colonies.

**Tables**
Depending on individual size, these corals may either resemble small circular lotus leaves or the gigantic ears of an African bull elephant.

**Brain**
These giant spherical corals feature an intricate network of meandering channels on their outer surface, resembling cerebral grey matter.

# Kayaking & Paddleboarding Around Drawaqa

WORK YOUR ROWING MUSCLES

The water-sports shed at **Barefoot Manta Resort** has a fleet of well-maintained kayaks as well as stand-up paddleboards that are free for guests to use through the daylight hours. You can kayak all around the island, although inexperienced rowers may want to avoid the Drawaqa Passage due to its strong currents. If you're a veteran kayaker, the island of Nanuya Balavu makes a fantastic excursion. You can row out of Drawaqa's southeastern bay, navigate south around the headland and then row in a westerly direction for about 30 minutes to the eastern shore of Nanuya Balavu, in the vicinity of the Mantaray Island Resort. Factor in winds and currents while calculating journey time, and always enquire with resort staff about prevailing weather and sea conditions before you go.

DON MAMMOSER/SHUTTERSTOCK ©

**Inset: Kayak, Drawaqa**

**GETTING AROUND**

The Yasawa Flyer usually moors on the western side of Nanuya Balavu to meet feeder boats from resorts in Nanuya Balavu, Drawaqa and Naukacuvu. The onward northbound calls in at 11.45am, while the returning southbound turns up around 3pm.

# YAQETA

Yaqeta is the first of the northern Yasawa islands, and forms its own clique in conjunction with the neighbouring islands of Matacawalevu, Nanuya Levu, Nanuya Lailai, Tavewa and Nacula. This cluster has one of the highest concentrations of resorts in all of the Yasawas, and attracts solitude seekers looking for nothing more than a few days of tranquillity, broken perhaps by the occasional snorkelling session in crystal-blue waters. There's also some celebrity associated with these islands: Nanuya Levu was the location where Hollywood film *The Blue Lagoon* was filmed in 1980.

Yaqeta and Matacawalevu have three villages between them where it's possible to go on cultural excursions. In the protected lagoon between the two islands, locals harvest *nama* (sea grapes), a type of seaweed that lends itself deliciously to salads and relishes and is regarded as a highlight of Fijian cuisine.

● Yaqeta

☆ Suva

## TOP TIP

If you're flying out of Fiji immediately after your trip to the Yasawas, always schedule a reserve day or two in Nadi. Sudden weather changes can affect ferry schedules. If you can't afford to miss your return flight, the only fix in such situations might be a costly helicopter charter out of Yasawa.

Nacula ○ 🏖 2
*Nacula Island*

Nalova Bay 🛏 9    Cobe Bay

🛏 6
*Tavewa*
🛏 5

○ Naisisili
Koronikelia Reef

🛏 7
🍴 4 🏖 1
○ Enadala

Matacawalevu ○
*Nanuya Island*

*Matacawa Levu*  Nasomo Bay   🛏 10

*Bligh Water*

🛏 8

Yaqeta
🏖 3

○ Matayalevu

*Yaqeta*

🧭 N  0 —— 2 km
      0 —— 1 miles

## SIGHTS
1 Enadala
2 Nacula
3 Yaqeta

## ACTIVITIES, COURSES & TOURS
4 Blue Lagoon

## SLEEPING
5 Coconut Beach Resort
6 Coralview Island Resort
7 Nanuya Island Resort
8 Navutu Stars
9 Oarsman's Bay Lodge
10 Turtle Island Resort

## ACTIVITIES AROUND YAQETA

**Diving**
The narrow ocean channel between the islands of Nacula and Nanuya Lailai has a few dive sites featuring coral walls, tunnels and swim-throughs.

**Kayaking**
The windy passage between Yaqeta and Matacawalevu is fabulous for advanced kayakers, while the many sheltered bays in the area are ideal for novices.

**Yachting**
Blue Lagoon is often used as a safe harbour and overnighting stop by many of the yachts touring through the northern Yasawas.

IMAGE PROFESSIONALS GMBH/ALAMY STOCK PHOTO ©

Yaqeta

# Snorkelling in Blue Lagoon

SEAGRASS BEDS AND COLOURFUL FAUNA

Snorkelling in the sheltered waters of Blue Lagoon is particularly delightful given the unique topography of its seabed. A fantastic seagrass garden thrives here, extending for about 50m from the shoreline into the lagoon, where the water is as clear as crystal. This makes for an unparalleled snorkelling experience: duck diving down to the floor (ranging 2m to 4m in depth), you can spot diverse fish and invertebrate species native to seagrass forests. The most striking among these are sea cucumbers that come in myriad colours and textures. Look out in particular for the elephant trunkfish, a giant sea cucumber featuring black stripes on a bright-orange exterior, or the prickly redfish, dotted with star-shaped spikes.

Swimming further out from the seagrass bed, you'll reach a deeper (3m to 4m) part of the lagoon, where you'll see isolated coral bommies on a sandy floor. These bommies are home to innumerable sergeant major fish schools, and snorkelling guides often throw bits of bread or fruit into the water to stir

## WHERE TO STAY IN & AROUND YAQETA

**Navutu Stars**
A pleasant and popular getaway featuring a string of restful sea-facing *bures* and surprisingly good Italian food on its à la carte restaurant menu. $$

**Turtle Island Resort**
This adults-only resort on Nanuya Levu (of *Blue Lagoon* fame) offers beachfront *bure* accommodation and several cultural experiences. $$

**Coralview Island Resort**
This party hot spot has a ripper bar, twice-weekly pit-roast dinners with fire shows, and delicious meals prepared from organic farm produce. $

up a tornado of fish darting in to feed on the scraps.

Blue Lagoon is located on the western side of Nanuya Lailai, looking out to Matacawalevu across the water. All resorts in the area arrange snorkelling trips to the lagoon, stopping en route at a nearby reef to spot tiny pipefish – a cousin of the seahorse – hidden in the crannies. A motorboat ride from Yaqeta to the lagoon takes 30 minutes.

# Village Interactions
MINGLE WITH THE COMMUNITY

Most resorts in Yaqeta and its neighbouring islands operate in close association with local populations. Some resorts lease their land from the community, while others employ staff and source produce directly from the villages. This symbiosis has resulted in strong bonds between resort owners and village residents. As a resort guest, you can venture into the villages to sample a slice of Fijian life. Village tours are a standard resort activity, and they include free transfers as well as *sevusevu* (gift ceremonies) where required.

Yaqeta, Enadala and Nacula are three of the most appealing villages to visit. On Sunday the children of **Yaqeta** arrive at Navutu Stars resort dressed in their best and sing hymns. For visits, the village is best accessed from the resort. Located on the eastern side of Nanuya Lailai, the hamlet of **Enadala** can be accessed from Blue Lagoon via a well-trodden inland track snaking over gently sloping hills. Catching a Sunday service at the chiefly village of **Nacula** is a real treat, as you can listen to vigorous and harmonic singing by the resident choir.

# Study the Night Sky
STARGAZERS' BALL

Located far from Fiji's urban areas, the Yasawas boast unpolluted skies and a complete absence of the visual interference that comes from the collective glow of artificial lights refracting against a night sky. For amateur astronomers, this is as good as it gets in terms of optimal stargazing conditions. If you come armed with charts of the southern skies, or have a GPS-enabled sky-viewing app on your phone, you can find yourself a nice spot on the beach after dusk and spend hours admiring planets and constellations as they slowly arc across a coal-black heavenly canvas.

**BEST BEACHFRONT RESORTS AROUND YAQETA**

**Coconut Beach Resort**
This former copra plantation sits on a gorgeous curving beach, with a vibrant marine sanctuary nearby that will impress the most discerning snorkeller. $$

**Nanuya Island Resort**
Located a short walk north along the sands of Blue Lagoon, this swish property boasts cosy treetop villas overlooking the lagoon's azure waters. $$$

**Oarsman's Bay Lodge**
Located by a fabulous slice of shoreline on Nacula, this property has beachfront *bures* (cottages) as well as an air-conditioned dorm for budget travellers. $

**GETTING AROUND**

If you want to visit only the northern Yasawas, a direct transport alternative from Viti Levu is the *Tavewa Seabus* catamaran service from Lautoka, 20km north of Nadi. Departing Lautoka at 8am, the *Tavewa Seabus* takes about three hours to complete its run to Tavewa via Yaqeta and Nanuya Levu. It returns to Lautoka by 4pm.

Yasawa Island

Yaqeta

# Beyond Yaqeta

The far north of the Yasawas are a playground of nature's forces, which have left their mark on the intriguing landscape.

If you have the time, tenacity and mindset to venture further north from Yaqeta, you'll arrive at Yasawa, the island from which the entire archipelago takes its name. A narrow strip of land 22km long, oriented in a northeast–southwest direction, this is the last island of the group. It lies beyond the reach of regular ferry services, all of which terminate in Tavewa and Nacula. And apart from some tiny villages and the odd isolated resort, it has few options in terms of accommodation and activities. The one compelling reason most people find to arrange an excursion here is to see the majestic Sawa-i-Lau caves, located to the southeast of the island.

## TOP TIP

Carry a waterproof torch if you want to swim into the smaller and darker cave at Sawa-i-Lau.

**Boat to Sawa-I-Lau Caves**

MATTHEW MICAH WRIGHT/GETTY IMAGES ©

RANI ZERAFA/GETTY IMAGES ©

Sawa-i-Lau caves

# Caves & Legends at Sawa-i-Lau

LIMESTONE GROTTOS AND HIDDEN LAKES

Over centuries, the movement of oceanic water carved the two **Sawa-i-Lau caves** out of a limestone island amid a string of outcrops formed by prehistoric volcanic activity. The limestone deposits here are thought to have formed a few hundred metres below the earth's surface and then been pushed up by seismic forces.

Through the day the gorgeous grottos attract boatloads of tourists. Access is via a precarious flight of stone steps carved onto a rock face. A short and steep climb brings you to an entrance that opens into the great hollow of a dome-shaped cave, its walls soaring nearly 15m above the water's surface. Shafts of daylight enter the cave from a vent at the top, and at the base is a mind-bogglingly beautiful natural pool where you can go for a swim. With an experienced guide and a little bit of courage, you can swim through an underwater passage linking the pool to another smaller pool in an adjoining chamber. Flashing your torch on the walls of this dark cavern, you can see prehistoric carvings, paintings and inscriptions of unknown meaning.

The caves are rich in legend. First, they're believed to be the final resting place of Ulutini, the 10-headed Fijian god. A popular tale tells of a giant hawk that lived in the caves that was killed after he kidnapped a princess from a nearby village. Another story recounts how a young chief hid the woman he loved in the caves after he learned that her parents wished to marry her to a rival chief.

## ESSENTIALS FOR MOTORBOAT EXCURSIONS

**Waterproof bag**
This is handy for shielding valuables such as mobile phones, cameras and wallets from spray during journeys on choppy waters.

**Hat and sunglasses**
The sun beats down very hard on clear days, and none of the motorboats used for local sightseeing trips have sunshades installed on them.

**Rain jacket**
It rains in these islands as frequently as the sun shines or the wind blows. Once again, the lack of cover on motorboats leaves you utterly exposed.

**GETTING AROUND**

All resorts in Yaqeta and its neighbouring islands organise boat safaris to Sawa-i-Lau. This is the best and most convenient way to visit the caves.

Levuka (P126)

# OVALAU & LOMAIVITI

## CRUCIBLE OF FIJIAN HISTORY

The rise and fall of Fiji's colonial history played out in this erstwhile nerve-centre of pan-Pacific trade.

Suva

In the 19th century, the Lomaiviti islands were a popular stopover for European merchant ships that crisscrossed the Pacific in search of commodities such as turtle shell, breadfruit and sandalwood. As trade prospered in the region, the scruffy port town of Levuka – which serviced the natural harbour on Ovalau island – gained a reputation as a boomtown at world's end. Its docks were laden with precious consignments of coconut kernel, sea cucumber and whaling products, and its streets were paved with opportunities that attracted prospectors and beachcombers, traders and freebooters, agents and intermediaries, carpetbaggers and crooks.

For a brief but tumultuous 50-year period, Levuka was also the stage of a political drama involving Western colonisers and chiefly Fijian communities that culminated in the cession of Fiji to the British Crown in 1874. Soon afterwards, power was shifted to the newly created capital of Suva, triggering a decline that saw Levuka slip from being the premier Pacific outpost to a simple port town going about its day's business in a far corner of the world.

Splendid in decay, Levuka is now a fabulous wormhole for history buffs interested in time-travelling through Fiji's colonial past. Beyond Levuka, Ovalau and the other Lomaiviti islands remain fairly unchanged by time or human endeavours, and they offer some fantastic outdoor excursions off Viti Levu's eastern seaboard.

Inset: Masonic Lodge, Levuka

THE MAIN AREAS

**LEVUKA**
Historical walking tour.
p126

**LELEUVIA**
Coral reefs and stargazing.
p133

# Find Your Way

Located within day-tripping distance of metropolitan Suva, the Lomaiviti islands are a breeze in terms of accessibility from Viti Levu. This makes the island group an ideal weekend destination for families, especially those travelling with children.

*Makogai*

*Nairgani*

*Wakaya*

Dawasuma

Rukuruku

*Ovalau*

Vatukalo

Vuma

*Bureta River*

Levuka

Lovoni

Tokou

Wainaloka

**Leleuvia, p133**
It's all about snorkelling, swimming, diving or just lazing on the golden sands with your loved ones in this picturesque island resort.

Nasauvuki

*Yanuka Levu*

*Caqalai*

*Moturiki*

Leleuvia

Kumi

Kasavu

Nausori

*Bird Sanctuary & Mangroves*

Nasilai

◆SUVA

*Nasilai Reef*

*SOUTH PASIFIC OCEAN*

Nabuna
Nathamaki
Nasau
*Koro*

Nakodu

## CARS & TAXIS

If you're not driving yourself, taxis from Suva will drop you at Natovi Landing, the jumping-off point for a twice-daily ferry to Levuka. The road trip takes 1½ hours. Taxis will also pick you up on your return journey if given notice.

### Levuka, p126

Amble around Fiji's atmospheric former capital, exploring its open-air museum of architectural relics thrown across a neighbourhood with a Wild West feel.

## FERRIES

Goundar Shipping's daily ferry to Levuka departs Natovi Landing at 9am and 5pm. Return trips are at 7am and 3pm. The journey takes about 1½ hours. Tickets can be purchased at the landing – be sure to arrive at least 30 minutes in advance.

*SOUTH PACIFIC OCEAN*

*Batiki*

Dalice Settlement

*Nairai*

## RESORT BOATS

To get to Leleuvia and Toberua, take a taxi to Viti Levu's Bau Landing and Nakelo Landing respectively, from where the resorts operate a twice-daily complimentary boat-transfer service, ferrying guests back and forth.

Qarani
Navukailagi
Sawaieke
Lamiti
*Gau*
Vadravadra

0 ———— 20 km
0 ———— 10 miles

# Plan Your Time

The Lomaiviti group can be easily explored within a few days. Ovalau, Leleuvia and Toberua are the most accessible islands, and can be visited either as stand-alone places or in combination, depending on the time you have.

Leleuvia (p133)

## If You Only Have One Day

● Departing Suva early, take the morning ferry from Natovi Landing and head for **Levuka** (p126) on Ovalau Island.

● Spend the morning on a slow pedestrian excursion through Levuka's charming old town, admiring its ramshackle monuments and memorials.

● After lunch, go on a scenic island drive around Ovalau, stopping en route to admire the picturesque traditional village of **Rukuruku** (p131), overlooking a serene bay. The drive-around is about 60km and takes three hours, factoring in photo stops at the many gorgeous viewpoints that afford sweeping vistas of the ocean and faraway islands on the horizon.

IMAGE PROFESSIONALS GMBH/ALAMY STOCK PHOTO ©

## Seasonal Highlights

June, July and August afford the coolest and driest weather for exploring the Lomaiviti islands. It's also when humpback whales use the scenic route nearby for their annual southward migration.

### FEBRUARY

Daytime temperatures become bearable for **hiking** at the end of the southern summer, but rain clouds hang heavy over the islands.

### MAY

After bucketing down nonstop for three months, the rains finally depart. The mercury dips as the dry season begins.

### JUNE

Glorious winter weather brings travellers to the islands in hordes. Advance bookings are a must, especially for big groups.

## A Long Weekend

● Spend your first day exploring Levuka and Rukuruku, then on your second day schedule a hike to **Lovoni** (p131), high in Ovalau's volcanic interior. Get familiar with native flora on the way, swim in a highland river, lunch on indigenous foods sourced from the wilds, then return to Levuka for the night.

● Take the morning ferry on the third day and return to Viti Levu. Arrange an advance taxi transfer from Natovi Landing to Bau Landing, and catch the ferry to **Leleuvia** (p133).

● Snorkel above beautiful coral reefs by day, and count stars spangled on a pitch-dark sky in the evening.

## Four Days or More

● After exploring Ovalau, bounce off Viti Levu and meander down the coast to Leleuvia on your third day.

● On day four, embark on a lazy boat ride in **Gavo Passage** (p139) to spy on resident dolphins and passing whales (in winter).

● Be intrigued by the legend of a sunken village, and visit hamlets on nearby **Moturiki** and **Bau** islands (p138) to meet some locals.

● With more time to spare, consider switching off and scoring some quality downtime in the peaceful island resort of **Toberua** (p139), tucking into delicious food and snorkelling above gorgeous hard coral colonies in the vicinity.

**JULY**

Peak window for possible humpback-whale sightings. Water visibility for **snorkelling and diving** is also at its best.

**AUGUST**

The shoulder season still sees plenty of visitors flocking to the Lomaiviti islands. The clear skies are ideal for **stargazing**.

**OCTOBER**

Visitor numbers surge briefly during the **Diwali** holidays. It's a good time to hike to Lovoni before summer rings in.

**DECEMBER**

Despite peak summer, tourist traffic hits its annual high through the Christmas and New Year holiday week.

# LEVUKA

Levuka started attracting foreign settlers after a whaling centre was set up in the 1830s. By the 1850s, as trade burgeoned, the town had gained a reputation for drunkenness, violence and immorality. By the 1870s, Levuka's expat population had boomed to around 3000, and the town infamously housed 52 hotels for the settlers and visiting sailors to revel in. The legend goes that ships could navigate their way into Levuka's harbour by following empty alcohol bottles floating out with the tide.

In 1874, following Fiji's cession to the British Crown, Levuka was briefly proclaimed the national capital. But after the government shifted to Suva in 1882, there was a rapid outflow of commerce. The town remained lost to the greater world until the 1950s, when the establishment of a tuna cannery and processing centre pumped vitality back into its veins. In 2013, Levuka was listed by Unesco as a World Heritage Site.

Levuka ●

☆ Suva

## TOP TIP

Levuka's half-dozen restaurants close between mealtimes and often down shutters by 9pm. Some remain shut on Sundays and public holidays. Unless you fancy surviving on instant noodles, make prior arrangements for food with your place of accommodation if you're visiting during a stretch of holidays.

MALOFF/SHUTTERSTOCK ©

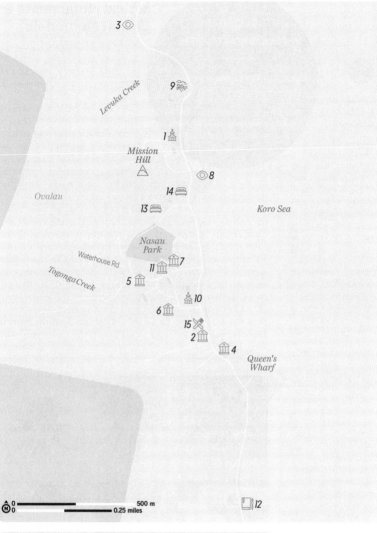

📖 12

## SIGHTS
**1** Anglican Church
**2** Bank of New South
Wales Building
**3** Gun Rock
**4** Levuka Museum
**5** Levuka Public School
**6** Marist Convent
School
**7** Masonic Lodge
**8** Niukaube Hill
**9** Original Levuka

Village
**10** Sacred Heart Church
**11** Town Hall

## ACTIVITIES,
## COURSES & TOURS
**12** Cession Site

## SLEEPING
**13** Levuka Homestay
**14** New Mavida Lodge

## EATING
**15** Kim's Paak Kum
Loong

Levuka

MALOFF/SHUTTERSTOCK ©

127

## CAKOBAU & THE CESSION

A powerful chief hailing from Bau island, Ratu Seru Cakobau (pronounced 'tha-kom-bau') rose to regional prominence in the 1820s after several villages in eastern Viti Levu swore their allegiance to him. By the 1850s he had gained enough political sway over the region to assert himself as the king of Fiji, although this claim wasn't accepted by all chiefs. After he unsuccessfully tried to form a government in Levuka 1871, Cakobau ran into huge debts. Economic and political trouble drove him to the British, with a bailout plea in exchange for ceding Fiji to the Imperial Crown. Despite widespread doubts regarding Cakobau's claim on Fiji, the British agreed. The Cession followed three years later.

### FOR NAUTICAL TOURISTS

Levuka, like **Savusavu** (p146) in Vanua Levu, is a nautical immigration point for yachts, sailboats and catamarans that ride the wind westward from the US to Fiji, or motor their way up north from Australia and New Zealand.

# Colonial Monuments & Quaint Memorials

WALK DOWN MEMORY LANE

Levuka's main sights are located along Beach St, and can easily be seen over a half-day walk. Most people begin their tour at the **Cession Site**, a 10-minute stroll south of town. The Deed of Cession, handing Fiji over to Britain, was signed here in 1874. The site is marked by a pair of ship anchors and three stone plaques commemorating visits by members of the British monarchy over time. Across the road are **Nasova House**, formerly the governor's residence, and the **Provincial Bure**, a venue for local council meetings that briefly doubled as the camp office of Prince Charles (now King Charles III) when he represented Queen Elizabeth II during Fiji's transition to independence in 1970.

Walking back into town past the **PAFCO tuna cannery**, you will arrive at the site of the original **pigeon post**, marked by a nondescript drinking fountain in the centre of the road. From here, pigeons provided the first postal link between Levuka and Suva. Two doors north on Beach St is the iconic 1868 facade of the former flagship **Morris Hedstrom** trading store, which sets the signature Wild West look of Levuka's main street. The building is home to **Levuka Museum**, which houses an interesting exhibition

ITPHOTO/ALAMY STOCK PHOTO ©

**Cession Site**

---

 **WHERE TO STAY & EAT IN LEVUKA**

**Levuka Homestay**
Noted for its garden-fronted rooms, lavish breakfast and super-affable hosts. In-house gardener Nok offers great walking tours of Levuka. **$**

**New Mavida Lodge**
A spartan yet comfortable hotel at the northern end of Beach St, with two superb 1st-floor suites featuring ocean views. **$**

**Kim's Paak Kum Loong**
This busy restaurant specialises in quasi Chinese dishes, best enjoyed on the covered balcony with complimentary ocean views. **$**

detailing the town's history, and is usually open weekday mornings.

Strolling north on Beach St, you will notice many more storefronts that reflect the 1850s boomtown aesthetic reminiscent of the American Gold Rush, including the 1909 wooden facade of the **Bank of New South Wales** (now Westpac Bank). Further up the road stands **Sacred Heart Church**, dating to 1858, visibly characterised by its rain-weathered steeple that once guided ships navigating the treacherous reefs of the Levuka Passage.

Located behind the church on Totoga Lane is the **Marist Convent School**, founded by Catholic missionaries in 1882. Further north on Totoga Lane stands the tiny weatherboard structure of Levuka's original **police station** (1874). Located across Totoga Creek from the police post is the **town hall** (now the town council), and immediately past it the stone shell of the South Pacific's first **Masonic Lodge** (1875). From the police station you can also go 100m west on Garner Jones Rd to visit **Levuka Public School** (1879).

Popping back on Beach St, continue north for five minutes to reach **Niukaube Hill**, a mound overlooking the harbour where Fijian chief Ratu Cakobau established his Supreme Court and Parliament House while trying to form a sovereign government prior to the Cession in 1874. The site is also where the first indentured labourers from India landed in Fiji in the 1880s.

ITPHOTO/ALAMY STOCK PHOTO ©

With more time and the inclination, you could continue further north past the 1904 **Anglican Church** to reach a towering outcrop called **Gun Rock**, so named after Western commodores pounded it with cannonball fire to impress local chiefs in the 19th century. The site is fronted by a placid bay where you can end your excursion with a dip in the cool water, and you may have the company of a few duck-diving locals harvesting seafood. To get to Gun Rock, you will pass the original **Levuka Village**. Remember to remove your hats and sunglasses as a mark of respect as you pass through (as you would in every traditional Fijian village).

Inset: Sacred Heart Church

## WHY I LOVE LEVUKA

**Anirban Mahapatra**, writer

Levuka is a playground for the imagination, and fires my mind with reveries as few other places do. Its main street oozes vintage appeal and reminds me of ramshackle one-horse mining towns in the spaghetti Western movies of my childhood. Drifting aimlessly through the town, I often imagine myself as a fortune seeker two centuries ago, sailing in from distant shores to seek my pot of gold at the end of the world. On my way into Levuka harbour by ferry from Viti Levu, I am often treated to the delightful sight of playful dolphins racing alongside the boat, especially in the lagoon of the inner reef fringing Ovalau's eastern shoreline.

## GETTING AROUND

The ferry vessel from Natovi Landing to Levuka can take a few cars on board. This allows self drivers to bring their vehicles over from Viti Levu to Ovalau if required. Alternatively, cars can be parked at an informal but secure parking area for a small fee at Natovi Landing for the duration of your visit to Ovalau. Taxis are readily available in Levuka for trips within town and around Ovalau.

# Beyond Levuka

Slip into your hiking boots – or behind the
steering wheel – and hit the track for some of
Ovalau's fascinating excursions.

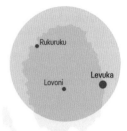

Ovalau is the largest island in the Lomaiviti group, and at its
centre are an extinct volcano and several towering hills that
offer some excellent day-hike options. Most popular among
these is the hike to Lovoni village, the former stronghold of
warriors fiercely opposed to Cakobau's chiefly aspirations as
well as the influx of Western settlers in the 19th century. Di-
agonally across the island from Levuka, on Ovalau's western
shoreline, is the breathtakingly beautiful island of Rukuruku,
set against forested hills and hemmed by a tranquil bay with
views of Viti Levu as a backdrop. Taxis from Levuka whisk
travellers to Rukuruku as part of the popular half-day road
trip around the island.

### TOP TIP

The drive around Ovalau
is best done clockwise, as
you'll drive downhill into
ocean vistas rather than
uphill and away from them.

IAN TROWER/ALAMY STOCK PHOTO ©

**Boats, Levuka**

# Hike to Lovoni Crater

HISTORY OF THE HEARTLAND

Edged by emerald rainforest in the bowl of an extinct volcano's crater, Lovoni is Ovalau's beating heart of indigenous culture. There's no accommodation here, but you can visit the legendary highland settlement on a guided day-hike from Levuka. The trailhead is a 25-minute drive out of town, from where a vigorous two-hour climb through wilderness will take you to a viewpoint on the crater's rim. Along the way, you will learn about natural medicines traditionally extracted from plants, uncultivated food and fruit sourced from the wild, as well as the intriguing history of Lovoni and its regional role in 19th-century power politics. From the viewpoint, it's a one-hour descent to the village.

Entering the 800-strong settlement requires visitors to present a *sevusevu* (gift) to the chief, which your guide will do for you. You can swim in the nearby river that gurgles down the extinct path of lava flow before being served a lunch of locally sourced wild yam, spinach, coconut cream and lemon-leaf tea. Lunch is usually followed by a storytelling session in which village elders narrate episodes from Lovoni's sombre history to guests. A 4WD vehicle will bring you back to Levuka at the end of the excursion.

The highly recommended **Epi's Tours** offers the hike as an all-inclusive experience tailored to the number of guests and their interests. Write in advance to Joanne at epistours@gmail.com to book a spot.

# Explore Rukuruku Bay

SWITCH OFF FROM THE WORLD

According to local lore, the village of Rukuruku was founded in the late 1940s to settle Fijian soldiers who had returned after their WWII service in the Allied forces' Solomon Islands campaign. Now home to about 400 islanders, it's easily one of the prettiest villages you can visit in the

Inset: Volcanic hills, Ovalau

### WARRIORS IN CHAINS

Lovoni's sovereignty was compromised in 1871 when its warriors came down from the safety of the village in good faith to make a truce with Cakobau, whose expansion attempts they had fiercely resisted for many years. Sadly, it was a trap: as the warriors began their meal, Cakobau's men caught them off guard and quickly captured them. To further their humiliation, Cakobau sold the warriors as slaves for £3 a head, using the earnings as capital to form his fledgling government. The only Fijian people ever to be enslaved, Lovoni's warriors were freed after Britain took over Fiji. The day of capture, 7 July, is commemorated as Lovoni Day, which village residents mark with stoic mourning.

## POPULAR STOPS ON THE DRIVE AROUND OVALAU

**Wainaloka**
From a roadside lookout you can enjoy lofty views of mangrove-draped Yanuca Lailai island across the channel.

**Arovudi**
In the vicinity are two viewpoints with ocean panoramas featuring Vanua Levu and Taveuni on the northern horizon.

**Vatukalo**
The most dramatic sight here is the decaying hull of a massive ship that was beached during Cyclone Winston in 2016.

JAMES R.D. SCOTT/GETTY IMAGES ©

**Longfin spadefish, Levuka**

## BEST ACTIVITIES IN RUKURUKU

**Snorkelling**
Rukuruku's bay has a superb coral wall that runs parallel to the shoreline, accessed by swimming about 50m out from the beach.

**Water slide walk**
A 30-minute walk into the hills takes you to a natural water slide draining into a plunge pool – perfect for a dip at the end of the hike.

**Sandbank trip**
The BayStay can organise a boat excursion to a nearby sandbank, complete with a barbecue lunch of fish caught along the way.

Lomaiviti islands, thanks to its million-dollar location on a serene bay that opens onto the sheltered ocean channel separating Ovalau from Viti Levu. The channel has a few coral reefs and sandbanks that promise a range of activities, such as snorkelling and picnics. Rukuruku is also one of the best places for doing absolutely nothing, apart from finishing that book you've long been intending to read.

Rukuruku is best explored by organising a visit through **The BayStay** (thebaystayfiji@gmail.com), a self-catering guesthouse located on the waterfront that works closely with the village community and offers guided tours, including *sevusevu* ceremonies at the chief's place. Accommodation (minimum two nights) is available in eco-chic cottages dotted around a leafy dale, and you can bring your own supplies to cook meals in the fully outfitted kitchen. There's a shallow reef of healthy coral not far from the beach (bring your own snorkelling gear), and the sheltered bay is great for some relaxed open-water swimming. Dog lovers will appreciate the joyful company of the many canine members of the host family.

### GETTING AROUND

If you're keen to visit Rukuruku before Levuka, you can ask The BayStay (thebaystayfiji@gmail.com) to send a village boat across the channel and pick you up directly from Natovi Landing. The journey takes about 30 minutes, and costs around $150 for up to six passengers. From Rukuruku, a taxi can transfer you to Levuka upon checkout.

# LELEUVIA

The resort island of Leleuvia offers a bouquet of oceanic activities in a modest and rustic setting where the vibe is somewhere between kids' summer camp and backpackers' paradise. What it lacks in creature comforts it more than compensates for with stunning ocean, gleaming stretches of golden sand and coral colonies sparkling in the shallows. Its rough-and-ready yet relaxed feel has made Leleuvia a favourite with budget travellers as well as families with young children.

Accommodation in the resort is in simple thatched *bures* (cottages) with basic furnishings – some units have sea views, while others are set in shady groves. Unless you're staying in one of the family *bures*, you'll have access to shared bath and toilet facilities. The set meals range from simple breakfasts to sumptuous dinners, while the beachside bar has an unending supply of chilled beer to fuel spirited conversations with resort staff and other guests.

Leleuvia
Suva

## TOP TIP

The kitchen at Leleuvia serves the three set meals included with the visitor package. If you fancy snacks or nibbles beyond these, carry some with you. Drinking water flows free, but take your own bottles to fill up. Coffee and tea are free too.

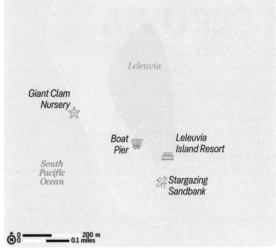

# LELEUVIA

Giant Clam
Nursery

*Leleuvia*

Boat
Pier

Leleuvia
Island Resort

South
Pacific
Ocean

Stargazing
Sandbank

0
0 — 200 m
0.1 miles

## BEST TIMES TO SNORKEL

**Early morning**
Dawn is the best time to have the reef to yourself. Fewer snorkellers means a quieter experience, and a greater concentration of reef life.

**Late afternoon**
The falling sun sets off a kaleidoscopic show of light and shadow among the coral reefs to the west of the island. A great time for those amazing reef photos.

**High tide**
Underwater visibility is typically better during the incoming tide. An hour either side of peak high tide offers the best visibility.

## Snorkelling & Swimming Around Leleuvia

AQUATIC ADVENTURES FOR ALL

Blessed with magnificent hard and soft corals at relatively shallow depths, Leleuvia is a fantastic place for guests of all ages and proficiencies to engage in diverse reef adventures. The daily tidal currents here are quite gentle compared to many other island getaways in Fiji, so children as well as novice swimmers should have little trouble negotiating the water, especially in the shallows along the western waterline on both sides of the boat pier.

The clump of mixed coral directly under the pier is particularly rich in marine life, where you'll find resident schools of elongated cornetfish, blue-and-green parrotfish, spiky sea urchins, vibrant angelfish and even the odd octopus conducting a masterclass in camouflage. Snorkelling along the shoreline north from the pier, you can see a spectacular garden of healthy soft coral. About 50m out west from the pier, a white buoy marks the site of Leleuvia's **giant clam nursery**, home to more than a dozen colourful oversized bivalves.

 **PACKING CHECKLIST FOR LELEUVIA**

**Headlamp or Torch**
The resort's generator stops between midnight and 7am, so a backup is a good idea.

**Sleeping Bag or Liner**
Supplied linen can be damp during periods of heavy rain. A liner will protect against insect bites.

**Sunscreen or Rash Vest**
Avoid sunscreens with zinc compounds. A SPF50 (or higher) rash vest is a good alternative.

Leleuvia

**OUTRIGGER CANOES**

The typical design of a traditional Fijian outrigger canoe comprises a long and narrow main hull, which seats rowers in single file, along with a shorter parallel support float called the outrigger, fastened to one side of the hull by two wooden poles. The outrigger, which acts like a proxy hull, provides added stability to the canoe by distributing its centre of gravity between the main hull and itself. Outrigger canoes have been documented as one of the earliest seaworthy vessels used by seafaring populations. Crafted by modern shipwrights to their near-unchanged historical design, outrigger canoes are still used widely by innumerable rural coastal populations across the South Pacific.

# Dive Among Soft Corals

OCEAN GARDENS GALORE

For some relaxed scuba action, head out with the resort's divemasters to the ocean channel on the eastern side of Leleuvia. The channel has a number of **dive sites** ranging in depth from 12m to 20m, where you can drop down among gorgeous colonies of hard and soft coral, sea fans, hydroids, multicoloured sponges and a diverse array of fish life. The low-to-moderate currents here make the diving suitable for people of all experience levels. The dive shop is well stocked with rental gear.

# Kayaking & Paddleboarding

ROW WITH THE FLOW

Leleuvia offers its guests complimentary use of one- and two-seater kayaks as well as stand-up paddleboards. The best place to flex your rowing muscles is on the waters to the west of the island. It's also possible to enjoy the unique experience of venturing out on a traditional Fijian outrigger canoe and learning to row in the way of ancient Fijian seafarers. The resort's watersports crew will happily give you a crash course in the basics of outrigger rowing.

# Stargazing Unlimited

STUDY THE SOUTHERN SKY

If your visit coincides with a window of clear weather, especially close to the new-moon phase of the month, set aside an hour or two in the evening to spy distant stars against a coal-black night sky. Best done before moonrise, stargazing is one of Leleuvia's best-kept secrets, and goes undiscovered by most people who visit the resort. The wedge-like southern sandbank forming a peninsula between the eastern and western banks is the best vantage point for a particularly immersive stargazing experience. Stand on the tip of the sandbank to feel a sense of ethereal awe as the sky descends to meet its own reflection on the watery mirror filling the darkness all around you. Look for the Southern Cross, the unwavering reference point for all constellations in the southern skies, and take it from there.

 **GETTING AROUND**

Depending on Leleuvia's in-house boat schedule, it's possible to request a pickup from Levuka and be transported directly to Leleuvia by sea. The hour-long journey through Gavo Passage is a beautiful experience, and prices can be negotiated with the resort depending on the number of passengers.

# Beyond Leleuvia

Wakaya Island
Leleuvia  Toberua Island
Bau Island
Moturiki Island

A sprinkling of islands in the channels around Leleuvia promise interactive village tours, up-close wildlife sightings and stylish resort living.

Many visitors build an extra day or two into their Leleuvia trip to explore the nearby islands, which are easily accessible by boat. Many of these islands are home to communities who have settled here over several centuries. You can visit the island's picturesque hamlets to learn about traditional rural Fijian life and culture, and be regaled by intriguing myths and the lore of land and sea, narrated by residents during the important social ritual of a kava session. Finally, if you are craving an indulgent time in the lap of luxury, the resort island of Toberua might be just the place to spend your final night (or two).

## TOP TIP

For max beach time, you can base yourself in Leleuvia and arrange day excursions to Ovalau (for Levuka, Lovoni and Rukuruku) by boat.

Bure, Toberua

# Visit Moturiki & Bau Islands

LOMAIVITI'S RURAL PULSE

## BEST SMALLER ISLANDS AROUND LELEUVIA

**Caqalai**
This currently uninhabited island has some dazzling coral reefs for snorkelling. It's located 10 minutes by motorboat from Leleuvia.

**Honeymoon Island**
Straight out of a fairy tale, this isolated palm-fringed outcrop is located in Gavo Passage and is easily visited on a picnic from Leleuvia.

**Yanuca Lailai**
Located beyond Moturiki, and closer to Ovalau than Leleuvia, this mangrove-lined island has a golden-sand beach and a few good snorkelling reefs.

Leleuvia has excellent relationships with the residents of its neighbouring islands. One of the most pleasant half-day trips to arrange during your stay here is to **Moturiki**, about 20 minutes by motorboat northeast of Leleuvia. Of the 10 villages on this island, the hamlet of **Uluibau** is the easiest to access. For a $50 donation, your boat driver–guide will perform a *sevusevu* (gift) ceremony for you at the chief's *bure.* Following this, you're free to walk around the village, or sit with a family and socialise over kava or coconuts.

Located 30 minutes southwest of Leleuvia from Bau Landing, **Bau** is a chiefly island where Cakobau originally hailed from. As a mark of respect to the great chief, outboard motors are revved down and hats removed as boats pass the island even today. The Bau community also owns Leleuvia, so if you wish to visit, simply let the resort know in advance. Excursions to Bau typically involve long storytelling sessions detailing Cakobau's reign in Fiji as well as the history of the Lomaiviti islands.

JAN BUTCHOFSKY/GETTY IMAGES ©

Toberua

 **WHERE TO DIVE IN TOBERUA**

**Shark Reef**
White-tip reef sharks glide among dramatic coral archways, overhangs and swim-throughs; 25m at its deepest.

**Playground**
Spot reef sharks, moray eels and turtles amid caves, crevasses and overhangs. For advanced divers.

**Bird Island Reef**
Dipping to 28m, this coral-draped site teems with turtles, tuna, sharks, barracudas, giant clams and eagle rays.

# Spotting Whales & Dolphins

GAVO PASSAGE BOAT SAFARI

The deep-blue waters of **Gavo Passage** extend along the southern side of Ovalau, triangulated between Leleuvia, Caqalai and Honeymoon Island. In July and August, humpback whales pass through on their migratory journey to the Antarctic, as they come up for air often, crossing paths with tourist boats. At other times of the year there's a fair chance of spotting pods of spinner dolphins, who frolic around the boat and swim alongside for a few minutes before going their own way.

The waters of Gavo Passage are considered sacred, and boat crew members may ask you to remove your hat and maintain silence while passing over them. The waters are said to be haunted by the spirits of an ancient hamlet that mysteriously sank to the depths of the passage, and stories of fishers hooking newly woven mats while fishing here are often whispered in local circles. Curious visitors peering into the water for a glimpse of the village are often rewarded with vibrant views of submerged coral.

# Relax at Toberua

STYLISH FAMILY HIDEAWAY

The island resort of **Toberua** is a favourite with families, many of whom return year after year to spend quality time in its peaceful folds. Accommodation on the tiny island is in smart villas with alfresco bathrooms and expansive views of the sea. The kitchen works up delicious gourmet meals (included in the stay package), and the tiny swimming pool – with its menagerie of shark and dolphin floaters – is a hit with children. The nearby reefs have some of Lomaiviti's best snorkelling and diving ($350 for a two-tank dive trip), and promise tons of vibrant multicoloured coral as well the odd encounter with reef sharks and turtles. Snorkelling trips to **Picnic Island** on Wednesdays and Sundays are a highlight on Toberua's activities list and must not be missed.

Getting to Toberua from Suva involves a 45-minute drive or taxi ride to Nakelo Landing, a few kilometres past Nausori airport. From here, a resort boat picks up visitors and transports them to the island in 30 minutes.

**THE PRIVATE ISLAND OF WAKAYA**

Located about 20km east of Ovalau, the island of Wakaya is historically famous as the first site where sugar-cane farming was (unsuccessfully) attempted in Fiji in the 1860s. The reefs around the island are protected for their incredible abundance of marine life. Sea turtles find sanctuary here, and manta rays also turn up in the shallow channels through the winter months of June, July and August. However, casual dips are not feasible as Wakaya is a privately owned island. The only way to sample the marine diversity is by booking a stay at **Wakaya Club & Spa**, the island's proprietary high-end resort.

**GETTING AROUND**

For a nominal fee, an informal but secure parking lot at Nakelo Landing offers self-drivers the option to park their car for the duration of their visit to Toberua.

# VANUA LEVU & TAVEUNI

## EMERALD FORESTS AND SAPPHIRE OCEANS

Step back in time to experience the prehistoric natural bounties of Fiji's northern islands.

Born out of intense volcanic activity in primeval times, Vanua Levu and Taveuni are home to some of Fiji's most dramatic landscapes. Separated by a sliver of deep ocean called the Somosomo Strait, these two heavily forested islands in the country's northern frontier feature mountain cliffs awash with ivory-white waterfalls, endless coastlines dotted with hideaway villages, steamy swathes of tropical rainforest with riotous growths of monster ferns and tropical wildflowers, sprawling plantations of copra and kava, a unique population of native bird species, and dazzling oceans resplendent with coral reefs and marine life. Arguably the country's most diverse region in terms of activities, Vanua Levu and Taveuni are an unopened goody bag of surprises for those keen on sampling the best of Fiji's outdoor offerings.

Quick and frequent air connections from Nadi and Suva, combined with a sprinkling of fabulous tourist refuges tucked away in amazing locations, make it easy to dip into these northern islands for either a short vacation or an extended stay, depending on your time and inclination. Take it slow, keep a smile on your face, and enjoy rural Fiji on its grandest scale.

DON MAMMOSER/SHUTTERSTOCK ©

**Inset: Jungle Myna**

## THE MAIN AREAS

| SAVUSAVU | SOMOSOMO | MATEI |
|---|---|---|
| Activities launchpad by a scenic ocean bay. | Taveuni's main town overlooking Rainbow Reef. | Base for exploring northern Taveuni's wilderness. |
| p146 | p156 | p163 |

DON MAMMOSER/SHUTTERSTOCK ©

Lavena village (p164)

# Find Your Way

Getting around in Vanua Levu and Taveuni requires some careful coordination between flights, ferries and road transfers joining the main towns to the outlying areas. Vanua Levu's southeastern bays are better accessed by boat from Taveuni across the Somosomo Strait.

### CAR & TAXI

Self-drive cars can be rented in both Savusavu and Somosomo. Vanua Levu has a tar-sealed all-weather road running from Savusavu to Labasa. Taveuni's main tarmac road connects Somosomo to Matei, giving way to gravelled surfaces beyond both towns.

### AIR

Savusavu and Taveuni have return flights from Nadi and Suva several days a week, operated by Fiji Airways and Northern Air. Labasa, one hour by road from Savusavu, has daily flights to Nadi and Suva.

### FERRY

Buca Bay in eastern Vanua Levu has a daily morning ferry service to Somosomo run by Taveuni-based Suncity Ferries. Goundar Shipping runs a ferry service from Savusavu to Somosomo (and onward to Suva) on Wednesdays and Sundays.

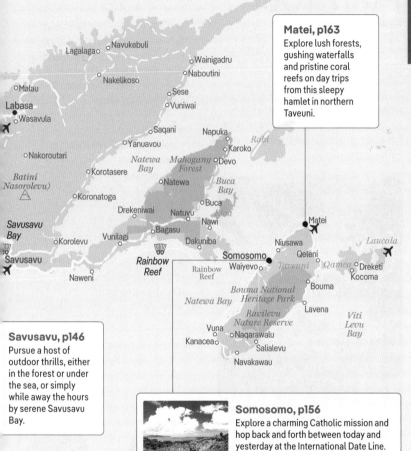

0 — 30 km
0 — 15 miles

**Matei, p163**
Explore lush forests, gushing waterfalls and pristine coral reefs on day trips from this sleepy hamlet in northern Taveuni.

Navukebuli
Lagalaga
Wainigadru
Nakelikoso
Naboutini
Malau
Sese
Labasa
Vuniwai
Wasavula
Saqani
Napuka
Yanuavou
Karoko
Rabi
Nakoroutari
Natewa
Bay
Mahogany
Forest
Devo
Batini
Nasorolevu)
Korotasere
Natewa
Buca
Bay
Koronatoga
Koiva
Drekeniwai
Natuvu
Buca
Savusavu
Bay
Bagasu
Nawi
Matei
Korolevu
Vunilagi
Dakuniba
Niusawa
Laucala
Savusavu
Rainbow
Reef
Somosomo
Qeleni
Naweni
Rainbow
Reef
Waiyevo
Taveuni
Qamea
Dreketi
Kocoma
Bouma
Bouma National
Heritage Park
Natewa Bay
Lavena
Ravilevu
Nature Reserve
Viti
Levu
Bay
Vuna
Naqarawalu
Kanacea
Salialevu
Navakawau

**Savusavu, p146**
Pursue a host of outdoor thrills, either in the forest or under the sea, or simply while away the hours by serene Savusavu Bay.

**Somosomo, p156**
Explore a charming Catholic mission and hop back and forth between today and yesterday at the International Date Line.

South
Pacific
Ocean

# Plan Your Time

It's easy to overstay your vacation in these stunningly beautiful islands, so plan your movements well. Pick one island (or even just one base) if you're pressed for time.

DONYANEDOMAM/GETTY IMAGES ©

**Lavena Costal Walk (p164)**

## If You Only Have a Weekend

● Look no further than Savusavu. Schedule your first day for a diving or snorkelling trip to the **Namena Marine Reserve** (p153), or the many dives sites in **Savusavu Bay and Koro Sea** (p147).

● On the second morning, consider a **pearl farm tour** (p151) to see how Fiji's famed black and green pearls take shape inside oysters, or book a **cocoa farm tour** (p151) to learn about local chocolate making, and buy some delicious bars to nibble on.

● Alternatively, if you prefer, book yourself an introductory **free-diving** (p148) lesson. In the afternoon, visit the **Nakama hot springs** (p148) and see locals cook dinner in the bubbling heat of Savusavu's natural geysers.

## Seasonal Highlights

May–September is cool and clement for hiking; November is good for spotting local flora. Diving occurs year-round, but certain months have better visibility than others.

**FEBRUARY**
As Fiji's wettest island, Taveuni gets drenched with rain, but its famed **waterfalls** are in full vigour.

**APRIL**
The **sailing** season kicks off, bringing yachts and sailboats from around the world to Savusavu Bay.

**JULY**
Divers in **Rainbow Reef** report stunning underwater visibility, sometimes up to 30m, which lasts until September.

## ne Week to Play

From Savusavu, visit the island **Nukubati** (p155) on Vanua vu's northern coastline, and end a few days exploring the lorn Great Sea Reef.

Alternatively, you could go east m Savusavu to pristine **Natewa y** (p154) and log a few coral es in Fiji's largest ocean bay.

En route, break your journey at **t Lake** (p154) for a kayaking cursion along a tidal creek lined h thick mangroves.

Next, take the morning ferry m Buca Bay and be transported Somosomo in Taveuni. From re, dive the famous **Rainbow ef** (p160), and then venture rth to Matei to discover **Tavoro aterfalls** (p164) and hike the cluded **Lavena Coastal Walk** 64).

## Ten Days or More

● For additional activities in Savusavu, acquaint yourself with a mind-boggling collection of palm species at **Flora Tropica Gardens** (p149).

● In Taveuni, make a day trip from Somosomo to the mesmerising **blowhole** (p157) and schedule a session of **bird-watching** (p157) on your way back to town.

● Schedule an extra day or two to dive the Rainbow Reef (160).

● Those keen on sweating it out in wild terrain could consider the steep hike to **Lake Tagimaucia** (p158).

● To end your vacation with some quiet time, seek refuge in the forested nooks of **Southeastern Vanua Levu** (p160), located within shouting distance of stunning Rainbow Reef.

**AUGUST**
Peak tourist season, when even isolated spots in remote parts of the islands see a fair number of visitors.

**SEPTEMBER**
A good time to explore the exuberance of **Namena Marine Reserve**, with visibility hitting 30m on good days.

**NOVEMBER**
Native *tagimaucia* flowers are in bloom, while the local **markets** brim over with fruits like pineapple, avocado and mango.

**DECEMBER**
The sailing season ends and the rains set in. Flight cancellations can be frequent in stormy weather.

# SAVUSAVU

Stretched along the arc of a serene and stunningly beautiful bay that was once the crater of a gigantic volcano, picturesque Savusavu began to attract merchants in the 19th century, who set up warehouses and trading posts on the bay for copra, sea cucumber and sandalwood. Now a clearinghouse for travellers and nautical tourists from around the world, this sleepy northern outpost is a melting pot for strangers meeting at the crossroads of their transcontinental adventures, and sharing flamboyant tales over beers in the town's ramshackle but charming waterfront taverns.

Savusavu makes a fantastic base if you wish to go after the innumerable activities that are on offer across Vanua Levu. Conversely, if you are addicted to the joy of doing nothing, you can spend all your vacation sitting on the dock of the bay, and waste your time watching the tide roll away.

Suva

## TOP TIP

The scenic coastal road leading east from Savusavu, called Hibiscus Hwy, has a string of fabulous resorts and guesthouses that offer easy access to Natewa Bay and Salt Lake. Hibiscus Hwy is routinely serviced by taxis from Savusavu, making connectivity a breeze.

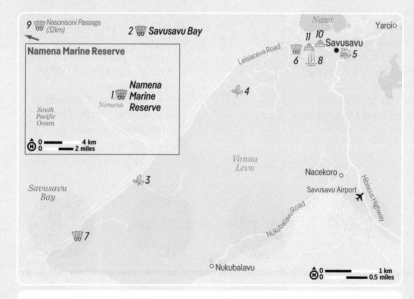

| HIGHLIGHTS | SIGHTS | ACTIVITIES, COURSES & TOURS | TRANSPORT |
|---|---|---|---|
| 1 Namena Marine Reserve | 3 Flora Tropica Gardens | 6 J Hunter Pearls | 10 Copra Shed Marina |
| 2 Savusavu Bay | 4 KokoMana | 7 Liquid State | 11 Waitui Marina |
| | 5 Savusavu | 8 Nakama Hot Springs | |
| | | 9 Nasonisoni Passage | |

DON YANEDOMAN/GETTY IMAGES ©

Savusavu

# Dive Savusavu Bay & Koro Sea

MULTITUDE OF FISH AND CORAL

Scuba divers visiting Savusavu are spoilt for choice when it comes to picking a dive site based on their underwater interests and dive certification levels. Despite being hit hard by Cyclone Winston in 2016, which bulldozed the shallow ocean bed of Savusavu Bay in the spell of a few hours, the hard coral reefs in the area have recovered quite rapidly. You can once again see some splendid formations in dive sites such as **Dungeons and Dragons** – with its towering maze of swim-throughs – and **Alice in Wonderland**, featuring massive bommies draped with diverse coral species. Also worth exploring is the magnificent soft coral garden at **Dreadlocks**, a dive site suited to divers of all levels. For a rendezvous with hammerheads and large schools of barracuda and jacks, drop down to the coral outcrop at **Dreamhouse**. On the other hand, thrill-seekers with advance diving skills might want to experience drift driving in the strong currents of nearby **Nasonisoni Passage**.

Diving in Savusavu takes place pretty much throughout the year, seven days a week, and dive shops operate boat trips up to three times a day (sometimes even a fourth trip for night diving). While factoring in the abilities of individual divers, dive sites are chosen depending on tides, currents and prevailing weather conditions. Dive sites within the bay are shallower and more sheltered from wind than those along the exposed Hibiscus Hwy in Koro Sea, where you can expect

## BEST DIVE SHOPS IN SAVUSAVU

### Jean-Michel Cousteau Diving

Founded by dive stalwarts Jean-Michel Cousteau and Don Santee. Expect top-shelf service, impeccable rental gear, nitrox refills and amazing guides.

### KoroSun Dive

Located in Savasi Island Resort, off Hibiscus Hwy, this outfit offers daily dive trips as well as certification courses up to divemaster level.

### Dive Savusavu

Located next to Koro Sun Resort on Hibiscus Hwy, this shop covers all dive sites in Savusavu Bay, Koro Sea, Namena and Natewa Bay.

## NAMENA DIVE TRIPS

The offshore **Namena Marine Reserve** (p153), known as one of Fiji's top diving destinations, is best accessed from Savusavu. For a fuel surcharge of about $75, all dive shops in town offer one- or two-dive trips to the reserve every week.

## WHERE TO STAY

**Gecko Lodge**
Pleasant and hospitable budget address on the waterfront, featuring colourful rooms and a communal kitchen that cooks up great meals. $

**Hot Springs Hotel**
Large modern establishment with clean and spacious rooms, a pleasant pool, decent dining, efficient service and fantastic bay views. $$

**Daku Resort**
Neat collection of comfortable *bures* amid manicured lawns, located across the road from a quiet pebbly beach opening onto the bay. $$

stronger currents and choppier surface conditions. Expect to pay between $275 and $340 for a two-tank dive in the area, depending on your choice of dive shop and dive sites.

# Learn to Free-Dive

HOLD YOUR BREATH

Opened in 2018, **Liquid State** is perhaps the only place in Fiji where aspirants can make a foray into what is currently one of the most Instagram-worthy water sports in the world. Priding itself on personalised service, the school works with small batches of four students or fewer at a time. On offer is a wide range of free-diving courses and certifications, such as a one-day 'discover free-diving' experience, a one-day, level-one certification down to 10m, and a three-day, level-two certification down to 20m. In-water training for all courses is conducted in the shallow and calm waters of Savusavu Bay, where the dive shop maintains a fixed buoy and mooring line. Prices for courses and experiences vary from $250 for one day to $700 for three days.

# Steaming Geysers Close to Boiling Point

VOLCANOES OF THE PAST

Less than 10 minutes by foot from Savusavu's main street is the fenced complex of **Nakama Hot Springs**, where a congregation of thermal geysers bubble away relentlessly as a constant reminder of Vanua Levu's seismic origins. The scalding hot water gushing out of these spouts is close to boiling point, and locals continue in the tradition of their ancestors to cook fish, tubers and sundry vegetables by steaming them in the geysers.

Once your nose has adjusted to the strong ammoniac smell and you can see through the plumes of hot steam that shroud the compound, spend some time reading the information plaques familiarising visitors with the science of tectonic plates, the creation of Fiji Islands as a result of volcanic activity, the formation of basalt columns and hot springs, and a map marking out more hot springs in other parts of Vanua Levu. Finally, be amazed when you learn that, in 2019, a bathymetric study conducted in Nakama confirmed the presence of several undersea hot springs in the vicinity of the bay area – the original giant crater – although it is yet to be determined whether these springs are active or dormant. The hot springs are open all day, and you can reach them by walking along the street that leads up the hill opposite Waitui Marina, between a fuel station and a convenience store.

 **WHERE TO STAY IN SAVUSAVU** —————————————————

**Jean-Michel Cousteau Resort**
Luxury resort attracting divers for its world-renowned owner, and families with children for its activities and complimentary babysitting. **$$$**

**Savasi Island Resort**
Elegant property with romantic *bures* located on an island connected to the Hibiscus Hwy by a causeway; a 10-minute taxi ride out of town. **$$$**

**Koro Sun Resort**
About 20 minutes out of town on Hibiscus Hwy, this upscale resort has a reputed spa, a nine-hole golf course and two tennis courts. **$$$**

# Palm Species from Across the Globe

A BOTANIST'S DELIGHT

The private **Flora Tropica Gardens**, sprawling over five acres of landscaped hillsides, is home to some 300 types of palm species collected painstakingly by its owners from around the world. For an entry fee of $25, you can spend hours on the timber boardwalk that goes around the tree-canopied gardens, and get acquainted with ghost palms from the Amazon basin, dwarf fishtail palms from Vietnam, cardboard palms from Mexico, as well as countless other varieties from countries as far as Madagascar, India and China. In the higher reaches of the boardwalk, you will arrive at a clearing from where you can appreciate fabulous views of Savusavu Bay below. En route, you will hear bird calls, spot butterflies and cross paths with slithery salamanders. The gardens are located about 4km southwest of town, and are open from 10am to 4pm daily.

## TOPSY TURVY

Seismological studies conducted in recent times have revealed a bizarre fact about Vanua Levu's geographic orientation. Apparently, the island was originally positioned in a northwest-southeast direction. But over millennia, the gradual shifting of the Pacific tectonic plate in relation to the Australian tectonic plate resulted in the entire island being turned anticlockwise by a full 90 degrees. Scientific data indicates that Udu Point – a narrow peninsula at the farthest eastern extremity of Vanua Levu – once pointed southeast, but is now positioned along a northeastern bearing. The neighbouring island of Taveuni also has volcanic pedigree, including the presence of a fault scarp where one tectonic plate has moved vertically in relation to its neighbouring plate.

CHAMELEONSEYE/SHUTTERSTOCK ©

Nakama Hot Springs

 **WHERE TO EAT IN SAVUSAVU**

**Captain's Table**
Restaurant with tons of ambience thanks to its vantage location on the marina; the multi-cuisine dinner menu is impressive to boot. **$$**

**Surf 'n' Turf**
Laid-back restaurant in a commercial complex with a decent wine list, tasty curries, hearty fish and meat dishes, and homemade ice cream. **$$**

**Chong Pong**
Cheap and tasty Chinese food combined with astonishingly quick service makes this 1st-floor restaurant a hit with the locals. **$**

## BEST TIMES TO VISIT THE MARINAS

**Breakfast**

**Copra Shed Marina** has a tasty and wholesome breakfast platter that sets you up for the day's adventures and the coffee hits the spot.

**Late afternoon**

A good time to socialise with nautical tourists, who usually gather at the pubs in both marinas to exchange notes after the day's chores on their boats.

**Sunday evening**

Live music and a hearty barbecue menu attract a crowd of laid-back locals and cheerful tourists to the beer garden at Copra Shed Marina every weekend.

Marinas

# Marinas by the Bay

HANG WITH YACHTIES

Every year between April and December, Savusavu's sleepy waterfront spurs to life, as dozens of sailboats and yachts call into the harbour every week and moor at one of the two marinas in town. Nautical tourism, though a nascent industry, is gathering momentum in the South Pacific, and this is evident in more and more sailing enthusiasts steering their floating homes to Fiji by either riding the trade winds blowing in from the US west coast, or navigating up from Australia and New Zealand.

Savusavu's principal hub for nautical activity is the **Copra Shed Marina**, a stylish multi-facility institution for visiting yachties – as well as walk-in tourists – that packs in two busy restaurants, a delightful pub by the water's edge, a travel agency and air ticketing office, a currency exchange desk, a convenience store for nautical gear and even a few 1st-floor rooms for short stays. The adjacent **Waitui Marina**, a rickety wooden establishment located about 100m west of Copra Shed Marina, is comparatively less busy but has loads of nostalgia from the rollicking days of high-seas adventure. As of 2023, a third under-construction marina (much larger and, arguably, more modern) is gradually taking shape across the water from the two existing marinas, presumably to cater to superyachts that are expected to come calling in the near future.

 **WHERE TO DRINK IN SAVUSAVU**

**Savusavu Yacht Club**
This delightful watering hole at Copra Shed Marina has chilled beer, tasty cocktails and a convivial mix of yachties and other travellers.

**Planter's Club**
Originally a thirst quencher for 19th-century planters in the colonial era, this charming relic does a range of sundowners and other mixes.

**Sea Lovers**
This well-stocked bottle shop and deli has wines from Australia and New Zealand, cheeses from Europe and coffees from around the world.

# Learn About Fiji Pearls

JEWELS OF THE SEA

Rare, expensive and globally renowned for their tonal lustre, Fiji pearls are produced by a unique species of black-lipped oyster endemic to the waters around Vanua Levu and Taveuni. Located in Savusavu's bay area, **J Hunter Pearls** is arguably the biggest name in Fiji's niche and high-end pearl industry.

The company's workshop is a five-minute walk west from Waitui Marina, where tourists are given a pearl-farm tour on weekday mornings for a $50 fee. The experience begins with an informative presentation on Fiji pearls, followed by a snorkelling tour (bring your own gear) in the bay where you can hover on the water's surface and spy the oyster lines descending into the depths, laden with giant pearl-bearing oysters left to age naturally for up to 18 months. If you visit in the 'seeding season' (April to May and October to November), you can observe visiting Japanese technicians implanting oysters with organic core pellets (around which pearls are formed by secretion of saliva), or even harvesting fully formed pearls from aged oysters.

# Tour a Cocoa Plantation

ORGANIC CHOCOLATES, ANYONE?

Sustainable agroforestry – the practice of growing a variety of crops by maximising land use while preventing the degradation of natural forests – comes to life in **KokoMana**, a brilliantly managed organic plantation located about 3km southwest of Savusavu. While it dabbles in a mix of crops such as yaqona (kava), vanilla, coffee, cardamom, cinnamon and ginger, KokoMana's true pride and joy is its cocoa farm. A guided tree-to-bar tour of the farm and the on-site chocolate factory explains each step involved in the process of making fine organic chocolate from local produce. Tours end with a tasting session, where you can sample as many as seven different varieties of chocolate produced by the farm, including a delicious 80% dark variety, a 70% bar seasoned with sea salt, and dark-chocolate bombs filled with candied ginger sourced from an organic farm in Viti Levu. On your way out, you can also purchase a few bars from the shop to savour through your vacation.

Farm tours at KokoMana are conducted at 10am on Monday, Wednesday and Friday. Each tour lasts about 90 minutes, and you'll have to buy a $30 ticket for the experience.

## WHAT MAKES FIJI PEARLS SPECIAL?

In a stark departure from black pearls farmed in other Pacific countries, such as Tahiti and Cook Islands, the black pearls of Fiji take on a unique sheen that ranges from green to golden. The dominant theory suggests this has to do with the nourishment that oysters derive from volcanic minerals present in Fiji's northern oceans. That said, the finest and most exacting step in producing Fiji pearls takes place at the seeding stage. After oysters have been implanted with core pellets, they are also grafted with a speck of tissue from a donor oyster identified for a specific colour, on the inside of its shell. The tissue transplant triggers the recipient oyster to replicate the colour of the donor oyster's shell in the pearl it eventually produces.

---

**GETTING AROUND**

A feeder bus service operated by Suncity Ferries leaves Savusavu bus stand at 6am daily to connect with the Taveuni-bound ferry from Buca Bay.

The road journey takes 90 minutes, and from there, it's another 90 minutes by boat to the pier just south of Somosomo.

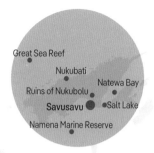

# Beyond Savusavu

The less-trodden path out of Savusavu takes travellers to isolated hideaways in the lap of unspoiled nature.

Very few travellers who visit Vanua Levu consider venturing out of Savusavu for a jaunt to the far extremities of the island, which is a plain shame. With a heart full of zeitgeist and a few extra days to spare, you could find yourself rowing your way through swathes of virgin coastal forests, exploring deserted ocean bays, or swimming with fishes on vibrant mid-sea coral reefs. Getting to these remote parts takes some advance logistical planning, but if you're willing to go the distance, you will be rewarded with a matchless natural experience that still reflects a sense of purity and innocence, fast becoming extinct in the world today.

**TOP TIP**

If you wish to self-drive around Vanua Levu, several agencies in Savusavu will rent you a sedan for around $120 per day, including fuel.

CHAMELEONSEYE/SHUTTERSTOCK ©

BRETT MONROE GARNER/GETTY IMAGES ©

Hawksbill sea turtle, Savusavu

# Fiji's Top Diving Experience

HUGE SUBMERGED BARRIER REEF

A two-hour speedboat trip south of Savusavu, the marine-protected area of **Namena Marine Reserve** has the most legendary diving around Vanua Levu, and possibly in all of Fiji.
Defined by a submerged barrier reef extending over almost
70 sq km in the ocean channel between Vanua Levu and Viti
Levu, Namena is Fiji's largest community managed marine
area. Over the years, a strict ban on fishing here has resulted in corals so vibrant, and marine life so plentiful that the
park has become the de-facto poster child for Fiji's underwater world.

To dive in Namena, you will have to pay an access fee of $30,
against which you will be issued a dive tag valid for a year's
diving in the park. The money raised from these tags goes directly into the welfare of the local community that safeguards
the reserve from illegal fishing and poaching.

Given its distance from Savusavu, dive boats only visit Namena once or twice a week, or whenever they have enough divers to fill a boat. There's also a surcharge of $75 involved, to
cover additional fuel burned during the longer run. Contact

**BEST NAMENA
DIVE SITES**

**Chimneys**

Two sheer towers
rising from a sandy
bottom at a depth
of 25m, home to
sea fans, gorgeous
colonies of soft coral,
white tip reef sharks,
and moray eels.

**Grand Central
Station**

This deeper dive
site is characterised
by a hair-raising
drop-off that plunges
into the abyss and
offers sightings of
hammerheads, manta
rays and mackerel.

**Save-A-Tack
Passage**

A deep, sand-
bottomed site
with drift-diving
opportunities,
featuring dogtooth
tuna, reef sharks,
giant groupers, and
schools of barracuda
and trevally.

 **OFFBEAT EXCURSIONS IN VANUA LEVU**

**Naweni**
A village where you can find
a unique species of prawns of
boiled-red colour, considered
sacred by the local population.

**Wasavula**
A site once used for
cannibalistic ceremonies, with
a head-chopping block and
a stone for presenting body
parts to the chief.

**Korovatu Beach**
The nearest stretch of sand
to Labasa town, which makes
for a decent side trip if you're
flying through Labasa airport.

## WAISALI FOREST WALK

In the mountains north of Savusavu, the 120-hectare **Waisali Rainforest Reserve** is home to thousands of birds, flowers, trees and plants, some of which are traditionally used in local medicines. There's a pleasant hiking trail that takes visitors through the untouched greenery of these pristine volcanic mountains, descending past a waterfall along the way (watch out for slippery deathtrap rocks). Depending on your walking speed and stops en route, the hike takes between 30 minutes and an hour.

The main gate to the park is 20km up the road from Savusavu going towards Labasa. A taxi ride from town takes 30 minutes. However, confirm in advance with your resort if the park is open, as landslides and path maintenance often result in temporary closures.

your preferred dive shop well in advance if you want to visit the park, so that they can confirm a few likely dates.

# Kayaking to Salt Lake
ROWING WITH THE TIDE

In the dense jungles north of Hibiscus Hwy is a tidal river that drains an inland reservoir – commonly called Salt Lake – into the ocean. Constantly ebbing and flowing with the tide, the waterway has become a popular kayaking route for those who fancy some relaxed action amid a paradise of tropical wilderness. If you align your visit with the incoming tide, you can simply sit back in your kayak and let the water carry you up the 2km mangrove-lined course all the way to the lake. After you have explored the flora and fauna in the lake's biosphere, ride the outflow down to your starting point, from where it's a 30-minute drive back to Savusavu.

**Immersion Fiji** conducts all-inclusive full-day trips to Salt Lake from Savusavu for $200 per person. The tour departs at different times every day, depending on the prevailing tide chart. Alternatively, you can stay a night or two at the secluded **Salt Lake Lodge**, located in the forest by the creek.

# Dive in Natewa Bay
LEARN ABOUT CORAL CONSERVATION

Owing to its remote location, Natewa Bay remains one of the least-visited scuba destinations in Fiji. However, those willing to make the schlep are rewarded with an

MARC ANDERSON/ALAMY STOCK PHOTO ©

**Blue starfish, Vanua Levu**

## OFFBEAT EXCURSIONS IN VANUA LEVU

**Floating Island**
An intriguing island in a pond – located east of Labasa – that apparently floats around on the water when a priest chants at it.

**Wainunu Bay**
A remote bay where the Wainunu river drains into the ocean, and where Fijian subsistence farmers grow timber and kava.

**Dakuniba**
South of Buca Bay, this forested village is the site of ancient petroglyphs considered to be of mystical or ceremonial significance.

154

underwater extravaganza of hard coral formations. Despite being Fiji's largest bay, Natewa Bay is well sheltered from the winds and swells of the open ocean, which makes diving a relatively comfortable and undemanding exercise. Often spotted here amid vast colonies of plate, table, brain, and staghorn corals are schools of white tip and grey reef sharks, snapper, trevally, mackerel and barracuda.

**Ocean Ventures Fiji**, a dive operation based in the bay, offers its clients fun dives as well as half-day coral conservation courses, on which you can get a first-hand feel of maintaining a coral nursery. It can arrange return transfers from Savusavu, but you could also stay midway at **Salt Lake Lodge** or Savasi Island Resort, especially if you're planning on diving multiple days.

# Escape to Nukubati

THE WILD WILD NORTH

The northern shoreline of Vanua Levu is guarded from the vastness of the Pacific ocean by the **Great Sea Reef**, also known as the third longest continuous barrier-reef system in the world. Stretching more than 200km, the reef has a mind-boggling biodiversity comprising more than half of all known fish species and three-quarters of all identified coral species in Fiji – including a dozen species currently listed as threatened.

The private island of **Nukubati**, perched off the shoreline and hemmed by the reef to its north, is one of the best vantage points from where you can witness the marine exuberance of the reef. A community tourism project uniting the island's owners and local villages who supply the island with produce and workforce, the salubrious resort island has five eco-chic *bures* that can be rented for a minimum three-night stay. Activities include diving (gear available for rental), muck snorkelling, kayaking, spearfishing, as well as interactions with the community over *tatavu* (barbecue) of fresh-caught reef fish.

Nukubati is two hours from Savusavu by road. (You can also access the island by flying to Labasa, from where the drive only takes an hour.) Ask the resort to arrange for a taxi that will bring you to the private landing on Vanua Levu's northern coast off Qumusea village, where the resort boat will be waiting to pick you up.

## RUINS OF NUKUBOLU

Deep in the mountains north of Savusavu lie the ruins of **Nukubolu**, an ancient Fijian village whose stone foundations and terraces have survived the spoils of time and remain in surprisingly good condition. The setting is picturesque, featuring a volcanic crater with steaming hot springs in the background. Local residents dry kava roots on corrugated iron sheets laid over the pools, and bathe in the mineral-rich waters as a healing aid. To get to Nukubolu, you will have to organise a day tour through your accommodation in Savusavu; you might need a 4WD in wet season. Remember to carry a *sevusevu* (gift) for the local village chief, whose permission you will require to visit the site.

**GETTING AROUND**

For an offbeat way of arriving in Vanua Levu, hop on to the thrice-daily ferry that connects Natovi Landing in Viti Levu to Nabouwalu

Landing on the western edge of Vanua Levu. From Nabouwalu, taxis can transport you to Savusavu in around 90 minutes.

# SOMOSOMO

Somosomo

✪ Suva

A long-winding, one-strip town of residences, conveniences and offices, Somosomo is the largest settlement on Taveuni. It's also of significant political and historical importance: the Great Council of Chiefs' meeting hall was built here in 1986 for the gathering of chiefs from all over Fiji. While not being the most beautiful part of Taveuni, Somosomo holds most facilities, and is a concourse for getting to several sights in the central and southern parts of the island. The southern neighbourhood of Naqara is where you will find a few supermarkets, budget hotels and the island's only bank with an ATM. Another 2km down the coast is Waiyevo, Taveuni's administrative centre with a hospital, a police station, the main ferry landing and a couple of resorts. About 2km further south is Wairiki, which has a general store, a hilltop Catholic mission and a playground that doubles as the island's main public area for sports competitions and festivities.

## TOP TIP

Naqara has a small collection of hotels, most of them boxy and practical. But you will also find a string of pleasant resorts and well-run guesthouses either between Waiyevo and Wairiki, offering easy access to the ferry landing, or along the secluded stretch of road past the Wairiki Mission.

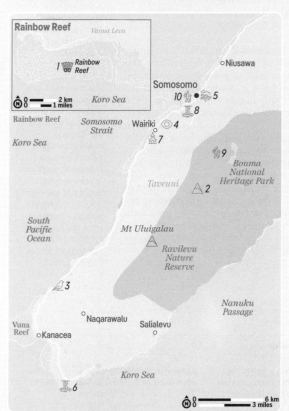

**HIGHLIGHTS**
1 Rainbow Reef

**SIGHTS**
2 Des Voeux Peak
3 Nabogiono Farms
4 International Date Line
5 Somosomo
6 South Cape Blowhole
7 Wairiki Catholic Mission
8 Waitavala Water Slide

**ACTIVITIES, COURSES & TOURS**
9 Lake Tagimaucia
10 Naqara

# Forlorn Cape with a Beauteous Natural Blowhole

SPECTACLE OF NATURE

The southern tip of Taveuni is guarded by a ruggedly beautiful coastline relentlessly sculpted out of volcanic rock by the ocean. All day and all night, angry waves crash with a deafening roar on the black stones lining the forlorn cape, and kick up a cloud of spray that hangs perennially in the air. A particularly awesome sight here is the natural **South Cape Blowhole**, which shoots up a column of seawater every time a breaking wave squeezes into the narrow cavern at its base, and is expelled upwards through the rocky spout. With strong breaks, the spray can sometimes erupt as high as 30m, dispersing in a million water droplets that refract the sunlight into misty rainbows.

Visiting this remote part of the island takes some logistical planning, although the sight is totally worth the trip. You can either self-drive, or rent a taxi in Somosomo to bring you here for a return fare of around $150 (the journey takes about 45 minutes each way). Leaving Somosomo, the tar-sealed road gradually gives way to a gravelled track that winds through forested hills, headed in a southwestern direction. After passing Vuna and Kanacea villages, the path veers left to continue southeast, until you reach an unmarked clearing on the seaward side of the road, which serves as the de-facto viewpoint for the blowhole down on the coast below. South Cape is also where the road grinds to an end, making the uninhabited wilderness of southeastern Taveuni completely inaccessible.

# Wing It with Taveuni's Birdlife

AN AVIAN OUTING

More than 20 species of birds thrive in the evergreen forests of Fiji's 'garden island', including silktails, red shining parrots, turtle doves, parrot finches, crowned flycatchers, and the rare orange dove. For a date with some of these native avian species all in one place, book yourself a one-hour bird-watching tour at **Nabogiono Farms**, a family-owned estate located midway on the road between Wairiki and South Cape. Sprawled across 40 hectares of farms, forestry and homestead combined, the property is a veritable hot spot for bird-watching. Tours – either in the early morning or late afternoon – are conducted by the informative Bobby, who owns the farm. The experience costs $40 per person (minimum two guests).

## BEST EXCURSIONS AROUND SOMOSOMO

**International Date Line**
A plaque-bearing pavilion in a field opposite Waiyevo Hospital, marking the axis along which the 180-degree meridian cuts through Taveuni, separating today from yesterday.

**Waitavala Water Slide**
A cascading waterfall in the forest (20 minutes by foot from Waiyevo), where frolicking locals slide down the narrow stony tract and plunge into the limpid pool below.

**Des Voeux Peak**
A bumpy one-hour drive by 4WD up to Taveuni's second-highest mountain, for panoramic bird's-eye views from its 1195m summit. You can hike back to Wairiki on the way down.

 **WHERE TO STAY IN SOMOSOMO**

**Aroha Taveuni**
Property on the northern edge of Wairiki with a collection of elegant beachside *bures* looking out over a black-sand beach. **$$$**

**Taveuni Dive Resort**
The island's premier dive resort, with a reputed dive shop on-site and eco-chic luxury *bures* built with sustainable material. **$$$**

**Nakia Resort**
Eco-themed resort with an in-house dive shop located midway between Somosomo and the northern settlement of Matei. **$$$**

To maximise your time at the farm and get a sense of other on-site activities, you could combine your bird-watching trip with a forest trek, followed by a farm-to-table lunch. This supplementary three-hour experience costs $80 per person (minimum two guests), and includes a sumptuous vegan sampling of the farm's own produce. If you still wish to linger, the farm has about 400m of private sea frontage, where you could take a dip in the ocean or indulge in a spot of kayaking.

Nabogiono Farms is best visited in conjunction with a trip to the blowhole. Tours are conducted seven days a week, but be sure to book a visit in advance.

## Hike to Lake Tagimaucia

TAVEUNI'S WILD HEARTLAND

Lake Tagimaucia is an old volcanic crater hidden behind dense forests in the mountains above Somosomo. Masses of vegetation float on the still waters of the lake (823m above sea level), and Fiji's national flower – a rare epiphyte called *tagimaucia* – grows wild on its swampy shores. This red-and-white flower blooms only from October to December, exclusively in its native habitat, and careful attempts to grow it elsewhere in the world have failed so far.

The final section of the trek is difficult, owing to its rough and overgrown trail (the initial approach road can be coursed by 4WD), and for the fact that the terrain around the lake can be very muddy. It will take you anywhere between three to four hours one way, so carry lunch, snacks and water, and allow for about eight hours to complete the round trip. Do not attempt this hike if you are visiting in the rainy season, as parts of the trail may be too slippery and dangerous. It is worth noting in this context that the flowering season of the *tagimaucia* is also the best time to attempt this trek, as the daytime temperatures are still bearable and the rainy season is still some weeks away.

The journey starts in Naqara, where – apart from stocking up on trek rations – you will need to arrange for a knowledgeable guide, preferably in advance. If you can't find a guide by yourself, ask your accommodation to book one for you. It is not recommended to do this hike without the supervision of an experienced local.

## WAIRIKI CATHOLIC MISSION

This faded colonial-era beauty has bags of architectural charm, and the setting is equally beguiling – standing on a hill slope peering over the Somosomo Strait. The mission's interior has an impressive beam ceiling and beautiful stained glass, reputedly from France. In the presbytery there is a painting of a legendary battle in which a Catholic missionary helped Taveuni's warriors defeat their Tongan attackers. The mission is worth a visit on Sunday when the congregation lets it rip with some impressive vocals. There are no pews here, though. The congregation sits on woven mats on the floor, a custom that requires you to take off your shoes before you enter.

## GETTING AROUND

Somosomo's main ferry pier at Waiyevo has morning connections to Vanua Levu's Buca Bay, which is serviced by road from Savusavu.

Tickets for the journey on board Suncity Ferries can be purchased from the Suncity supermarket in Wairiki.

# Beyond Somosomo

Somosomo

Rainbow Reef

Beneath the waters off Taveuni's west coast, not far from Somosomo, is an undersea garden famous for its soft corals.

Somosomo is a convenient jumpoff point for travellers looking to explore Vanua Levu's southeastern shoreline which, given Taveuni's geographic position, is only a short speedboat ride from town across the Somosomo Strait. This remote shoreline drops sharply into the ocean channel, where strong water currents bring rich supplies of plankton and microorganisms for soft corals to feed on and thrive. Over time, this nutritive abundance has resulted in the formation of a reef system spectacularly laden with innumerable species of soft corals, spanning a diverse colour palette that has gained it the moniker Rainbow Reef. This is coral diving at its absolute best, and promises mesmerising underwater encounters that few other places in the world can guarantee.

## TOP TIP

Some deep dives in Rainbow Reef are only possible around neap tide every month, at low slack tide when water levels are at their lowest.

Vuna Reef, Somosomo Strait, Taveuni

JASON EDWARDS/GETTY IMAGES ©

FLICKETTI/SHUTTERSTOCK ©

**Great White Wall**

### BEST DIVE SHOPS IN TAVEUNI

**Taveuni Dive**

One of the island's longest-running and most reputed dive operations, which can combine dive trips with classy accommodation packages in its proprietary resort.

**Garden Island Dive Centre**

A trusted and well-run dive shop located within Garden Island Resort, offering a good range of rental gear and nitrox tanks for certified divers.

**Taveuni Ocean Sports**

Located midway between Matei and Somosomo, this eco-minded operation does marine biology briefings during dive trips to educate divers about reef ecology.

# Dive Rainbow Reef

SOFT CORALS UNLIMITED

Lending credence to Fiji's reputation as the soft-coral capital of the world, Rainbow Reef is a supernova of dazzling colours displayed by the most splendid array of soft-coral species you could possibly encounter anywhere on the planet. The story goes that the reef was discovered by diving legend Jacques-Yves Cousteau, and over the years, more than 20 dive sites were identified along the relatively short length of the reef. There are more than 300 species of soft coral here (and another 100 or so species of hard coral), along with schools of large pelagic fish, such as barracuda, jacks, dogtooth tuna, sharks, rays and mackerel.

According to one's individual diving expertise and experience, it is possible to do three types of dives here. The most challenging but exciting are wall dives, where divers catch a drift current and glide along the face of undersea cliffs plunging into the blue abyss. Time and tide permitting, experienced divers take a shy at exploring the **Great White Wall**, where a hairy descent through a narrow

 **OTHER DIVE SITES TO EXPLORE IN RAINBOW REEF**

**Purple Wall**
Adjacent to the Great White Wall, this site promises heaps of purple soft coral, with tons of fish and invertebrate species.

**Zoo**
One of the farthest sites from Taveuni, on the far western end of Rainbow Reef, best dived at low slack tide due to its depth.

**Sam's Point**
A shallow site with mild current, laden with colonies of soft coral and sea fans, usually done as a second dive after a deeper first dive.

cavern spits divers out into a big blue void at nearly 30m. Looking behind, even while drifting with the ebbing tide, you see a massive wall draped with soft coral the colour of fresh snowflakes. In the bottomless depths below, dolphins and tiger sharks often make an unexpected entry. A matchless display of otherworldly nature, the Great White Wall is often ranked among the top 10 dive sites in the world, so have a go at it if you can.

Less nervy than wall dives are pinnacle sites, such as **Annie's Bommies**, where a bunch of rocky towers layered with soft coral rise from the seabed, allowing divers to meander through them at leisure. Sloping reef sites, on the other hand, are usually the least demanding in terms of currents and depth, and are suited to divers of all levels. One of the most popular sloping reef sites visited by dive boats is **Jerry's Jelly**, where a gentle drift takes you past pinnacles of white soft coral before transporting you to the sheltered side of the reef. **Fish Factory**, another frequently visited site, is aptly named, thanks to its schools of parrotfish, Napoleon wrasses, trevally, Spanish mackerel and countless other species. Finally, if a dramatic hard-coral panorama is what you fancy, ask the boat to make a stop on **Cabbage Patch**, where a shallow drift dive takes you over a vast field of giant cabbage coral spread over a sand patch nearly the size of two tennis courts.

If you're keen to explore Rainbow Reef but are unable to dive, you might consider snorkelling on some of the shallow sites. Unless they are specifically headed to deep dive sites on neap tide days, dive boats will typically take on snorkellers. Bear in mind that snorkelling in the channel is also subject to currents, so you'll often be following the same course as the divers below you, while the boat drifts alongside towards the endpoint of the dive.

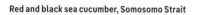

Red and black sea cucumber, Somosomo Strait

## LEGEND OF TAGIMAUCIA

Fiji's floral emblem, the *tagimaucia* (pronounced 'tan-gee-mouth-ya') grows above 600m in Taveuni and isolated areas of Vanua Levu. The rare flower hangs off a vine and has white petals with a layer of red petals underneath. As Fijian legend goes, there once lived a young girl who fled into the forest and climbed a vine-covered *ivi* (Polynesian chestnut) tree. The higher she climbed, the more entangled she got in the creepers. Unable to break free, the girl began to weep, and her tears, as they fell on the vines below, turned to beautiful *tagimaucia* flowers. Calmed by the sight of the flowers, the girl finally managed to escape from the forest and return home.

## GETTING AROUND

An end-to-end boat ride across the breadth of Somosomo Strait can take between 30 and 45 minutes, depending on your start and end points. Resorts in southeastern Vanua Levu can arrange a boat transfer for guests to/from a pier close to Matei airport, bypassing Somosomo's Waiyevo pier.

# MATEI

A residential area on Taveuni's northern cape, Matei offers access to Taveuni's only airport, and is therefore preferred by many travellers as their base on the island. The main road runs along the beach, passing a string of manicured resorts and leafy guesthouses before arcing around the airport and heading down Taveuni's isolated northeastern shoreline. The airport is tiny, and if you are travelling light, you can literally step off the plane and wander into the locality in five minutes. Matei also makes a fantastic base for accessing the northern dive sites of Rainbow Reef, and for making forays into the wilderness of northeastern Taveuni for a mixed bag of adventures on land and in water.

## TOP TIP

Pull out enough cash from the ATM at Naqara before coming to Taveuni, as there are no cash machines or banks in this part of the island. You will find a couple of decent supermarkets near the airport, so don't feel compelled to stock up on conveniences before heading north.

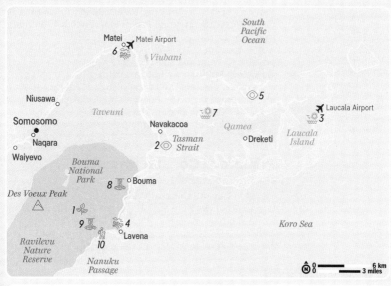

## SIGHTS
1 Bouma National Park
2 Civa Pearl Farm
3 Laucala
4 Lavena
5 Matagi
6 Matei
7 Qamea
8 Tavoro Waterfalls
9 Wainibau Waterfall

## ACTIVITIES, COURSES & TOURS
10 Lavena Coastal Walk

**Wainibau Waterfall**

## OFFSHORE ISLANDS NEAR MATEI

### Qamea

This island close to Taveuni's northeastern shore is riddled with deep bays and lined by white sand beaches, its interior rich with bird life.

### Matagi

Formed by a submerged volcanic crater, this tiny island has a northern bay facing the open ocean, and a fringing reef to the southwest.

### Laucala

Playground of the rich and famous, this private island is home to an ultra-luxury resort reputed to be one of the world's most exclusive getaways.

# Tavoro Waterfalls Hike

ENCOUNTER TAVEUNI'S GRAND WILDERNESS

Pristine **Bouma National Park** covers about 150 sq km of rainforest and coastal greenery in upper Taveuni. A convenient way to experience the green abundance is to hit the forest trail along the course of the majestic three-stage **Tavoro Waterfalls**. From the roadside visitor centre, it's a 90-minute hike through a magical forest alive with the sound of birdcalls, gurgling water and leaves rustling in the wind. At the first and lowest stage, about 10 minutes from the starting point, the waterfall plunges dramatically down a 25m cliff into a pool of clear water, where it's possible to swim and snorkel. The second stage is reached via a steep 40-minute climb, involving a rock-hopping river crossing. The third and highest stage is another 40 minutes up the trail; if you bring your snorkel gear, you can see hundreds of prawns at the pool here.

The visitor centre is 20 minutes by road from Matei, on Taveuni's east coast.

# Primordial Coastal Greenery

BEACHES AND WATERFALLS

The 5km **Lavena Coastal Walk** starts from **Lavena** village and follows the edge of a forest along the stunning white-sand Lavena beach. Through most of this two-hour walk, the clearly marked and well-maintained trail keeps close to shoreline while passing peaceful hutments and

## WHERE TO EAT IN MATEI

**Dive Cafe**
Strong espressos, hearty meals and yummy desserts are on offer through the day at this relaxed cafe located right on the water's edge. $

**Tramonto**
Cheerful restaurant hard to beat for its gigantic pizzas, chilled beer and sweeping panoramic views of Somosomo Strait. $$

**Suncity**
A surprisingly well-stocked supermarket close to the airport, with an impressive selection of hard cheeses, chocolates and ice creams. $

skirting around thick coastal greenery. Past Naba settlement, the path spills onto the beach and crosses a stream, then crosses a suspension bridge to eventually ascend the ancient valley of Wainibau Creek. Walking through a landscape straight out of *Jurassic Park*, clambering over rocks and swimming through two small pools, you finally arrive at the **Wainibau Waterfall**, where two cascades plunge at different angles into a deep pool with sheer walls. Given the lay of the terrain, the path can be tricky to walk during spells of heavy rain, when violent flash floods may occur. It is not recommended to do this walk alone – you can hire a local guide at the visitor centre.

Lavena village is 40 minutes from Matei, 20 minutes past Tavoro Waterfalls (p164) on the same road. Boat tours can be arranged to visit the waterfall by sea.

# Pearls & Corals

TOUR A PEARL FARM AND SNORKEL A STUNNING SHALLOW REEF

Located in the coastal expanse midway between Lavena and Matei, **Civa Pearl Farm** harvests exquisite crops of Fijian black pearls in the waters adjacent to the protected Waitabu Marine Park. You can contact them in advance to arrange a pearl farm tour, usually conducted at 2pm on weekdays depending on visitor numbers. Civa's guest centre is a stilted shed that stands in a shallow reef about 100m off the coast. The tour here includes a lecture-demonstration on how Fiji pearls are produced, the characteristics of black-lipped oysters and a Q&A session related to pearl farming. This is followed by a 15-minute snorkelling trip in the farm's house reef, which is easily one of the best-preserved shallow coastal reefs you can ever set your eyes on.

DON MAMMOSER/SHUTTERSTOCK ©

**Oyster shells at a pearl farm, Vanua Levu**

## BEST PLACES TO STAY IN MATEI

**Maravu Plantation Resort**
This sprawling resort offers a mix of well-maintained private *bures* as well as shared accommodation in its palm-shaded hillside premises. $$

**Tides Reach Resort**
Intimate, modern and minimalistic, this seaside resort features four elegant *bures* with private wooden decks looking onto the ocean. $$$

**Taveuni Palms**
Each villa in this breathtakingly beautiful resort has its own private beach and pool. It offers complimentary nights for stays longer than six days. $$$

---

## GETTING AROUND

Public transport in Matei is scarce, and it is advisable to hire a dedicated car for exploring northern Taveuni. Every resort in Matei can arrange a vehicle for day trips. Expect to pay around $200 for a full-day hire.

Great Astrolabe Reef (p172)

# KADAVU & LAU

⭐Suva

## FIJI'S FAR-FLUNG FRONTIERS

Secluded, remote and untouched, Kadavu and Lau lure
intrepid souls to venture off the beaten tourist track.

A long chain of interconnected undersea mountain ranges marking the southern and far eastern extents of Fiji's territory, the island groups of Kadavu and Lau are among the country's least-explored regions. Visiting these distant parts poses several challenges in terms of logistics and transport, and the lack of adequate tourism infrastructure means that only a few travellers eventually get the chance to set foot here. However, those who are resilient and patient enough to venture out to these outlying parts are rewarded with unparalleled close encounters of the natural kind, while indulging in a magical holiday far from the trappings of modern urban life.

The main reason to make a trip to Kadavu is a chance to see the magnificent

Great Astrolabe Reef, the fourth-largest barrier reef on the planet. Lau, on the other hand, promises turquoise ocean waters, impenetrable tropical jungles and traditional villages that still preserve elements of antique Fijian (and Tongan) life. Sandwiched between the two groups is a third cluster of islands called Moala, even more tricky to access, where travellers with tons of endurance can rock up to experience a natural environment that harks back to historical times.

If you are planning a holiday in these islands, you must note that these groups are all very far from each other to cover in a single trip. A convenient (though expensive) workaround is to book yourself on a cruise ship that drops anchor at different islands while doing a circuitous trip around Fiji.

Inset: Lau banded iguana, Lau (p181)

THE MAIN AREAS

**GREAT ASTROLABE REEF**
Corals as far as the eyes go.
p172

**VANUA BALAVU**
Fiji's first port and botanical gardens.
p180

# Find Your Way

Kadavu's only airstrip is at Vunisea village. Vanua Balavu and Lakeba in Lau have fair-weather grass airstrips. Government ships service Lau islands once or twice a month, but departures can sway widely from schedule.

### AIR

Serviced by Fiji Airways, Vunisea has a return flight to Nadi five days a week, and one direct flight to Suva every Monday. For Lau, there's one weekly return flight from Suva to Vanua Balavu on Wednesdays, and Lakeba on Thursdays.

### FERRY

Goundar Shipping has two weekly overnight ferries from Suva to Vunisea on Tuesdays and Fridays. However, delays and cancellations are not uncommon, and crossing the open seas can be rough in bad weather.

### CRUISE

Captain Cook Cruises has a leisurely 11-day itinerary starting from Port Denarau and going around Fiji Islands. The luxury cruise ship drops anchor along the way at several spots in Kadavu, Moala and Lau.

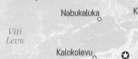

**Great Astrolabe Reef, p172**

This gigantic undersea barrier reef is a grand amphitheatre for marine life sightings and coral odysseys.

DENNIS SABO/SHUTTERSTOCK ©

Buca

Matei

Bagasu

Somosomo

Bouma

Kocoma

Laucala

Taveuni

Lavena

Navakawau

**Vanua Balavu, p180**

The biggest settlement in northern Lau, where laid-back residents play cricket when not going about their relaxed lives.

Malima

Vanua Balavu

Kaibu

Nukutolu

Kanacea

Lomaloma

Munia

Vatu Vara

Mago

Katafaga

Tuvuca

Lomati

Tuvuca

Cicia

Viti Levu Bay

Nayau

Liku

SOUTH PACIFIC OCEAN

Lakeba

Tubou

Vanua Vatu

Aiwa

Nasoki

Ororua

Moala

Tavu Na Sici

Komo

Namaku-i-Lau

Vuaqava

Totoya

Kabara

Udu

Matuku

Qalikarua

Fulaga

0  50 km
0  25 miles

# Plan Your Time

Always factor in reserve days while visiting Kadavu and Lau. Flights and ferries can be cancelled at short notice due to bad weather, and it may be a while before you are put on the next connection.

BCAMPBELL65/SHUTTERSTOCK ©

Coral reef, Lau (p181)

## Less Than a Week

● If you have only a few days, limit your explorations to within **Kadavu** (p173).

● Book an air ticket to **Vunisea** (p179) from Nadi or Suva; the flight takes less than an hour.

● From Vunisea, have a resort boat pick you up and take you to a resort of your choice – the most popular and accessible destinations are **Matava** (p174), **Oneta** (p175) and **Kokomo** (p176).

● Base yourself in one of these places, and make the most of your time to explore the marine wilderness of the **Great Astrolabe Reef** (p172), and catch up on some quality alone time.

### Seasonal Highlights

Trips to Kadavu and Lau in the rainy season (November to March) may coincide with the odd cyclone that is likely to blow in. The winter months (May to August) are great for cruises.

**JANUARY**
The ocean is warmer than the rest of the year, but water visibility is low, due to wind and swells.

**MARCH**
There is a high chance of rain playing spoilsport and messing with your travel plans, particularly flights.

**MAY**
Trade winds begin to blow in from the southeast. The mercury dips as the dry season kicks off.

BOTTOM, FROM LEFT: MALOFF/SHUTTERSTOCK ©, BRIDGET CALIP/SHUTTERSTOCK ©, BCAMPBELL65/SHUTTERSTOCK ©

# One Week to Play

● It would still be prudent to remain within **Kadavu's islands**, for the simple fact that it is the most accessible from Viti Levu.

● Get an overdose of diving, see **manta rays** (p174) in their natural habitat, go **surfing** (p175) on the impressive reef breaks, and **snorkel** (p175) above shallow reefs in sheltered lagoons.

● Take the time to engage in inland activities on Kadavu's main island, such as **bird-watching** (p178) and swimming in the plunge pools of **Naikorokoro Waterfalls** (p179).

● If you're feeling particularly adventurous, consider a **sea-kayaking** (p176) trip around Kadavu for a few days.

# Ten Days or More

● Time (and, more importantly, endurance) permitting, you can try exploring the **Lau** group on your own.

● Fly to **Vanua Balavu** (p180) from Suva, and spend the rest of the week (or two weeks) soaking up the restful nature of this sleepy far-eastern settlement.

● If you're willing to push the frontier even further, you could visit the distant chiefly island of **Lakeba** (p181) to travel back in time and relive its historical significance as a meeting point for merchants and emissaries from different countries.

● Alternatively, you could just sit back in a vessel of floating luxury and enjoy a multiday **luxury ship cruise** (p181) through these isolated islands.

| JULY | AUGUST | OCTOBER | NOVEMBER |
|---|---|---|---|
| The driest month in the islands, promising the most stable weather conditions for flights and ferry crossings. | Usually the best time for visibility, as well as cooler water temperatures for **scuba divers** and **snorkellers**. | The trade winds begin to fall, while the dry season makes a slow transition into the rainy months. | Annual rising of **balolo** (tiny sea worms) in Lau's Vanua Balavu, a week after the full moon. |

# GREAT ASTROLABE REEF

Suva

Great Astrolabe Reef

Snaking its way around the outer edge of Kadavu and spanning almost the entire length of the island group, the Great Astrolabe Reef is an undersea wonderland home to hundreds of species of corals, reef life and pelagic creatures of the deep. Named after a 19th-century French exploratory ship, the barrier reef fosters a rich and abundant marine biosphere in the deep channels on the outer side of the barrier. In the relative lack of human presence and interference, these waters are a paradise for divers who want to spy on marine animals in their wild habitat. Given its exposed location facing the open waters of the South Pacific, the Great Astrolabe Reef is severely affected during cyclones. Following devastating storms in 2016 and 2020, large patches of coral were destroyed and are yet to revert to their original exuberance. As climate change intensifies in the region, the reef becomes more susceptible to destructive acts of nature.

## TOP TIP

Several tourist operations in Kadavu were either permanently closed or went on long hiatus following cyclone damage in 2016 and 2020, and the COVID-19 pandemic. As of 2023, less than half a dozen resorts were operational across the island group, and these were the only places one could actually visit.

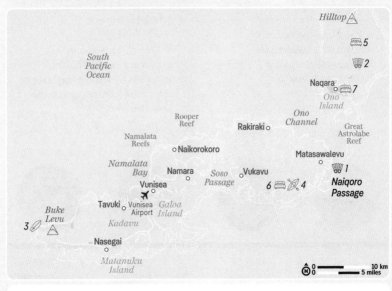

| HIGHLIGHTS | ACTIVITIES, COURSES & TOURS | 4 Tamarillo Active Travel | SLEEPING |
|---|---|---|---|
| 1 Naiqoro Passage | 2 Buliya | | 5 Kokomo |
| | 3 Cape Washington | | 6 Matava Resort |
| | | | 7 Oneta Resort |

Great Astrolabe Reef

# Dive the Coral Reefs

CARNIVAL OF COLOUR

Innumerable dive sites have been identified over time along the length of the Great Astrolabe Reef, all of which are crammed with colourful coral colonies as far as the day's visibility (sometimes up to a flabbergasting 40m) will allow you to see. The **Naiqoro Passage** – which bisects the reef midway and is subject to strong currents – is home to brilliantly coloured soft and hard coral, as well as a fantastic assortment of tunnels, caverns and canyons for divers to pass through. There's also **Eagle Rock**, a dive site that features a group of rock pinnacles with abundant hard corals and masses of fish life including pelagic species. **Broken Stone**, another popular dive location, is known for its beautiful underwater landscape comprising a maze of swim-throughs, caverns and tunnels. Yet another recommended site, simply known as the **Corner**, promises encounters with scowling turtles and nurse sharks snoozing on the sloping sea bed. For a different experience, visit the artificial wreck of **Pacific Voyager**, a tanker purpose-sunk in the 1990s that now shelters several species of marine

## WHY I LOVE KADAVU

**Anirban Mahapatra**, writer

As a scuba professional, I have a very special place in my heart for the untamed wilderness of the Great Astrolabe Reef. Diving here is vastly unpredictable, from the vagaries of prevailing weather to the sightings (or a lack thereof) on any given day. But therein lies the unparalleled charm of diving in Kadavu. I will never forget that special dive when, expecting to see nothing in the water made turbid by strong current, I suddenly spotted a massive manta ray – almost 4m from tip to tip – emerge from the dark depths of the outer reef and glide gracefully by, blocking out the sun for a few seconds as it passed directly overhead. It remains, till this day, the single most spectacular encounter I have experienced at depth.

**PRETRAVEL CHECKLIST FOR KADAVU & LAU**

**Cash**
Settle major payments by credit card in advance, and bring enough cash for smaller payouts. There's virtually no ATM access here.

**Power bank**
Some resorts only run on solar power and have limited charging points in the common areas, which are shared by all guests.

**Medicines**
Do not forget your prescription medicines. Also carry a few essential over-the-counter meds for fever, diarrhoea, aches or injuries.

## MATAVA: ACTIVITY CENTRAL

A social, comfortable and impeccably run place, **Matava Resort** is located in the most strategic spot as far as access to dive sites, surf breaks and other activity zones is concerned. Built on eco-chic principles, powered by the sun and operating sustainably in the wilderness, Matava has its own vegetable garden and enforces strict recycling policies. The gourmet meals here taste outright delicious, and are impeccably presented at mealtimes in the communal dining area. The bay in front is great for kayaking, and there's a shallow reef extending to the pretty offshore island of Waya that's amazing for snorkelling. Matava is the best resort to stay for divers keen on visiting Manta Point (a $55 boat surcharge applies ,though).

DAVID FLEETHAM/ALAMY STOCK PHOTO ©

**Manta rays, Kadavu**

life within its metallic chassis slowly being reclaimed by nature. A two-tank dive will cost you $250–300, including gear rental.

When choosing where to dive, remember that the southern extent of the reef promises more exciting encounters with marine species as well as a flourish of coral, whereas sites along the northern section have more clement surface conditions, thanks to being sheltered from the incoming winds. Staying at a resort in the dive zone of your choice significantly cuts down on daily journey times, allowing you to enjoy more time within the resort premises.

## Serenade Manta Rays

SWIM WITH WINGED BEAUTIES

Unlike in the Yasawa islands – where they migrate to feed in the winter months – manta rays are permanent residents in Kadavu's waters. However, it takes some patience and luck to spot them here, to the extent that dive resorts cannot guarantee a manta dive unless you are staying for a minimum of four or five days. The trick is to go spying for them on a day when weather conditions are neither too windy nor too still, and the current's not too strong but not too weak either. The best spots to cross paths with them are at 'cleaning stations' – patches of reef where parasitic fish species pluck bacteria and dead tissue off the skin of pelagic animals dropping in for a bit of salon time.

There are two well-known locations in the Great Astrolabe Reef for manta ray sighting. The first is **Manta Point**, due

### PRETRAVEL CHECKLIST FOR KADAVU & LAU

**Rain jacket**
Your movements within the islands will involve journeys in open boats. It is not uncommon for the skies to open up when you are out on the water.

**Adventure gear**
You may not always find a rental dive mask, wetsuit, dive computer or surfboard that is either a good fit or to your liking. It's best to bring your own.

**Memory cards**
There are no shops here to buy camera cards, and there is no guarantee that a fellow guest will have a spare card to lend you.

southeast of Vunisea on the slopes of the outer reef. You will have to dive to see them here, as the cleaning stations are among coral bommies at depths ranging between 12m and 18m. With some luck, you might also spot an oceanic manta ray – a cousin of the reef manta ray – which can grow to a whopping 7m from tip to tip. The other viewing area is located off **Buliya**, a tiny island to the north of Ono island, where it's also possible to see them while snorkelling. Chances of sightings are higher in poorer visibility, as more suspended plankton promises a bigger feast for these graceful, winged giants.

## Snorkel in the Shallows
CORAL, FISH AND MORE

The inner channels of the Great Astrolabe Reef – as well as the shallow parts of some dive sites in the outer reef – promise fantastic snorkelling for people of all experience levels. Each of Kadavu's resorts also has nearby lagoons where you can simply wade out with a pair of flippers, a mask and a snorkel and soothe your eyes on fantastic arrays of hard coral. On the outer reef, where it's possible to snorkel in water a few metres deep, you can duck dive to the bottom and see the impressive expanse of coral that would otherwise only reveal itself to scuba divers.

## Surfers' Paradise
RIDE THE MASSIVE BREAKS

Thanks to its remoteness, Kadavu remains largely unexplored by surfers from around the world. So if you come this far to catch a wave, chances are you will be surfing it all by yourself, without a dozen other surfers bobbing in the shoulder to spoil your ride. In theory, the best surfing here is found around **Cape Washington**, located on the far southwestern tip of Kadavu island. It gets plenty of swell around the year, and has a particularly impressive left break called **King Kong Left**, off Nagigia island. In practice, however, Cape Washington poses a logistical challenge to visit from the resorts located on the opposite end of the island, unless you are willing to pay the resort a substantial fuel surcharge for the long trip and make the excursion worth their while.

The most accessible breaks from all the resorts – particularly Matava – are around the **Vesi Passage**. This channel has powerful surf, and a mix of left- and right-hand breaks, although some of the waves tend to get blown

### ONETA: SPOT OF SERENITY

Located northeast of Kadavu's main landmass, Ono island is home to the stylish **Oneta Resort**. Sitting in an artfully landscaped garden complete with fruit trees and organic vegetable beds, and fronted by a lush white-sand beach, Oneta has an assortment of architecturally classy thatched *bures* with hardwood floors, woven walls and louvred netted windows. In addition to its bouquet of outdoor activities, Oneta scores in terms of its proximity to Buliya island, where one can enjoy the unique experience of snorkelling with manta rays. A community oriented property, the resort maintains close relations with nearby villages on Ono, where one can go on a village tour or attend church on Sunday.

**PRETRAVEL CHECKLIST FOR KADAVU & LAU**

**Camera batteries**
You may not always have the chance to charge batteries overnight, so it's best to carry a backup cell for an extra day's photography.

**Books**
Paperbacks (or e-books) are a great way to pass the idle hours on days when the weather prevents you from venturing outdoors.

**Insect repellent**
An absolute must for keeping winged pests at bay while lounging in common areas, and to ensure a comfortable night's sleep.

out from time to time. A daunting break here, called **Board Breaker**, attracts only the most advanced surfers. **Naiqoro Passage** also has a tall right-hand break suited to expert surfers. Less experienced surfers, on the other hand, could try tackling the gentle left-hander at **Soso Passage**.

## Sea-Kayaking Safaris

ROW AS YOU GO

DESIGN PICS INC/ALAMY STOCK PHOTO ©

Sea-kayaking has a niche following among people who appreciate the sense of unbridled adventure associated with navigating their way through the ocean powered by nothing but their own arms. Organised sea-kayaking day trips take place in all of Kadavu's resorts, which main-  tain small fleets of two-seater kayaks free for guests. For a more compelling experience, you could also have your resort organise a sea-kayaking safari through **Tamarillo Active Travel**, a New Zealand–based adventure company with operations in Kadavu. To cater to people with limited experience, the excursions are conducted through sections of the reef protected from wind and swell, and each group is accompanied by knowledgeable guides to keep the rowers on course.

Tailored to suit your time in hand, sea-kayaking safaris can be a one-day affair, or extend over a week. On the longer itineraries, you will return every evening to the comfort of a resort room, and continue with your adventure after a good night's sleep. If you fancy the thought of overnighting in a village for a night, homestays can also be arranged with prior notice.

### KOKOMO: LAP OF LUXURY

Located on a speck of forested land north of Buliya, **Kokomo** is a private island resort that sets a contemporary benchmark in hinterland luxuries. The property has a collection of one-, two- and three-bedroom villas, all appointed in the most elegant and premium fashion, as well as five sprawling residences for larger groups that are situated on prime viewpoints with sweeping views of the ocean. Kokomo island is located very close to the manta snorkelling area, and the resort also runs the Kokomo Manta Conservation Project in an effort to generate awareness about manta rays and protect the native population of the animal in the Great Astrolabe Reef.

### GETTING AROUND

All resorts in Kadavu have in-house motorboat services to pick up and drop off passengers arriving or departing by flight from Vunisea airport. Skimming over shallow ultramarine lagoons within the reef, the boats take about 45 minutes to reach Matava, an hour to call at Oneta, and about 80 minutes to get to Kokomo.

# Beyond Great Astrolabe Reef

Kadavu has some activities on dry land that are well worth pursuing after you've overdosed on marine thrills.

Great Astrolabe Reef

Naikorokoro Waterfalls

Vunisea · · Kadavu Koro

Most people hastily presume that Kadavu has little to offer them beyond oceanic adventures. However, that's not true. Once you have rinsed the salt off your skin after your time in the water, you can very well schedule a day or two on dry land to explore Kadavu's forested interior. In this lush tropical terrain, hidden rivers snake lazily through dense layers of mangroves, exotic bird species chirp away from tree canopies, and dazzling waterfalls cascade down rocky crags to plunge into emerald pools. There's no method to planning a holiday around these attractions, but excursions can be arranged by all the resorts upon short notice, and you will most likely find other resorts guests tagging along with you for company.

## TOP TIP

The northern shoreline of Kadavu island has a couple of isolated resorts where you can spend a few reclusive days.

JOSHUA FAWCETT/SHUTTERSTOCK ©

## KADAVU KORO

Not far from Matava, on the edge of a river-mouth shaded by tropical vegetation, stands the minuscule village of Kadavu Koro. An interesting way to get here is by kayaking west along the mangrove-lined coast from Matava, which takes about 30 minutes (or you could just ride the resort motorboat). Following a brief introduction session by your resort guide, you can wander through the village, stopping at homes to socialise with residents, or studying elements of rural Fijian life, such as tin-sheet *tatavu* (barbecue) grills and heaps of freshly procured cassava or kava. The village is en route to the Naikorokoro Waterfalls, and can be visited together as a half-day excursion.

EAQIVEN/GETTY IMAGES ©

**Waterfall, Kadavu**

# Spot Kadavu's Avians

BIRDS OF LAND AND SEA

Kadavu is home to four endemic bird species – Kadavu fantail, Kadavu honeyeater, Kadavu musk parrot and the whistling dove. Bird-watchers with enough time and inclination to wander the bushes can set themselves up for a meeting with not just one of these rare creatures, but also two-dozen-odd other winged species native to Kadavu's interior and coastal areas. Among these, the Fiji goshawk often piques the interest of serious bird-watchers. A mid-sized bird of prey with grey plumage and a dull pink collar, this goshawk species is endemic to Fiji, and is closely related to the brown goshawk found in Australia and New Caledonia. You may also spot several species native to the Pacific region, such as Fiji woodswallow, Fiji white-eye and the Polynesian triller.

All of Kadavu's resorts can organise a bird-watching trip, with the services of an in-house guide if required. Usually conducted in the early mornings or late afternoons, the walks follow trails in the rainforests contiguous to the

 **OTHER PLACES TO STAY ON KADAVU ISLAND**

**Papageno**
A low-key eco-resort on the northern coastline of Kadavu island, with a mix of dark-wood *bures* and garden rooms surrounded by greenery. $$

**Tiliva Resort**
This stylish resort occupies a vantage location on the isolated northeastern cape of Kadavu, very close to the manta snorkelling site at Buliya. $$

**Homestays**
A few families in Vunisea rent out basic rooms to the odd (and rare) passing traveller who fancies staying in the village for a night. Enquire upon landing. $

resort area, and last for a couple of hours. If you can pull yourself out of bed in the small hours of the morning, you might even luck out and see one or more of these birds perched on trees right within the resort premises. However, remember to bring your own binoculars, as the guide may not always have a pair to lend you. If you are a photography enthusiast, try to bring a telephoto lens (300mm and higher) with a relatively wide aperture opening (eg f2.8), so that you can shoot in shaded groves where natural light may be inadequate.

# Discover Naikorokoro Waterfalls

SWIMMING IN ROCK POOLS

On the outskirts of Kadavu Koro village, not far from Matava, the stepped waterfalls of Naikorokoro burst forth from sheer cliffs and tumble into deep pools of placid water, creating a magical atmosphere that's straight out of a *Jumanji* filmset. There are few swimming spots in Fiji that are so amazing, and getting to the waterfalls is an adventure in itself. Keeping Kadavu Koro to your right, your boat will float up the creek to the end of the village, where you will have to clamber about 20ft up a bouldery wall to access the lower rock pool, fed by the flow of the first waterfall. Children from the village often play here on weekends, and pull off daring plunges from stony ledges high up on the cliffs.

Once you've cooled off in the water, it's time for the second part of the adventure. Swim across the pool and begin a precarious 15ft ascent by stepping on stony footholds through the wash of the waterfall. It's a demanding climb that will require you to rely on all four limbs, but your guide will tell you exactly where to step so as not to get battered by the water. At the end of the climb, tip yourself over a rim of smooth rock and slide straight into the jade-green waters of the upper pool, filling the base of a cavernous hollow. On the far end of the hollow, you'll see the second waterfall – many times taller than the first – descend with a deafening roar from a gash in the rocks, through which you can spy a sliver of Kadavu's unpolluted skies above.

## PASSING THROUGH VUNISEA

A blink-and-miss-it settlement straddling a narrow neck of land in the centre of Kadavu island, Vunisea comes to life once a day five days a week, when the day's flight from Viti Levu calls in at the airstrip. For the rest of the week, the place is on snooze mode, and apart from a few casual homestays, cafes and grocery stores, there's little here to appeal to travellers. Transiting between the flight and your resort boat, you will want to spend very little time in Vunisea. On the day of checkout, always have your resort confirm that your flight is on schedule before heading towards Vunisea. Overnighting here is not the most promising plan-B in the event of your flight being cancelled.

**GETTING AROUND**

The airport in Vunisea is tiny, and the matchbox-sized terminal building has little more than a check-in counter, a bare-bones waiting area and a row of toilets. Island resorts arrange their pickups and drops based on the day's flight arrival and departure information.

If the weather forecast is tricky, the boat will likely drop you at the airport and rush back well before the skies open up, leaving you sitting at the airport for a couple of hours, with no access to amenities.

# VANUA BALAVU

The largest island in the northern Lau group, forlorn Vanua Balavu averages about 2km in width, and resides with eight other smaller islands within a barrier reef. The interior of Vanua Balavu is scattered with rugged hills, while pristine sandy beaches ring the group's perimeter. Vanua Balavu's largest village is Lomaloma on the southeastern coast. In the mid-19th century, the neighbouring kingdom of Tonga conquered the island, and the village of Sawana was built next to Lomaloma. Descendants of early Tongan settlers still live in Sawana, and houses with rounded ends show the influence of Tongan architecture.

At one time, merchants ships conducting trade in the Pacific regularly visited Lomaloma, and the village had the first port in Fiji. In its heydays, the settlement had many hotels and shops catering to sailors and merchants, as well as Fiji's first botanical gardens, though little now remains of its grandeur.

Vanua Bala

★ Suva

## TOP TIP

The Bay of Islands, also known as Qilaqila, sits in Vanua Balavu's northeastern pocket and is a fabulous site for snorkelling, kayaking and swimming. The bay has been traditionally used by ships as a cyclone shelter, and is still occasionally used by visiting yachts and cruise ships to drop anchor.

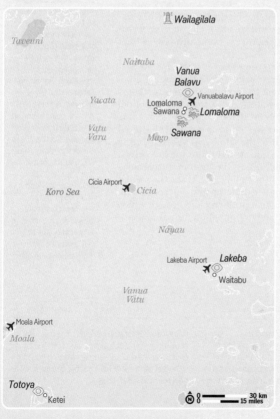

# Island Cruises

CONVENIENCE AND
COMFORTABLE

Given all the logistical complexities associated with traveling to Lau (scant connections, unpredictable schedules, unforeseen delays etc), travellers often bypass the DIY schlep to these far-flung islands and simply sign up for a luxury cruise instead. Most of Fiji's island cruises depart from Port Denarau. The number of cruise days varies from package to package, but those going as far as Lau are usually about 11 days long. Charting a circular course around Viti Levu, the vessels stop at a new island each morning. Passengers are allowed to alight and engage in watersports and cultural activities through the day, before returning to their luxurious cabins for the night and heading off to the next destination.

The first stop in Lau is **Wailagilala**, home to the ruins of an old lighthouse and turtle nests. The next stop is usually the traditional cyclone shelter of **Qilaqila**, where snorkelling in the spectacular bay is one of the trip's highlights. The cruise then visits **Vanua Balavu**, **Lakeba** and other smaller Lau islands such as **Fulaga**, which has an amazing lagoon rife with coral. From here, the ship changes course to head east to **Totoya** in the Moala group, before returning to Denarau via Kadavu.

If you're not among the intrepid few who – for the compelling sake of adventure – would rather spend weeks plodding across these islands by hitching rides on rickety boats and sleeping in austere lodgings, an island cruise is arguably the nicest way to visit Fiji's distant islands.

**Inset: Sailing, Lau**

## LAKEBA ISLAND

Lakeba – a roughly circular volcanic island that serves as the hereditary seat of Lau's chiefs – is the most important island in southern Lau. In days of yore, the islanders lived in an interior hilltop fort, far from marauding invaders. Today, they live in eight coastal villages connected by a road circling the island. To the east is a wide lagoon enclosed by a barrier reef.

Lakeba was historically a meeting place for Fijians and Tongans. It was also the place where Christian missionaries first entered Fiji via Tonga and Tahiti. Two missionaries, named Cross and Cargill, developed a system for written Fijian here and produced the first printed book in the language. The island has a few caves worth a visit, especially the ones with huge columns of limestone stalactites and stalagmites.

---

## GETTING AROUND

Despite being in the same island group, Vanua Balavu and Lakeba don't have regular or frequent transport connections between them. Unless you are on a cruise that calls on both destinations as part of its itinerary, you are likely looking at a fishing boat to haul you across open ocean (not recommended).

# Beyond Vanua Balavu

At the far southeastern rim of Fiji's geographical presence is a slim necklace of tiny islands collectively known as the Moala group.

The three islands of the Moala group – Totoya, Matuku and Moala – are geographically removed from Lau, but administered as part of the same Eastern Division. The islands are eroded tops of previously submerged volcanic cones that lifted more than 3km to the sea's surface over several millennia. Among the three islands, Moala, approximately 65 sq km in size and located about 160km from Suva, is the largest and most northerly of the group. Totoya's horseshoe shape is the result of a sunken volcano crater forming a landlocked lagoon. Matuku bears marks of its seismic history in the form of rich volcanic soil, steep wooded peaks and a submerged crater on its western side.

## TOP TIP

Telephone connectivity is patchy to nonexistent in the Moala group. Some islands rely only on satellite phone connections.

MIKE ROBINSON/ALAMY STOCK PHOTO ©

Tovu Village, Totoya

Lau Islands

# Escape to Moala

FAR SOUTHEASTERN OUTPOST

All of Moala's islands have villages on them, although **Matuku** is virtually inaccessible to visitors, due to its scant connectivity. **Moala** itself can be visited, and the best option is to take the weekly flight from Suva, operated by Northern Air, which lands in the island's grassy airstrip every Tuesday and flies back within an hour. A sleepy island with little to see or do for tourists, Moala makes for an offbeat cultural exploration at best. For geology enthusiasts, the highest peak in the island rises 460m above sea level and has two crater lakes.

The island has very fertile soil, thanks to volcanic eruptions of the past, which supports nine villages where residents grow coconut and banana as their chief source of subsistence. Moala has no tourist infrastructure, and although you don't need a formal invitation to visit, your only option for accommodation is to prearrange a homestay with a family in one of the villages. This is much easier said than done.

Owing to the fact that cruise ships drop anchor at **Totoya** as part of their voyage around Fiji, this is, without doubt, the most accessible island in the Moala group. Less than 30 sq km in area, Totoya traces the semicircular shape of the sunken volcanic crater around which it is formed. The reef that protects the island on its exposed sides has some impressive breaks that draw a handful of daring surfers through the year.

## CRICKET IN LAU

Unlike the rest of Fiji, where rugby is the number-one public sport and passion, people in the Lau islands have a fondness for cricket. The sport was introduced in Fiji by the British in the 1880s, and islanders from the east showed a heightened interest and flair for the game compared to residents in other parts of the country. Over time, Lau became the heartland for the growth and development of cricket in Fiji. Such is Lau's contemporary dominance in the sport that six of nine regional affiliates of Cricket Fiji (the country's governing body for the sport) are from islands across the Lau group. It is not uncommon for villages here to have their own cricket teams.

## GETTING AROUND

Bear in mind that if you choose to travel to Moala by the weekly flight from Suva, you will have to stay on the island for at least seven days, until the next week's return flight. In case of an unforeseen situation leading to that flight being cancelled, your stay in Moala would be extended by a whole week.

# TOOLKIT

The chapters in this section cover the most important topics you'll need to know about in Fiji. They're full of nuts-and-bolts information and valuable insights to help you understand and navigate Fiji and get the most out of your trip.

**Arriving**
p186

**Getting Around**
p187

**Money**
p188

**Accommodation**
p189

**Family Travel**
p190

**Health & Safe Travel**
p191

**Food, Drink & Nightlife**
p192

**Responsible Travel**
p194

**LGBTiQ+ Travellers**
p196

**Accessible Travel**
p197

**Nuts & Bolts**
p199

**Language**
p200

**Boat cruise, Yasawa Islands**

# Arriving

Fiji's central location in the South Pacific makes it one of the main airline hubs in the region. The principal gateway into Fiji is the international airport in Nadi, with a smaller international airport in Nausori near Suva.

### Visas

Visitors' passports must be valid for at least six months after departure. 100+ nationalities can obtain a four-month visa on arrival. Visit immigration.gov.fj for more information.

### Airlines

Fiji Airways is the country's main airline. Neighbouring countries' airlines include Air Niugini, Air New Zealand, Air Vanuatu, Solomon Airlines, Jetstar, Qantas and Virgin Australia.

### Sea Routes

Travelling to Fiji by sea is difficult unless you are on an international cruise ship, or on your own yacht. The main designated ports of entry are Suva, Savusavu, Levuka and Lautoka.

### SIM Cards

Vodafone and Digicel have kiosks in the arrival lounge of Nadi airport, where you can readily buy a phone SIM with 100GB-plus data packs starting at $50 per month.

## Taxis from Airports to Destination Hubs

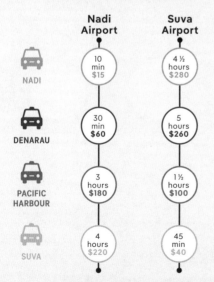

| | Nadi Airport | Suva Airport |
|---|---|---|
| NADI | 10 min $15 | 4 ½ hours $280 |
| DENARAU | 30 min $60 | 5 hours $260 |
| PACIFIC HARBOUR | 3 hours $180 | 1 ½ hours $100 |
| SUVA | 4 hours $220 | 45 min $40 |

## BIOSECURITY & QUARANTINE

Apart from food products, Fiji has a long list of items that are not okay to bring into the country, owing to potential biosecurity and contamination threats. These include animal parts such as shells, hide, feathers and bones (often used to design jewellery); souvenirs made of wood, bamboo, cane or straw; and outdoor sports equipment such as fishing rods, reels, tents and bicycles that can act as vectors for pests and diseases. It is easy to forget declaring such everyday objects upon arrival, yet not doing so may land you in a spot with airport customs.

# Getting Around

Organised public transport is scant in Fiji except within big towns and populated urban areas of its main islands. Unless you're very long on time, opt for taxis or self-drive vehicles.

## TRAVEL COSTS

Rental
**$100-150/day**

Petrol
**$2.60-2.80/
litre**

Taxi ride in town
**$5-10**

Domestic flight
**$100-200**

### Air Links

Nadi and Suva are connected to small towns by local flights. The farther and smaller the destination, the fewer scheduled flights. Remote places may have grass airstrips for small aircraft. Bad weather may cancel the week's only flight.

### Taxis

Metered radio taxi are plentiful in Viti Levu, and work well. They are fast, clean, comfortable, not too expensive and flexible. Taxis are also available in Vanua Levu (out of Savusavu and Labasa) and Taveuni (out of Somosomo and Matei).

**TIP**

A few transport companies rent out chauffeur-driven cars (costly but comfortable and convenient) in Viti Levu and Vanua Levu.

### LONG DRIVE KNOW-HOW

Queens and Kings Rds (Fiji's only trunk roads) are two-lane thoroughfares, with no median between you and oncoming traffic. There are passing lanes at regular intervals to allow overtaking, but you could spend a long time stuck behind slow vehicles between passing lanes. Road repairs on the road surface take place year-round, and can create traffic bottlenecks. There are amenities such as toilets, restaurants and cafes between Suva, Nadi and Lautoka, but are scant along the rest of the circuit.

### DRIVING ESSENTIALS

Drive on the left.

**30**

Speed limit is 30km/h in villages, 50km/h to 60km/h in towns and 80km/h on major roads.

### 3 MONTHS

Foreign driving licences printed in English are good for use for three months from arrival.

## Self-Drive/ Rental Vehicles

A rental car is a great idea if you want to improvise, making stops and detours along the way. You can readily hire 2WD sedans and 4WD SUVs in Nadi, Suva and Savusavu. Present your driving licence, put down a refundable security fee of a few hundred dollars and drive out.

## Buses & Minivans

Public buses and minivans are most common in Viti Levu than other islands, and are only practical along Kings Rd and Queens Rd – particularly between Nadi and Suva where they are most popular. They are rare on Sundays and virtually entirely unavailable on public holidays.

## Boats

Boats in Fiji range from precarious canoes fitted with an outboard motor carrying a dozen-odd people, to massive passenger-turned-cargo carriers that visit remote islands once or twice a week (or month). In between are fast and comfortable catamaran services ferrying tourists on busy circuits such as the Mamanuca Islands.

# Money

## CURRENCY: **FIJI DOLLAR ($)**

### Credit Cards

Primarily Mastercard and Visa are widely used for accommodation, activities, vehicle rentals, restaurants meals and shopping. Most Fijian businesses add a 3% surcharge, both for online and POS transactions.

### ATMs

ATMs are plentiful in Nadi, Suva and Lautoka. The top banks are ANZ, Westpac and BSP. Take enough cash into remote areas. There are no cash machines in Mamanuca, Yasawa, Kadavu and Lau. All of Taveuni has only one ATM (in Somosomo.)

### Cash

Cash is preferred for settling small purchases, especially away from big urban centres. Common paper money denominations are 100, 50, 20, 10, five, plus commemorative seven-dollar notes.

### Tipping

Tipping is neither expected nor overtly encouraged in Fiji. However, if you are pleased with service, you can always leave behind a small amount, which is greatly appreciated.

### HOW MUCH FOR...

Cappuccino
**$5**

Movie ticket with popcorn
**$20**

Haircut
**$10**

Restaurant dinner for two
**from $80**

### HOW TO... SECURE BOOKINGS

If you are pretty much sure you would be purchasing a certain service along your way, always pay for it in advance. This guarantees your reservation, and ensures you get your room upon arriving at the hotel, or a seat on a ride upon turning up at the venue. If you have to cancel or defer last minute, don't worry – Fijians are extremely accommodating with unforeseen changes of plan.

### LOCAL TIP

The seven-dollar commemorative notes are issued in limited numbers, and thus have value as collectibles. A commemorative 50-cent coin with the Fijian flag on one side, embossed in colour, is also sought after.

## PRICE ALERT

Goods and services in Fiji – especially in the tourism industry – are not cheap, for good reason. Firstly, most of Fiji's supplies are imported by ship from distant countries, which bumps up costs to begin with. Any unforeseen disruption in supply chains creates acute shortages, which spikes prices further.

More importantly, a significant part of the revenue charged to tourists goes into community welfare, whether to pay for leases or wages, or to support initiatives in education, healthcare and capacity building.

# Accommodation

## Package Deals

A classic Fijian holiday is all about finding a resort of your dreams. From sprawling mini-cities with hundreds of lavish rooms to elegant hideaways on remote islands, Fiji has plenty of resort-style properties to choose from. Most places require you to book and pay in advance. The norm here is to go for a package deal including full-board meal plans.

## Rooms in Town

Regulation hotels are usually confined to big urban centres like Nadi and Suva. However, demand far outstrips supply, and hotels can be booked out year-round. Advance booking is once again the name of the game – don't step off a bus and go looking for a room like you would elsewhere, as you will likely not find one.

## Go Eco, Go Chic

Fiji has a niche supply of eco-chic resorts in its outlying islands, which combine responsible living with plenty of style. They are far cheaper than luxury properties, and while you will sleep in rustic *bures* (thatched cottages) powered with solar energy, the food will be delicious, the ambience irreverent and lively, and your access to the outdoors simply unbeatable.

### HOW MUCH FOR A NIGHT IN...

a five-star resort
$600-1000
(full board)

an eco resort
$200-400
(full board)

a homestay
$100-150
(full board)

### Dorm Digs

Out in the islands, many luxury resorts have a limited number of shared beds to accommodate budget travellers. Enquire at the time of booking if shared accommodation is available.

Picking a good resort with dorm beds means you will sleep on the cheap, yet eat well and have access to all of the resort's common facilities.

## Stay at Home

If you're travelling on a budget and want to keep your lodging options flexible, opt for homestays for at least a part of your vacation. Fijians are great hosts and welcome you easily into their homes. Take advance note of village protocols that may apply, and bring a gift (a bundle of kava, for example) to break the ice upon arrival.

### MAKE YOUR MONEY COUNT

Regardless of their pricing category, many resorts in Fiji operate in close association with village communities and the environment. A browse through a property's website will tell you how deeply it is invested in supporting local economy or protecting the natural heritage. Try to pick a property that contributes positively in terms of sustainability and regenerative tourism. The flip side is that the tariffs will be marginally higher, but your tourism revenue will go directly into making a difference to the land and its people.

# Family Travel

Fiji is a kids' own adventure story writ large. The swimming and snorkelling is spectacular, there's a bunch of rides and slides to keep them happy, there are caves and jungles to explore, as well as enough slush pits and mud pools to satisfy every get-grubby urge. And the Fijians – who famously adore children – have smiles and hugs for every little visitor.

## Children's Health

In the unfortunate case of children falling ill, you may be stretched to find prompt and effective medical care outside the big cities. Carry essential medications for common conditions such as fever, flu, allergies, diarrhoea, as well as cuts, bruises and aches. Insect repellent is a must if you're venturing into the wilderness. Pharmacies are usually shut on Sundays and public holidays.

## Food & Drink

Most restaurants and resort kitchens will have kid-pleasing items, such as hamburgers and pasta dishes, on the menu – if not a dedicated kids' menu section. Some restaurants in cities, and well-equipped resorts in touristed regions, have highchairs for young ones, but they are uncommon elsewhere. Fijian food is usually not spicy and goes down well with children.

### Packed Goodies

If your child is a fussy eater, do a supermarket run to stock up on backup tins or packs of their favourite snacks. Long-life milk is readily available, as is bottled water and fruit juice (both sweetened and without added sugar).

### Resort Finder

Not all resorts in Fiji accept children. Many that do have kids' clubs (usually for children aged 4 to 12) and child-friendly pools. In these places, babysitters can also easily be arranged for the day or overnight for a reasonable hourly rate.

### KID-FRIENDLY PICKS

**Blue Lagoon (p116)**
A magical place to snorkel and spot creatures like sea cucumbers and pipefish.

**Big Bula Waterpark (p56)**
Water rides and splash pools in Denarau for kids to roll and tumble.

**Moon Reef (p85)**
Make friends with cheery dolphins who swim up to the boat from the deep.

**Kila World (p74)**
Kids can't get enough of the giant swing at this adventure park in Viti Levu.

**KUATA (P106)**
Children get to snorkel with harmless reef sharks in a shallow ocean channel.

## INDOOR ENTERTAINMENT

Since Fiji is all about the outdoors, there's always a chance of kids getting bored if the weather closes in on the day's adventures – or if a child simply has no desire to frolic in the great wide open. To keep children occupied indoors, check with the resort management if the playroom has board games and puzzles. Better still, carry a few table games with you (chequers, dominoes, or anything your children might like to play). Fiji's resorts have decent wireless internet, so streaming films and kids' shows on your tablet is another good way to keep them entertained.

# Health & Safe Travel

## INSURANCE

Always have your trip covered with health insurance, including evacuation. Fiji has no multi-speciality or super-speciality hospitals. In case of an emergency or critical medical condition, patients may have to be evacuated to Australia for treatment. There is a hyperbaric chamber in Suva for treating decompression sickness in divers, but you'll want to have dive insurance if such a need arises.

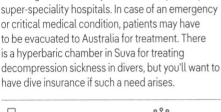

### Healthcare

Everyday healthcare in Fiji ranges from government hospitals, private clinics and laboratories to private dentists, opticians and general physicians. The further you get from the cities, the more basic these services tend to get. Many private chambers may remain shut on Sundays and public holidays. For late-night emergencies, your best bet are doctors on call at the nearest government hospital.

### Vaccinations

Apart from proof of mandatory COVID-19 jabs, there are no compulsory vaccinations needed for Fiji. But the World Health Organization recommends that travellers be covered for diphtheria, tetanus, measles, mumps, rubella and polio. If you have been in a country affected by yellow fever within six days of your arrival in Fiji, you will have to produce a vaccine certificate to be allowed entry.

### Water

The municipal water supply in Suva, Nadi and other large towns is chlorinated and safe to drink. However, always use discretion regarding the sanitary conditions of the plumbings through which the water might reach the tap. In small towns and villages, drink only bottled water, unless the resort has a dedicated water-filtration plant for supplying potable water to its guests.

### MEDICAL SUPPLIES

Over-the-counter medication is both cheap and widely available in Fiji's private pharmacies. Also available are a wide range of skincare lotions and creams, personal hygiene products, prophylactics, and food and drink supplements. Most supplies find their way in from India and Australia. Private pharmacies are not allowed to dispense listed drugs without a prescription.

### SOLO TRAVEL

Women usually feel safe travelling alone in Fiji. Incidents of harassment, assault or mugging are rare, though snatching and burglary can happen.

191

# Food, Drink & Nightlife

## When to Eat

**Breakfast** (7am–10am)
Common breakfast foods include bread, roti, pancakes, doughnuts, eggs and fruits. Tea and coffee are widely consumed.

**Lunch** (1pm–2pm)
Midday staples include cassava, rice, curried or fried vegetables, and fish or meat. Sandwiches are popular too

**Dinner** (6pm–9pm)
Dinner menus don't vary much from lunch offerings, but extend to popular Chinese, Indian and European platters.

## The Year in Food

### SPRING
Many coastal areas witness a brief spike in the harvest of crabs, and the annual rising of sea worms such as *balolo*. Beverages like kumquat juice and lager step in as thirst quenchers.

### SUMMER
The markets run low on vegetables, as temperatures soar in the South Pacific. However, there's an explosion of mango and pineapple, as local plantations burst into seasonal bloom.

### AUTUMN
Imported fruits and vegetables complement the scant local produce through the shoulder season. But avocado trees go berserk and bear huge volumes of fruit, sold in heaps by the roadside.

### WINTER
The cool season is the best time for vegetarians and vegans to feast on local produce. The clement weather also allows people to dig into carb-rich Fijian food and sumptuous *lovo* spreads.

## HOW TO... Book a Table

The need for booking a table is usually confined to upscale restaurants in busy tourist hubs, such as Nadi and Denarau.

To reserve a table, simply call the establishment and leave your name and number. If you are headed to a beachside restaurant, specify at the time of booking that you would like a table with views, as these are the first ones to go. If you have children with you, leave a note in advance asking for highchairs.

Fijian restaurants take your word for what it's worth, and assume that you will turn up to honour your reservation. If you are late or change your plans along the way, it is polite to call and let the management know, especially during peak dining hours when there may be other walk-in groups waiting to secure a table.

## DRINKING MEASURES

**Handle**
A small glass of beer, usually around the 200mL mark.

**Can**
Standard lager cans in Fiji measure 330mL.

**Stubby**
Australian terminology for a small bottle of beer, usually 355mL.

**Pint**
Expect about

350mL, less than the global standard, shy of the half-litre mark.

**Jug**
A monster serving of draught beer, usually about 1.5L.

**Glass of wine**
A standard serving of house wine, around 125mL.

**Bowl of kava**
Half of a coconut shell; the exact volume varies with size.

FROM LEFT. ANDYD/GETTY IMAGES ©, STUDIOBYTHESEA/SHUTTERSTOCK ©

## HOW MUCH FOR A...

roadside
snack
$5

food court
lunch
$12

all-you-can-eat
buffet
$45

pint of
beer
$8

glass of
wine
$12

cocktail
$18

slice of
dessert
$12

## HOW TO... Eat at a Food Court

Fast-moving food courts can be convenient for travellers to refuel on the move. They vary in form and size, from fan-cooled cafeterias to an agglomeration of steel tables and chairs in air-conditioned halls within shopping complexes.

The defining factor is the presence of several food stalls – usually covering the main culinary traditions of Fijian cuisine, such as Chinese, Indian and European-inspired fast food – that belt out wholesome and cheap food at short notice.

Food courts open around 9am, and serve food until around 9pm. The busiest hour is between 1pm and 2pm, when swarms of office-goers queue up for their midday serving of food. Cash is usually the preferred mode of payment, and menus behind the counter prominently feature pictorial representations of the most popular dishes (which can vary considerably from the real serving). All menus are printed in English.

The dining area typically has a few dozen small tables seating four diners each. Tables are shared among the stalls, and during peak hours it is customary for strangers to eat at the same table as long as there's an empty chair. Leave your crockery and plate at the table after you finish, as food court staff routinely make rounds to clean tables for the next group of diners to swoop in. Eating at food courts is also a popular family activity on weekends.

TOOLKIT

### Sharing a Meal

Fijian servings are big – you will see diners around you putting away large quantities of food with ease. Feel free to order one portion and ask for an extra plate and cutlery set to share a serving between two people.

## NIGHTLIFE TIPS

Urban centres in Fiji have a variety of nightlife spots to liven up your evening. You can pick from sophisticated whiskey bars catering to malt connoisseurs; sports bars with free-flowing beer and rugby, football or cricket playing on giant screens; happening bars with loud music that morph into impromptu dance floors as the evening progresses; stylish nightclubs with neon-laced interiors, laser lighting and groovy music churned out by popular DJs; and down-and-out dives where young men gather to shoot the breeze and have a laugh over several rounds of drinks.

Going out at night is relatively safe in Fiji. It might get loud and raucous at times, but the environment is usually peaceful. Drunken revelry or bar brawls are

rare, and you will usually be in the company of friendly and cheerful drinkers who may want to socialise with you without any malicious intent. Some nightspots have pool tables and dart boards, and provide a fantastic opportunity for strangers to become friends over games.

Disarming as the experience may be, it is advised that you keep your wits about you at all times, as you would anywhere else in the world. Don't get too drunk, or lose track of your belongings, or take up on offers to go someplace else with strangers. Always hail a cab to take you back to your room after you call it a night – they are available around the clock. It is not recommended to walk alone at night, even if you are not far from your hotel.

# Responsible Travel

## Climate Change & Travel

It's impossible to ignore the effect we have when travelling, and the importance of making changes where we can. Lonely Planet urges all travellers to engage with their travel carbon footprint. There are many carbon calculators online that allow travellers to estimate the carbon emissions generated by their journey; try resurgence.org/resources/carbon-calculator.html. Many airlines and booking sites offer travellers the option of offsetting the effect of greenhouse gas emissions by contributing to climate-friendly initiatives around the world. We continue to offset the carbon footprint of all Lonely Planet staff travel, while recognising this is a mitigation more than a solution.

## Regenerative Tourism

A significant part of the revenue brought into Fiji by mass tourism goes into regenerative activities to support and empower rural communities, thereby decreasing internal migration and the pressures of overpopulation in urban areas.

## Coral Reefs

With a sudden and prolonged spike in sea temperature, corals expel symbiotic algae (their main colour component) and turn white. Fiji's coral reefs are healthier than in many other parts of the world, but remain vulnerable to ocean warming.

## Fossil Fuels

Fiji is still heavily reliant on fossil fuels. Electric vehicles have not yet made a foray, and many of the outer islands meet their electricity demands with generators burning diesel that is supplied by tanker ships.

Many of Fiji's rural resorts operate along sustainable lines, where rooms are powered by solar energy, food is prepared largely from local produce, natural waste is composted, and plastic is recycled or reused using innovative ideas.

Most common sunscreen brands contain zinc components, which can leach from the skin while swimming and severely harm coral health in the shallows. Using reef-safe sunscreen during watersports helps alleviate the effect on reefs.

## RESOURCES

**Talanoa Consulting**
talanoa-consulting-fiji.com
Consults on climate change, food security and agribusiness.

**Mangroves for Fiji**
mangrovesforfiji.com
Conservation efforts to protect Fiji's mangrove forests.

**NatureFiji-MareqetiViti**
naturefiji.org
Biodiversity conservation and sustainable management of natural heritage.

## Plastic Bottles

Bottled water sourced from artesian wells is arguably Fiji's most popular merchandise worldwide. However, more sales also mean a greater buildup of plastic bottles, one of the biggest pollutants currently present in nature.

## Rainforests

Tropical rainforests comprise some of the world's most important biospheres. Even after years of deforestation and logging, Fiji retains a significant portion of its primal rainforest cover, and tourism revenue encourages its sustained conservation.

## Vegan Dining

Vegan food is increasingly becoming popular in Fiji, and gives diners a chance to sample freshly harvested local produce while easing the demand for imported vegetables and fruits, thereby decreasing the overall carbon footprint.

## Cyclones

Cyclones in the Pacific can be intense and severely destructive, and are Fiji's main environmental concern in the era of global warming. Category 5 cyclones in 2016 and 2020 have shown that the worst may be yet to come.

## MARINE CONSERVATION

Vulnerable marine species, such as sharks, dolphins and manta rays, are now included within conservation models that generate tourist revenue to incentivise the protection of these animals and their natural habitats by stakeholder communities.

Treated tap water in big restaurants is safe to drink, and diners can always request topping up their bottles to go.

Air-conditioning is redundant in Fiji (except in peak summer), especially at night and for rooms opening to the sea.

### Mangroves

Fiji has concentrated mangrove forests lining the shores of many of its islands. Mangroves are among the best-known carbon sinks present in nature, and also work as a barrier during natural disasters, such as cyclones and tsunamis.

## 53

Fiji ranks 53rd on the list of countries in the 2022 Global Sustainability Index. The government has committed to a five-year national development plan and a 20-year strategic vision to achieve its sustainable development goals.

# ⭐ LGBTIQ+ Travellers

Fiji is one of the more progressive countries in the Pacific region when it comes to same-sex relations. Laws banning discrimination based on sexual orientation were introduced following the implementation of the 2013 constitution. There is a strong LGBTIQ+ movement in Fiji, and the local scene – which has been fairly closeted in the past – is slowly opening up to the winds of change.

## Hotels & Nightclubs

Cohabitation by same-sex couples is widely accepted in contemporary Fijian society. Hotels and resorts make no discrimination based on the gender of their guests, so there will never be problems finding accommodation anywhere in the country. A large number of LGBTIQ+ men and women work in the hospitality industry. There are few dedicated nightlife spots for LGBTIQ+ guests, but bars and nightclubs in Lautoka, Nadi, Suva and Savusavu are extremely LGBTIQ+-friendly.

### THIRD GENDER

There's an age-old social custom in Fiji, where some young boys are brought up as girls within families. Upon reaching adulthood, many of these individuals identify as women, and their transgender identities are socially recognised by the term *vakasalewalewa*.

### GETTING HITCHED

Same-sex marriages and civil unions are still not recognised in Fijian family law. This means visiting LGBTIQ+ couples will sadly not be able to merge their dream Fijian holiday with reading their wedding vows on one of the country's pristine white-sand beaches.

## Public Affection

Fiji is socially conservative, despite its tolerance towards same-sex relations. Public displays of affection are generally frowned upon. For LGBTIQ+ couples, the risk of receiving unwarranted attention for outwardly affectionate behaviour in public remains high. Also use your discretion depending on the locale; an adults' resort on a private island may be more open towards displays of affection than a restaurant catering to families.

## SUPPORT GROUPS

### Haus of Khameleon
hausofkhameleon.com

Social justice organisation that advocates transgender rights in Fiji and the greater Pacific region.

### Rainbow Pride Foundation
mangrovesforfiji.com

Engaged in policy, research, safety, inclusion, mental health and capacity building for LGBTIQ+ people.

### Drodrolagi Movement

Facebook group (*drodrolagi* is Fijian for 'rainbow') that encourages advocacy and dialogue for LGBTIQ+ rights.

# Accessible Travel

In Pacific countries, people with disabilities are an integral part of the community, looked after by the family where necessary. As time goes by, more and more establishments in big cities are gearing themselves with accessibility features, though Fiji's wild landscape often poses challenges in this regard, especially as one ventures out of urban centres.

## Plan Your Travel

If accessibility is an issue, limit your explorations within the urban stretch of Viti Levu. Travelling to the islands would involve taking boats that are not outfitted with any mobility features.

### Airport

The international airport in Nadi has elevators, ramps and handrails in the terminal building, as well as wheelchair service. None of the other airports in Fiji have such fixtures, and flying there mostly involves journeys in small propeller planes.

### Accommodation

Enquire at the time of booking if your resort of choice has accessibility features installed. Many of the big resorts and hotels do, especially in Nadi and Suva, and you can request services in advance if necessary.

## LIFT CHECK

Elevators equipped with Braille-imprinted buttons are becoming more common in hotels, shopping arcades and office buildings in the urban centres. Many low-rise buildings in Fiji – especially those less than four levels – don't have elevators installed by design.

## ISLAND RESORTS

The undulated terrain on most islands is a serious contraindication to accessible travel. Most resorts are stretched along hill slopes, and are accessed from boats via shallow waters or sandy beaches.

## Suva's Streets

Downtown Suva has broad pavements and walkways that are wheelchair-friendly. The top-end hotels in this part of town have ramps, handrails and elevators, and also have valet service to help people with impaired mobility.

## Road Travel

Bus stands are short on accessibility features. Commuting by taxis or self-driven cars, you will still face issues like finding public toilets en route that accommodate wheelchairs or have safety fixtures installed.

## RESOURCES

**Fiji Disabled Peoples Federation** *(fdpf.org)* is a Suva-based organisation that has been around since the 1970s as a support group for people with disabilities. It has several affiliate bodies looking into spinal injuries, visual impairment, hearing impairment and psychiatric issues. The organisation is actively involved in awareness and advocacy programmes, and may be able to help with pre-trip planning advice if required.

Scan this QR code for FDPF advice and information

### DENARAU

The highest concentration of resorts with accessibility features are in Denarau. The marina and shopping complex at Port Denarau has a wheelchair-friendly promenade for accessing the seafront as well as restaurants and shops.

# ⚖️ Local Laws

Fiji is a relatively hassle-free country to travel through, and few tourists ever get tangled up with police or the law. Nonetheless, there are some regulations one must be mindful of, going by the basic assumption that what may be fine in one country may not be so in another. It is also worth noting that many smaller nations don't have a diplomatic mission in Fiji that could be approached by visiting citizens in the unlikely case of a civic, criminal or medical emergency.

## CASUAL EMPLOYMENT

Fiji does not allow casual employment on a visitor visa. If you wish to find employment during your stay, make prior enquiries with the Fijian mission in your country. Digital nomads could potentially work remotely during their holidays, as long as their earnings are not generated within the country.

### SEX WORK

Commercial sex work is not legal in Fiji, including acts of offering, soliciting or procuring sex in exchange for money. Engaging in the services of a commercial sex worker (male or female) or giving the impression of being interested in buying sexual services, especially in public, is not advisable.

### Speed Limit

The speed limit along open sections of Queens Rd and Kings Rd is 80km/h. This drops to 50km/h or slower while passing through village settlements. Speeding is heavily monitored by speed cameras along the road at regular intervals, and perpetrators will have to cough up hefty fines.

### Drink Driving

Fiji has a zero-tolerance policy regarding driving under influence; police vans stationed in random spots along the road often flag down passing vehicles for Breathalyser tests for blood alcohol. Always have a designated driver if you plan to drink on a road trip. Better still, hire a taxi.

### DRUG USE

Recreational drug use is entirely illegal in Fiji. Stay away from narcotics of any kind. Even possession of very small quantities of prohibited substance – from chemical drugs to natural substances such, as opium, coc and marijuana – can result in huge fines and jail time.

## FOOD FOR THOUGHT

Fiji has strict biosecurity rules regarding food items – these are diligently enforced by airport officials. Items such as meat and plant products, fruits and vegetables in raw or dry form, dairy products (especially unprocessed or unpasteurised) and honey are prohibited. You could get into a lot of trouble if the airport X-ray machines detect any such item tucked in a corner of your suitcase. Even if you are carrying processed foods like chocolates, branded cereals and snacks in their original sealed packages, declare it on the customs form prior to presenting yourself at immigration. Leave all half-eaten food and drink in the airplane before disembarking.

# Nuts & Bolts

## OPENING HOURS

Opening hours are hard-set for government offices and big businesses. Smaller businesses may keep 'Fiji time', which depends on various factors. On Sunday, assume that everything will be closed (on public holidays, it most certainly will). Lunch hour in Fiji is 1pm to 2pm, when some shops and offices stop work.

**Banks** 9.30am to 4pm Monday to Friday

**Post offices** 8am to 4pm Monday to Friday

**Restaurants** 11am to 2pm and 6pm to 9pm or 10pm daily

**Supermarkets** 8am to 9pm daily

### Postal Services

Post Fiji, the statewide postal service, is prompt with actual deliveries, even if a bit slow at the counters. There are post offices across the country. For international mail, Post Fiji uses the EMS network. However, you will need to present the contents of your parcel for inspection before booking it; the packaging must be done at the counter. DHL and FedEx have offices in Suva, Nadi and Lautoka. DHL has kiosks in some shops where you can drop a souvenir bound for home after purchase.

### Electricity 240V/50Hz

240V/50Hz

## GOOD TO KNOW

**Time Zone**
GMT/UTC +12 (+11 in northern summer)

**Country Code**
679

**Emergency Numbers**
917 (police)
911 (ambulance)

**Population**
900,000

## Weights & Measures

Fiji uses the metric system, but imperial measures (feet, pounds etc) are casually used in speech.

## Bargaining

Bargaining is not common in Fiji, although some merchants can be open to negotiations.

## PUBLIC HOLIDAYS

Fijians celebrate a variety of festivals. Exact dates of some holidays vary from year to year, but are declared by the Fiji government on their website (fiji.gov.fj) by the beginning of each calendar year. Annual public holidays include the following:

**New Year's Day**
1 January

**National Sports Day**
March

**Eid ul-Fitr**
March/April

**Easter Weekend**
April

**Prophet Muhammad's Birthday**
September/October

**Fiji Day (Independence Day)**
10 October

**Diwali**
October/November

**Christmas Day**
25 December

**Boxing Day**
26 December

# Language

Most Fijian locals you're likely to come in contact with speak English, and all signs and official forms are also in English. However, English is not the mother tongue for almost all local people, – at home, indigenous Fijians speak Fijian and Indo-Fijians speak Fiji-Hindi (also known as Fijian Hindi or Fiji Hindustani).

## NUMBERS

| | |
|---|---|
| 1 | dua |
| 2 | rua |
| 3 | tolu |
| 4 | vaa |
| 5 | lima |
| 6 | ono |
| 7 | vitu |
| 8 | walu |
| 9 | ciwa |
| 10 | tini |
| 100 | dua na drau |

## Basics

**Hello.** *Bula!*
**Hello.** (reply) *Io, bula./Ia, bula.* (more respectful)
**Goodbye.** (if you don't expect to see them again) *Moce.*
**See you later.** *Au saa liu mada.*
**Yes.** *Io.*
**No.** *sega.*
**Please.** *Kerekere.*
**Thank you.** *Vinaka.*
**Sorry.** *(Ni) Vosota sara.*
**What's your name?** *O cei na yacamu(ni)?*
**My name is ...** *O yau o ...*
**Do you speak English?** *O(ni) kilaa na vosa vakavaalagi?*
**I don't understand.** *Saa macala.*

## Directions

**Where's (the (main) bus station)?** *I vei na (basten)?*
**I want to go to ...** *Au via lako i ...*
**How do I get to ...?** *I vei na sala i ...?*
**Can I walk there?** *E rawa niu taubale kina?*
**Can you show me (on the map)?** *Vakaraitaka mada (ena mape)?*

## Time

**What time is it?** *Saa vica na kaloko?*
**yesterday** *nanoa*
**today** *nikua*
**tonight** *na bogi nikua*
**tomorrow** *nimataka*
**Monday** *Moniti*
**Tuesday** *Tusiti*
**Wednesday** *Vukelulu*
**Thursday** *Lotulevu*
**Friday** *Vakaraubuka*
**Saturday** *Vakarauwai*
**Sunday** *Sigatabu*

## Emergencies

**Help!** *Oilei!*
**Go away!** *Lako tani!*
**I'm lost.** *Au saa sese.*
**Call the police!** *Qiria na ovisa!*
**Call an ambulance!** *Qiria na lori ni valenibula!*
**Call a doctor!** *Qiria na vuniwai!*
**Where's the hospital?** *I vei na valenibula?*
**I need a doctor.** *Au via raici vuniwai.*
**I'm diabetic.** *Au tauvi matenisuka.*
**I'm allergic to penicillin.** *E dau lako vakacaa vei au na penisilini.*

## Shopping & Services

**What time does it open/close?** *E dola/sogo ina vica?*
**I'm just looking.** *Sarasara gaa.*
**How much is it?** *E vica?*
**That's too expensive.** *Au sega ni rawata.*
**I'm looking for a/the ...** *Au vaaqaraa ...*
**church** *na valenilotu*
**market** *na maakete*
**museum** *na vale ni yau maaroroi*
**police** *na ovisa*
**post office** *na posi(tovesi)*
**public toilet** *na valelailai*
**tourist office** *na valenivolavola ni saravanua*

## WHO SPEAKS FIJIAN?

### Viti
(FIJIAN)

name indigenous Fijians used for
i before the arrival of Europeans
hose mispronunciation gave Fiji
its current name)

The many regional dialects found in Fiji today all descend from the language spoken by the original inhabitants. All the people in this vast area speak related languages belonging to the Austronesian family. There are some 300 regional varieties of Fijian, but they fall into two major groups: broadly divided into the areas East and West of Viti Levu. The eastern dialect has been adopted as the standard form of Fijian. This standard form of Fijian is popularly known as vosa vakabau (Bauan). It's used in conversation among Fijians from different areas, on the radio and in schools, and is the variety used in this chapter.

### 'Fijinglish'

Some English phrases are used in Fijian with slightly different meanings.

**grog** – kava
**bluff** – lie, deceive
**chow** – food, eat
**set** – OK, ready
**step** – cut school, wag
**Good luck to ...!** – It serves ... right!

### Kerekere
(FIJIAN)

**Custom of unconditional giving
based on the concept that time and
property is communal;
also means please**

### WHO SPEAKS FIJI-HINDI?

Fiji-Hindi is the language of all Indo-Fijians. It has features of the many regional dialects of Hindi spoken by the Indian indentured labourers who were brought to Fiji from 1879 to 1916. Some people call Fiji-Hindi 'Bhojpuri', but this is the name of just one of the dialects that contributed to the language.

Some people say that Fiji-Hindi is just a 'corrupted' version of standard Hindi. In fact, it is a legitimate dialect with its own grammatical rules and vocabulary unique to Fiji.

54
Percent of the
population
speak **Fijian**

37
Percent of the
population speak
**Fiji-Hindi**

Fiji ●

# STORYBOOK

Writer, Anirban Mahapatra, delves deep into different aspects of Fijian life

### A History of Fiji in 15 places

Voyages and migrations have marked the beginning and end of important chapters in Fijian history.

**p204**

### Meet the Fijians

Smile and be welcomed – Fijians are a warm, easygoing and happy population, with great regard for the small joys of life.

**p208**

### Voyages - Past & Present

Is there a community that can identify as being truly Fijian, or is it merely a matter of who got here before the others?

**p210**

### Speak. Share. Drink. Repeat.

Conversations fuelled by kava are the lifeblood of Fijian social interactions, whether among Fijians themselves or with visitors.

**p214**

### Towards a Greener Future

Fiji draws on traditional practices and vast reserves of ancient wisdom to design sustainable policies for the years ahead.

**p216**

Indigenous Fijian man outside his *bure*, Navala village
CHAMELEONSEYE/SHUTTERSTOCK ©

# A HISTORY OF FIJI IN
# 15 PLACES

Voyages and migrations have marked the beginning and end of important chapters in Fijian history. Over centuries, even millennia, people from faraway corners of the world arrived to Fiji's islands in search of fortune, prosperity and a better life. These journeys are documented in the tales of different settlements that evolved through time across the country.

**FIJI WAS FIRST** settled by waves of Polynesian and Melanesian seafarers – from Papua New Guinea and New Caledonia – who had descended from earlier Austronesian migrants from Southeast Asia. It is theorised that a thousand years later, new arrivals from Melanesia assimilated, displaced or killed the descendants of the earlier colonists, and that it was the blending of these two cultures that gave rise to the indigenous Fijian culture of today.

Cut to the 19th century: at a time when Fiji was dominated by two chiefly confederacies named Rewa and Bau, the first lot of European explorers came looking for natural resources. Christianity steadily made inroads into Fijian culture; gunpowder and muskets changed the fabric of feuds and warfare; and the country's trajectory took a whole new path when Fiji became a British colony in 1874.

A new political landscape dawned a century later in 1970, when Fiji became independent and emerged as a multicultural nation with a large population of naturalised Indo-Fijians alongside the native iTaukei people. A protracted period of ethnic tensions followed, interspersed by the occasional military coup, but Fiji came out stronger on the other side with stable governance and communal harmony achieved through the early decades of the 21st century.

## 1. Sigatoka
CRADLE OF COMMUNITY

The so-called Lapita people – one of the world's first seafaring communities – possibly arrived in Fiji from New Caledonia more than 3000 years ago. One of their first settlements was near the modern-day town of Sigatoka, on Viti Levu's southern coast. In the vicinity of Sand Dunes National Park, where ocean winds have sculpted giant dunes along the coast, the Lapita had one of their largest settlements as well as a mass burial site. Excavations in recent times have unearthed pottery fragments as well as human remains harking back to the early days of the Lapita settlement.

*For more on Sigatoka, see p65*

## 2. Somosomo
CHIEFS & MISSIONARIES

The largest village on the island of Taveuni, Somosomo has historically served as the headquarters of Tui Cakau, the high chief of the northern Cakaudrove province.

Somosomo's southern borough of Wairiki gained religious prominence after a Catholic mission was established here in 1907, in honour of a French missionary who provided invaluable counsel to Taveuni's forces in a vital battle against invading Tongans. Somosomo has become an important tourist hub in recent times after a string of spectacular dive sites were discovered along the soft-coral-draped Rainbow Reef in the ocean channel (aptly named Somosomo Strait), located not far from town.

*For more on Somosomo, see p156*

### 3. Vanua Levu

VOYAGES PAST & FUTURE

Several medieval European voyagers made cartographic notes on Vanua Levu while passing the island on their trans-Pacific journeys. Most notable among them were Abel Tasman in 1643 and William Bligh in 1789 (from a canoe while fleeing his commandeered ship HMS Bounty). The island's rich supply of sandalwood attracted traders to prospect its forests in the early 19th century, and copra plantations were set up by settlers from Australia and New Zealand in the 1860s. In 2012, the neighbouring island nation of Kiribati acquired 5000 acres of land on the island as a future

**Holy cross, Somosomo (p156)**

KHABAROV IURII/SHUTTERSTOCK ©

resettlement colony for people who could be displaced due to rising sea levels. town.

*For more on Somosomo, see p156*

### 4. Kadavu

OUTPOST IN THE SOUTH

Kadavu was sighted by William Bligh (of HMS Bounty fame) in 1792 during his second Pacific voyage on board HMS Providence. The Great Astrolabe Reef, which fringes Kadavu's islands and is the fourth-largest barrier reef in the world, takes it name from a curious incident in 1827, when a French horse-transport barge turned exploration vessel named Astrolabe was nearly wrecked on its treacherous reef outcrops. Kadavu faces open ocean to the south, and its exposure to nature's unrestrained forces has seen it bearing the brunt of severe cyclones over time, most recently in 2016 and 2020.

*For more on Kadavu, see p173*

### 5. Savusavu

NORTHERN TRADING HOTSPOT

Thanks to a serene bay that served as a natural harbour for merchant ships, Savusavu gained prominence in the late 19th century as a trading hub for copra, sea cucumber and sandalwood. It was around the same time that European merchants began to settle in Savusavu and run copra plantations that were central to the production of coconut oil. The Nakama hot springs in town were documented for the first time in 1864, and a Roman Catholic mission was set up on the town's outskirts in 1870. The copra trade dwindled in the mid-20th century, but Savusavu gained prominence as a tourism hub thereafter.

*For more on Savusavu, see p146*

### 6. Lakeba

CHRISTIANITY'S ENTRY POINT

The hereditary seat of the Tui Nayau chiefs of Lau province, Lakeba was historically a meeting place for Fijians and Tongans, and evidence of this confluence still manifests in its local culture and architecture. Christian missionaries had tried to make inroads into Fiji since 1825. But it was only in 1835 that David Cross and William Cargill – two

Wesleyan missionaries accompanied by their spouses and a team of Tongans – succeeded in landing in Lakeba after a circuitous journey via Tonga and Tahiti. Cross and Cargill also pioneered a system for written Fijian, and produced the first printed book in the Fijian language.

*For more on Lakeba, see p181*

## 7. Lovoni
### SLAVERY'S DARK EPISODE

Lovoni has a singular mention in Fiji's history as its people are the only to have ever been enslaved. In 1870 and 1871, the warriors of this highland village fought repeated battles with Cakobau – refusing subordination to the Bau chief's claim as the king of all Fiji – and the settlement of Levuka was sacked several times over. In 1871, Lovoni fell into a deceitful trap set by Cakobau, when the chief ostensibly invited them down from their mountain stronghold to break bread and make peace. Lovoni's men were captured, enslaved and sold to the British, who eventually freed them after Fiji was ceded to the Imperial government in 1874.

*For more on Lovoni, see p131*

## 8. Levuka
### FROM BOOM TO BUST

The first and foremost of Fiji's European settlements, Levuka gained notoriety through the 19th century as a bolt-hole for dreamers, darers, drunks and the debauched. As the hub of pan-Pacific trade, the docks along its harbour were heaped with commodities bound for Western markets, and its streets were lined with hotels and pubs crammed with sailors and traders. Levuka's fortunes dwindled post-1874, soon after it deferred to Suva as national capital. Levuka was also where Indian indentured labourers called Girmitiyas – brought by the British to work in sugarcane fields – first set foot in Fiji in 1879.

*For more on Levuka, see p126*

## 9. Nabutautau
### LEGEND OF THE HIGHLANDS

A remote village located high up near the source of the Sigatoka River in the mountainous heart of Viti Levu, Nabutautau has an infamous place in Fijian history. It was the village where Reverend Thomas Baker – a British missionary tasked with spreading Christianity among rural Fijian communities – was killed and eaten by the Vatusila people in 1867. The legend of Thomas Baker is widely referenced in the narration of Fijian history; the Fiji Museum in Suva prominently exhibits utensils that were used in the cannibal feast of Baker's corpse, as well as the well-chewed remains of his shoe (which eventually proved inedible).

*For more on Nabutautau, see p86*

## 10. Suva
### POLITICAL NERVE CENTRE

Shortly before being proclaimed national capital in 1874, Suva had a false start in town-building when Australian businesses (unsuccessfully) tried to grow sugarcane in its recently drained swamplands. Suva's modern history in post-colonial times is inevitably linked to the coups that threw the city into chaos. The two 1987 coups tested the country's ethnic tolerance, while in 2000 its parliament buildings became the site of another drama when 36 government officials were held hostage for almost two months. A fourth coup in 2006 was followed by a stable political landscape through several rounds of democratic elections, the latest taking place in 2022.

*For more on Suva, see p75*

## 11. Ba
### SUGAR & FOOTBALL

Located around the northwestern corner of Viti Levu, Ba developed as a town hand in hand with the growth of the local sugar industry. In 1884, narrow-gauge railway tracks were laid in its surrounding areas to cart harvested sugarcane into town for processing at the sugar mill, which was operational since 1866. The modern town was formally established in 1939, and its economy continues to revolve around sugar production. In a marked departure from Fiji's general fascination with rugby, Ba has a strong football culture. The town's main football stadium was inaugurated in 1976, and was used to host numerous football tournaments over the years.

*For more on Ba, see p60*

Denarau (p55)

## 12. Lautoka
SUGAR BOWL OF FIJI

According to legend, Lautoka's name derives from a battle cry meaning 'spear-hit'. Apparently, it was here that a chief once cried out 'lau toka' after spearing his rival to death. Lautoka is Fiji's second-largest city, and was designated as a town in 1929. However, it grew in size and population after 1970, and its recent history is entwined with the fortunes of the regional sugar industry centred around the settlement – hence its other moniker, Sugar City. Lautoka now has more than 50,000 residents, a substantial number of whom are descendants of the Girmitiyas who were settled here to work in sugarcane plantations.

*For more on Lautoka, see p57.*

## 13. Tavua
SLEEPY MINING TOWN

Tavua is a small, quiet agricultural town in northern Viti Levu with lots of temples, churches, mosques, a scattering of old houses, and an air of faded glory. Its fortunes rose and fell with the Emperor Gold Mining Company, which mined the precious metal here from the 1930s up until 2006, when the mine was closed. During the mine's heydays, most of its workers lived in Vatukola, a purpose-built town south of the modern settlement of Tavua, which was declared as a town in 1992. The mine was reopened on a much reduced scale in 2008, but Tavua never quite regained its former glory.

*For more on Tavua, see p93*

## 14. Nadi
FIJI'S MAIN TRANSPORT HUB

Nadi was established as a township in 1947, on the building blocks put in place by the US Navy who had built a naval base here during WWII. Businesses and offices soon moved into town, taking advantage of Nadi's importance as a transport hub, thanks to an airstrip that was built by New Zealand in the early days of the war. Heavily used by US bombers to attack Japanese targets in the Pacific Theatre, the airstrip was gradually developed into an airport after the war ended. It was finally handed over to Fijian authorities in 1979 to serve as the country's primary international airport.

*For more on Nadi, see p52.*

## 15. Denarau
OASIS OF LUXURY

Denarau is a satellite settlement contiguous to Nadi, perched on a beautiful lagoon and connected to Viti Levu by a short causeway. Once an ignored patch of island with a rich growth of mangroves, it was conceptualised as a resort development project in the 1970s – the first luxury hotel was inaugurated soon after. A massive amount of foreign investment flowed in through the 1980s, triggering a spur in urban development. Over the years, the mangrove forests of the island made way for a sprawling golf course as well as a string of hotels, resorts and a marina lined with designer stores.

*For more on Denarau, see p55.*

207

# MEET THE FIJIANS

Smile and be welcomed – Fijians are a warm, easygoing and happy population, with great regard for the small joys of life. ANIRBAN MAHAPATRA introduces the society he currently lives in.

**FAMILY, RELIGION AND** community constitute the most important pillars of Fijian society. The tenets of iTaukei culture are deeply rooted in the villages, where life is governed by complex rules of etiquette and ownership, and hereditary chiefs still wield great influence over their clans. Traditional customs, from drinking kava to abiding by village laws, all remain crucial to maintaining iTaukei identity in the wake of globalisation and 24-hour media culture.

As a *kaivalagi* (foreigner; literally 'people from far away'), you will be instantly made to feel at home with a toothy grin and a cheery *bula* (Hello! Welcome! Here's to life!) greeting. This is the first word you will pick up in the iTaukei language, and possibly the most important one too. You will soon learn to offer *bula* back with as much fervour and as broad a grin. This gregarious presentation on your part will magically open doors and allow you into homes and hearths like a long-lost member of the family.

Apart from the iTaukei people, you will notice the presence of a notably different culture and community, harking back to the Indian subcontinent. Ever since they arrived to work in Fiji's sugar plantations in the 1880s, the Indian diaspora has grown to almost 40 percent of Fiji's entire population. Needless to say, this garnishes Fijian culture with the dazzle of multicoloured saris and the heady aroma of cooking spices. Fijians also love Bollywood, and the latest Hindi blockbusters are usually released to packed houses of popcorn-munching audiences.

There are some distinct Chinese notes to Fiji's multicultural identity as well. Thanks to merchants who arrived over the years from China to do business in Fiji, there's a robust Chinese community here, which would explain some really delicious Chinese food you might tuck into during your holiday.

Fijians are deeply religious. Churches across the nation come alive with hymns and recitals on Sunday mornings, and the entire country shuts down to celebrate Christmas with prayer, homecoming and feast. Fiji also breaks into rapturous celebrations during festivals marked by the Indo-Fijians. Diwali promotes great bonding between communities, when Fijians and Indians celebrate over food, sweets, bursting of firecrackers and overall good cheer.

A small caveat about everyday life: time melts in Fiji like a Dalí painting, and clocks keep 'Fiji time' – which varies considerably from the satellite-calibrated hour-minute display on your smartphone. Eons might pass before a flight eventually takes off, or a meal order makes it to a restaurant table, or the proverbial light-bulb gets fixed. Fijians have their own coping mechanism to deal with such delays – a joke and a laugh. And in most cases, approaching a problem with a sense of humour resolves it in the quickest possible manner.

## WHO & HOW MANY

Fiji is a nation of around 900,000 people. More than half of this number are native iTaukei people, while those of Indian descent make up nearly 40% of the population. Other minority groups include people of Chinese and European origin.

### I LIVE IN FIJI & IT'S FASCINATING

Having travelled through every continent and lived or worked in a dozen different countries, I arrived in Fiji to find the cosmopolitan utopia I had always been looking for. I was welcomed by warm and friendly souls on my very first day, and barely a year into my stay I became an integral part of the community.

People are all just humans here, regardless of colour, race, ancestry or livelihood, and everyone is welcome to join the glorious confluence of cultures and customs that defines Fijian society. Living here also comes with the intangible benefit of accessing the magnificent outdoors. Fijians love sports

and activities, and come together during excursions into Fiji's highlands and oceans. It didn't take me long to find my own creed, either on a tennis court or a mountain trail or aboard a dive boat, and the resulting camaraderie only increased my sense of belonging to this country and its people.

# VOYAGES
# PAST & PRESENT

Who does Fiji belong to, really? Is there a community that can identify as being truly Fijian, or is it merely a matter of who got here before the others? By Anirban Mahapatra

**TO FIND AN** answer to these questions, one would have to delve into the pages of a grand anthropological narrative that spans three millennia of human migrations. And whichever route one takes in navigating through its pages, all academic inquisitions would lead to the eventual conclusion that Fiji may well be one of the most cosmopolitan countries on the face of the planet, the fabric of its society woven by the multicoloured yarns of the many communities who migrated from far corners of the world to call the islands their home.

## First Peoples

According to oral folklore, the indigenous Fijians of today are descendants of a chief named Lutunasobasoba, who along with his companions reached Vuda (near Lautoka on the western seaboard of Viti Levu) in their canoe *Kaunitoni*. Though this story has not been independently substantiated, it is promoted with much fanfare, and

many tribes today claim to have descended from Fiji's first chief. Historical evidence, on the other hand, points to the fact that Fiji was first settled by a people called the Lapita, who had ventured eastward from their prehistoric homes in Southeast Asia in search of new lands. Navigating across thousands of kilometres of open ocean in their canoes, with stopovers in Papua New Guinea and New Caledonia, they finally arrived in Fiji. The assimilation of the Lapita people with Melanesians – who arrived a thousand years or so later – resulted in an indigenous Fijian population, which evolved over time to be known as the iTaukei people native to Fiji's islands.

Around 500 BCE, a shift from coastal fishing lifestyle towards an agrarian way of life resulted in the formation of inland habitations. Along with continued immigration from other parts of Melanesia, this led to the creation of diverse clans and communities (who were not

**Fijian man in ceremonial dress**
MICHELE WESTMORLAND/GETTY IMAGES ©

always at peace with one another). Fiji was by then part of a well-developed network of western Polynesian islands. Its Samoan and Tongan neighbours were sources of trading goods, cultural exchange and intermarriage. Travel between the island countries was made possible by enormous double-hulled canoes called *drua*. The largest of these canoes reached over 30m, could carry over a hundred people, and were a source of great chiefly prestige, apart from being vehicles of war.

## Arrival of Europeans

It wasn't until the 19th century, at the peak of European colonialism, that Fiji experienced its next major social upheaval. European seafarers of the 17th and 18th centuries – voyaging through the Pacific in search of terra australis incognita, or the unknown southern land – had occasionally bumped into Fiji along the way. English captain James Cook had in fact stopped over on Vatoa in the southern Lau islands during a voyage in 1774, and his countryman William Bligh had rowed his way to safety through the ocean passage between Viti Levu and Vanua Levu after being bumped off the commandeered *Bounty* by mutineers. So it was only a matter of time before European explorers began turning up in greater numbers, scoping Fiji for natural resources such as sandalwood and beche-de-mer (sea cucumber), and bringing gunpowder and the word of their Christian god.

By the 1820s, Fiji's sandalwood forests had been heavily logged, with beche-de-mer reserves also beginning to dry up by the 1850s. However, an estimated 5000 muskets had been traded in the meantime, resulting in a spike in tribal warfare. Ironically, in the wings of violent tidings, Christianity was making a steady foray into the hearts of Fijians, and its early adoption meant that the new religion was infused with traditional spirituality rather than replacing it outright. More than 60% of Fiji's population is now Christian, yet ancient legends and lore – along with customary social beliefs – remain entrenched.

## Colonial Fiji

Western (more particularly British) influence in Fiji ramped up after 1874, when the country was ceded to the Imperial government by Cakobau, chief of the Bau confederacy and self-proclaimed king of Fiji. Sweeping changes following the Cession resulted in British administrative, legal, educational and financial structures being put in place alongside traditional Fijian systems. Fijians were introduced to the English language, which today serves as the nation's lingua franca among different ethnicities.

Fourteen years into Fiji's British rule, the authorities entered into negotiations with the Indian colonial government to hire indentured labourers for the country's booming copra and sugar plantations, which required vast amounts of cheap labour in order to turn profits. After working in Fiji on a five-year contract, the labourers (known as *girmitiyas*, derived from the word 'agreement'), would be free to return home. Fair as it may sound, many today infer that indenturing was a lopsided form of employment tilted heavily in favour of the employer – a sugarcoated version of forced labour at best. Unbeknownst to anyone at the time, this would bring about one of the most important migrations into Fiji in modern times.

## Indo-Fijians & Chinese Fijians

In 1879, the first ship carrying more than 500 indentured Indian labourers set sail from Calcutta (Kolkata) and arrived in Levuka after a four-month journey. By 1916, some 60,000 *girmitiyas* were transported to work in Fiji, and after the government ended indenturing in 1920, a significant number of labourers chose to stay behind and begin life afresh far from their native India. Once their presence in Fiji had been recognised, more Indians voluntarily ventured out of the subcontinent to seek business opportunities in Fiji, and their combined presence resulted in the formation of the country's second-largest ethnic group, the Indo-Fijians. Needless to say, the Indians brought with them many colourful aspects of Subcontinental culture that added new dimensions to Fijian society over time. Indian food items such as roti and dhal are now ubiquitous in Fijian diets across the country, while Fiji Baat – a version of Hindi mixed with several other Indian languages and dialects – is widely spoken in the country, thanks to some 40% of the population bearing Indian ancestry.

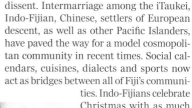

Predating Indo-Fijians as far as their presence goes, Chinese merchants regularly visited Fiji since the 1850s in search of sandalwood and bêche-de-mer. Starting from the mid-1990s, Fiji also saw a steady influx of Chinese, mostly from the Guangdong (Canton) province bordering Hong Kong. Within a few years, Chinese-run businesses – from general stores to restaurants – established themselves prominently in Fijian marketplaces. Current estimates peg the number of Chinese Fijians around the 8000 mark, or approximately 1% of the country's total population.

## Independence & Beyond

In recent decades, notably after independence from British rule in 1970, ethnic tensions between the iTaukei and the Indo-Fijians reached fever pitch from time to time. Much of this unrest was based on a fundamental imbalance arising from the fact that Indo-Fijians controlled a majority of business operations in Fiji, and thereby had their fingers on the purse strings, while the iTaukei had exclusive ownership to land, whether as individuals or as a community. Two back-to-back military coups in 1987 – and a third one ostensibly led by a businessperson in 2000 – were carried out in the wake of elections where political parties with Indio-Fijian representation had won majority votes. Members of the Chinese community, on the other hand, were occasionally mired in controversies ranging from immigration fraud to online scams.

However, in the long run, communal bonding has gained a distinct advantage in its arm-wrestling match with partisan dissent. Intermarriage among the iTaukei, Indo-Fijian, Chinese, settlers of European descent, as well as other Pacific Islanders, have paved the way for a model cosmopolitan community in recent times. Social calendars, cuisines, dialects and sports now act as bridges between all of Fiji's communities. Indo-Fijians celebrate Christmas with as much aplomb as the iTaukei celebrate Diwali, while popular Chinese delicacies are lapped up by the populace with as much gusto as a traditional Fijian lovo pit roast.

## Into the 21st Century

It is interesting to note how Fiji's attitude towards communal harmony and multi-ethnic democracy has directly affected its relations with the greater world in the recent past. The 1987 coups (which saw a significant number of Indo-Fijians leaving the country in fear of persecution) led to Fiji being briefly expelled from the Commonwealth. In 2009, the country was once again briefly suspended from the Commonwealth for failing to hold democratic elections further to yet another coup in 2006 (the elections were finally held in 2014).

In December 2022, amid a huge wave of optimism, Fiji held its latest round of elections, which resulted in the formation of an inclusive coalition government (the unmissable irony lies in the fact that the current prime minister was at the helm of the 1987 coups in his then capacity as a military officer). However, public opinion seems well-stacked in favour of the new government with the popular confidence that it will usher in a golden age of multiracial harmony in the years to come.

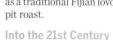

European explorers arrived in greater numbers, lured by natural resources such as sandalwood and bêche-de-mer, bringing gunpowder and the word of their Christian god.

**Above: Sacred Heart Catholic Church, Levuka (p129)**

# SPEAK. SHARE. DRINK. REPEAT.

Conversations fuelled by kava are the lifeblood of Fijian social interactions, whether among Fijians themselves or with foreigners.
By Anirban Mahapatra

With its roots buried deep in the sub-soil of Fijian culture, the ancient custom of *talanoa* can be loosely defined as a constructive exchange of ideas and perspectives between people who may not always come from the same school of thought. Ranging from a brief chat about the week's weather to several days of intricate negotiations in state-craft, a *talanoa* session can either be casual, involving friends at home or strangers at a bus station; or formal, bringing together clan chiefs keen on resolving matters of administrative import.

Whatever its scope, form or theme, the objective of *talanoa* is for both parties to hear each other out and achieve a unified form of thought that is greater than the sum of its parts. *Talanoa* sessions have historically played an important role in fostering interaction between Fijians and foreigners, and facilitating the process of strangers becoming friends. The practice continues to play a vital part in business meetings, social assemblies and administrative conferences in Fiji.

You will likely partake in various forms of *talanoa* during your stay. From resort staff and taxi drivers to shop owners and boat hands, everyone you meet will engage you in conversations potentially ranging in topic from the steep price of tomatoes in Fijian markets to the number of siblings, children and grandchildren you have back home. Such enthusiasm to engage rank strangers in conversation might feel like an intrusion into your personal space – especially if you come from a culture in which people keep to themselves in shared public areas such as buses and shops – but remember that the success of a talanoa session depends on both parties meeting each other halfway. The more you give to the energy of the conversation, the more rewarding the exercise will be.

In its most ceremonial form, a *talanoa* experience accompanies a *sevusevu* ceremony, when you as a traveller would be required to present a gift to a village chief before being granted permission to enter the village. This is also when you would likely taste your first bowl of kava, the social grease of all Fijian gatherings. The custom of kava drinking is umbilically linked to a *talanoa* session, and not merely because it is a rite of passage where both parties share the ceremonial drink while introducing themselves to each other. A mild sedative that produces a pleasantly numbing effect on the body, kava is a natural relaxant that allows people to let it all hang out over a good laugh. This ensures that both parties come to the table with their guard down and exchange ideas in an upfront and uninhibited manner.

The kava ritual starts with village residents pounding yaqona roots with a metal pestle. The powder is bundled into a cloth and repeatedly strained in a wooden *tanoa* (a conical vessel with a wide rim mounted on four short legs) to produce a turbid solution that looks like muddy water. This grog is then poured into drinking bowls made of coconut shell in a high-tide (full) or low-tide (half) measure, and passed on to drinkers one bowl at a time. It is customary to clap once in acceptance of the bowl, consume the drink (preferably in one go) and then clap three times after handing back the empty bowl. From here, you are free to politely decline a second serving or gleefully continue to gulp copious amounts of kava throughout the evening. A *talanoa* session does not end until all the kava has been consumed, and it can stretch into the wee hours of the night.

Kava tastes pretty much like what it looks like: muddy water. But many drinkers eventually acquire a taste for it. If you find that you do, too, you'll be able to buy commercially packaged kava ready-mixes to take back home at the end of your holiday.

> Kava contains a mild sedative that produces a pleasantly numbing effect on the body and is a natural relaxant that allows people to let it all hang out over a good laugh.

**Inset: Setting up the tanoa for a kava ceremony in Vorovoro**
Opposite top left: A tanoa filled with kava; top right and bottom left: Fijian men performing kava ceremony; bottom right: Kava root powder

215

# TOWARDS A
# GREENER FUTURE

Fiji draws on traditional practices and vast reserves of ancient
wisdom to design sustainable policies for the years ahead.
By Anirban Mahapatra

**RELYING ALMOST ENTIRELY** on its natural
heritage for sustenance, Fiji was quicker
than many other countries to realise that
nature's bounty is not infinite and that the
wilderness will eventually be depleted if conservation and regeneration measures are not
put in place. While this is easier said than
done in an era of ever-growing human con-
sumption, Fiji has achieved some degree of
success in turning back the clock in favour
of nature – and it has done it in a relatively
short span of time.

Much of this accomplishment stems
from Fiji's age-old social customs, which
revolve around community-based resource
management. Fijian society traditionally comprises various *mataqali* (groups
of families sharing a common livelihood
or marital bonds), with two or more *mataqali* forming a greater unit called the
*yavusa*. It is customary for each *mataqali* to stick together and look after its members through unified approaches that are
decided by the senior members of each community. A key management aspect relates
to agricultural land or fishing waters that
are traditionally owned by each *mataqali*
and accessed by members of the community
for their livelihood. Implemented over several centuries by successive generations of

**Local fishers**

community members, these localised management practices have made each *mataqali* richer by accruing a huge corpus of knowledge about geological, climatic and oceanic patterns (or vagaries) crucial to the management of their land and waters.

In the 1990s, after many years of unregulated harvesting had depleted Fiji's oceanic resources, unified thinking by the government and environmental agencies led to the realisation that the country's vulnerable marine biospheres could be effectively safeguarded and restored if the reins of their management were handed over to their original guardian communities and if *mataqali* members were included as stakeholders within each localised conservation model. This led to the formation of several community-managed marine areas (CMMAs) across the country, where community elders draw on traditional wisdom to formulate management policies for each biosphere. A variety of regenerative strategies have been adopted, ranging from periodic fishing bans to allow adequate regeneration of fish populations to demarcating clear no-take areas where revenue can be generated from alternative activities, such as scuba diving. Three decades later, it's no surprise that some of Fiji's most remarkable coral-reef biospheres – such as Vatu-i-Ra and Namena Marine Reserve – fall within protected waters spreading across CMMA projects, and feature a mind-boggling abundance and diversity of marine life.

Community ownership also goes a long way in protecting Fiji's terrestrial biospheres. Nearly 90% of all terrain in Fiji is classified as iTaukei (indigenous Fijian) land owned by communal units and comprising village sites or reserved land (including forests). Development on such land is permissible only through a lease that must be obtained through a statutory trust that oversees the de-reservation of land for commercial use. In other words, given the limited availability of land in an island nation, Fijian customs ensure that land is never opened up for uncontrolled development, and that a balance is maintained between preserving natural wealth and embracing regulated initiatives in urban development or the logging industry. Sustainable agroforestry projects have also sprouted in recent times to maximise the use of forested land by dovetailing the growth of mixed crops, such as cacao, yaqona and coffee. These are then sourced directly from villagers to make small-batch products, such as craft chocolates, kava and packaged coffee.

> Fijian customs ensure that land is never opened up for uncontrolled development.

Last but not least, tourism plays a key role in fostering sustainability in regenerative activities in Fiji. In many of the forests and marine protected areas, tourism revenue directly supports welfare activities among guardian communities, thereby incentivising the protection of their showcase natural heritage. In several places across the country, tourist resorts lease land from communities and employ people from nearby villages to work as service staff. This not only generates income for families but also builds capacity at the grassroots level by training workers in the ways of the tourism industry.

**Sugar cane plantation**

LEFT: YUVIS STUDIO/SHUTTERSTOCK © RIGHT: WORCHI ZINGKHAI/SHUTTERSTOCK ©

# INDEX

**A**

abseiling 74
accessible travel 197
accommodation 189
  Coral Coast 65
  Drawaqa 112
  Levuka 128
  Matei 165
  Moon Reef 85
  Nadi 53, 58
  Pacific Harbour 70
  Sunset Strip 66
  Suva 76–7
  Yaqeta 116
activities 40–4, 50, 107,
  101–2, 116, 153, **43–44**, *see*
  *also individual activities*
  Kuata 107
  Mamanuca 101–2
  Vanua Levu 153
  Yaqeta 116
adults-only retreats 10
adventure park 41
agroforestry 217
air links 187
airlines 186
airport, Nausori 84
Albert Park 32, 78
ATMs 88, 188

Map Pages **000**

**B**

Ba 33, 60
Baker, Thomas 77, 86–7
Balolo Rising Harvest 35
Bau 125, 138
Beachcomber Island 101
beaches 8–9, 26, 28, 62, 67,
  137, 153, **9**
bee farm 33
Beqa Lagoon 28, 70
Big Bula Waterpark 27, 56
biosecurity 186
bird-watching 31, 41, 59, 74,
  83, 145, 157, 171, 178,
  Great Astrolabe Reef 178
  Kadavu 171
  Lau 171
  Nabogiono Farms 157
  Somosomo 157
  Vanua Levu 145
Bligh, William 76
blowhole 19, 31
Blue Lagoon 116
boats 187
bookings 188
books 37
botanical gardens 26, 30,
  58, 145–49
botany 26, 58, 60, 78,
  83, 149
Bouma National Park
  31, 164
Bounty Island 101
budget 188
Bula Coffee 67
Bula Festival 35, 53
bull sharks 26, 70, 107
buses 187

**C**

Cakobau 77, 128, 138
cannibalism 32–3, 77,
  86, 153
Captain Cook Cruises
  41, 101
Caqalai 138
car rental 187
Castaway 103
caves 19, 27, 119
  Sawa-i-Lau 119
Cession Site 128
Charles III, King 128
charters 102
chauffeurs 187
children, travel with 11, 41,
  108, 139, 190, **11**
chocolate 30
Christmas 34–5, 51
churches 129
Civa Pearl Farm 165
climate 34
climate change 194
Cloud 9 26, 102
Cloudbreak 105
cocoa farm 144
Colo-i-Suva 83
colonial era 32
community-based tourism
  59
conservation 30, 33, 217
Cook, James 212
Copra Shed Marina 150
coral 14, 27, 28, 30, 31,
  33, 194
Coral Coast 64–7
  accommodation 65
  food 67
  costs 188
  country code 199

courses 11, 28, 30, 41
  cooking 74, 102
  surfing 41
crafts 79, 83
credit cards 188
cricket 78
cruises 102
culture 20, 23, 86, 131, 208,
  210, 212–17
  Chinese Fijians 208, 213
  Fijian 214
  Indo-Fijian 208, 212
  iTaukei 208, 210
  kava 216–17
  Lapita 210
  Lovoni 131
  *mataqali* 216
  *sevusevu* 215
  *talanoa* 214
  village 215
Cuvu Bay 66
cyclones 35, 131, 195

**D**

dance show 54
Denarau 27, 55–6
Denarau Golf & Racquet
  Club 27, 56
Des Voeux Peak 157
disabilities, travellers
  with 197
dive shops 147–60
dive sites
  Alice in Wonderland 147
  Annie's Bommies 161
  Bird Island Reef 138
  Bird Rock 103
  Broken Stone 173
  Cabbage Patch 161
  Chimneys 153

dive sites *(continued)*
  Corner 173
  Drawaqa 113
  Dreadlocks 147
  Dreamhouse 147
  Dungeons & Dragons 147
  Eagle Rock 173
  Fish Factory 161
  Fish Market 103
  Gotham City 103
  Grand Central Station 153
  Great Astrolabe Reef 173
  Great White Wall 160
  Jerry's Jelly 161
  Lau 171
  Leleuvia 136
  Lomaiviti 125
  Naiqoro Passage 173
  Namena Marine Reserve 153
  Nasonisoni Passage 147
  Natewa Bay 154
  Ovalau 125
  Pacific Voyager 173
  Playground 138
  Purple Wall 160
  Rainbow Reef 160
  Salamanda 103
  Sam's Point 160
  Save-A-Tack Passage 153
  Savusavu Bay 147
  Shark Reef 138
  Sherwood Forest 103
  Toberua 138–39
  Yaqeta 116
  Zoo 160
diving 12–3, 28, 30, 32–3, 40, 42–3, 70, 80, 99, 103,
Diwali 34–5, 51, 125
dolphins 32–3, 41, 85, 102, 139
domestic flights 187
Drawaqa 27, 111–14, **111**
  accommodation 112
  itineraries 27
Drawaqa Passage 112
drink driving 198
drinking & nightlife 26–7, 30, 39, 102, 192, 215
driving 83, 187, 198
drugs 198

Easter 34, 50
ecotourism 33, 189
Ecotrax 41, 66–7
electricity 199
emergency numbers 199
environmental agencies 217
equipment 14, 16, 19, 61

etiquette 18, 23, 36, 60
experiences
  Bula Coffee Tour 67
  dolphin spotting 32–3, 41, 85, 102, 139
  Ecotrax 41, 66–7
  horse riding 40, 63
  shark diving 70, 108
  skydiving 54
  whitewater rafting 73

family travel, *see children, travel with*
festivals & events 34
  balolo rising harvest 35
  Bula Festival 35, 53
  Fiji Regatta Week 35
  Hindu 53
Fiji Museum 32, 66, 76
Fiji Regatta Week 35
films 37, 76
fishing 40, 103
flora 83
Flora Tropica Gardens 145, 149
food 22, 38–9, 192
football 78
forests 57, 60, 72
free-diving 30, 144, 148
frescoes 53
Frigates 63
Fulaga 181

game fishing 103
Garden of the Sleeping Giant 26, 58
Gavo Passage 125, 136, 139
gay *see LGBTIQ+ travellers* 196
geology 19, 83, 217
geothermal pools 58
geysers 30, 57, 148
giant swing 74
Girmit history 76
GJ Marks 78
golf 27, 56
Grand Pacific Hotel 32, 79
Great Astrolabe Reef 170, 172–79, **172**
  accommodation 178
  Broken Stone 173
  Buliya 175
  cyclone damage 172
  Eagle Rock 173
  Kadavu 178
  Kadavu Koro 178
  Kokomo 176
  Manta Point 174
  Naikorokoro Waterfalls 179

Naiqoro Passage 173
Pacific Voyager 173
travel within 179
Great Sea Reef 155
Great White Wall 160
Guns of Momi 62

health 191
highlights **8–23**
  beaches 8
  children, travel with 11
  diving 12
  food 22
  hiking 16
  history 20
  romantic 10
  snorkelling 14
  surfing 15
  walking 16
  waterfalls 18
hiking 16–7, 32, 41–3, 59, 65, 74, 83, 85–6, 107, 110, 113
  Colo-i-Suva 83
  Drawaqa 113
  Joske's Thumb 83
  Kuata 107
  Nabalasere Waterfall 85
  Nabutautau 86
  Rukuruku 132
  Sigatoka Sand Dunes 65
  Vatuvula 110
  Waya 110
Hindu festival 35
history 20–1, 28, 32, 62, 76–7, 83–4, 86, 124, 128–9, 131, 138, 204–7, 210, 212–3
  1987 coups 213
  2006 coup 213
  Independence 213
  Ba 206
  Cakobau 77
  cannibalism 206
  Cession site 128
  Chinese Fijians 212
  colonialism 212
  Commonwealth 213
  democracy 213
  Denarau 207
  European 212
  Fiji 204–207
  First Peoples 210
  Girmit 76
  Gun Rock 129
  Guns of Momi 62
  HMS Bounty 76
  Indo-Fijians 212
  Kadavu 205
  Lakeba 205
  Lapita 204, 210
  Lautoka 207
  Levuka 206
  Lomaiviti 138

Lovoni 206
Nabutautau 86, 206
Nadi 207
Ratu Finau 76
Savusavu 205
Sigatoka 204
Solomon Islands campaign 131
Somosomo 204
Suva 77, 206
Tavua 207
tribal 84
Vanua Levu 205
WWII 83, 131, 207
HMS *Bounty* 76
holidays 34, 50
  Christmas 34, 35, 51
  Diwali 34, 35, 51, 125
  Easter 34, 50
homestay 23, 189
Honeymoon Island 138
horse riding 40, 63
hot springs 148

immigration points 128
Indo-Fijians 35, 212
insurance 191
International Date Line 157
island hopping 101
islands
  Bau 138
  Caqalai 138
  Honeymoon Island 138
  Laucala 164
  Matagi 164
  Moturiki 138
  Nukubati 155
  Qamea 164
  Yanuca Lailai 138
iTaukei 22, 208, 217
itineraries 26–33, 50–1, 98–9, 124–5, 144–5, 170–1, **27, 29, 30–1, 33**

jet-ski 102
J Hunter Pearls 151
Joske's Thumb 83

Kadavu 28–9, 40, 167–83, **168–9**
  accommodation 178
  activities 171
  climate 170
  cruise 171
  essentials 173–5
  Great Astrolabe Reef 172–9
  itineraries 28–9, 170, 172

Great Astrolabe Reef
*(continued)*
navigation 168–9
packing 173–75
travel seasons 170
travel within 168
Vanua Balavu 180–3
weather 170
Kadavu Koro 178
Karthingai Deepam 53
kava 39, 87, 214–5
kayaking 26–7, 30, 40
Drawaqa 114
Kuata 107
Leleuvia 136
Salt Lake 154
Wayasewa 107
Yaqeta 116
Kila World 41, 74
Kings Rd 33
Kingsford Smith, Charles 78
KokoMana 151
Kokomo 29, 170, 176
Koro Sea 144, 147
Koroyanitu National Heritage Park 59
Kuata 26, 106–10, **106**
activities 107
itineraries 26
travel within 108, 110
Kulukulu village 66

**L**

Lake Tagimaucia 31, 145, 158
Lakeba 171, 181
land management 217
landscapes 19,
language 37, 200–1
Lapita 66
Lapita pottery 66, 76
Lau 167–83, **168–9**
activities 171
climate 170
essentials 173–5
Great Astrolabe Reef 172–9
itineraries 170–1
navigation 168–9
packing 173
travel seasons 170

travel within 168
Vanua Balavu 180–3
weather 170
Laucala Bay 81
Lautoka 33
Lavena Coastal Walk 31, 145, 164
legal matters 198
Leleuvia 29, 41, 125, 133–9, **134**
essentials 134
itineraries 29
packing 134
travel within 136, 139
lemon shark 107
lesbian *see LGBTIQ+ travellers 196*
Levuka 32, 124, 126–132, **127**
accomodation 128
immigration point 128
itineraries 32
memorials 128
travel within 129, 132
Levuka Museum 128
Levuka Village 129
LGBTIQ+ travellers 196
Lomaiviti 32, 120–39, **122–3**
climate 124–5
itineraries 32, 124–125
Leleuvia 133–139
Levuka 126–132
travel seasons 124
travel within 122
weather 124
Lomaiviti islands 41
Lovoni 125
Lovoni Crater 131
Lovoni village 32

**M**

Malolo 26, 101–2
itineraries 26
travel within 100
Malolo Fisher Sports 102
Malolo Island Resort 102
Mamanuca 94–119, **96–7**
accommodation 101
activities 101
itineraries 98–9
travel within 97, 103
Mana 101
mangrove forests 67, 81, 83, 195
manta rays 26–8, 81, 99, 112
marinas 55, 150
Marist 7s rugby 35
markets 38, 79, 145
ROC Market 79
Suva Municipal Market 79
Taveuni 145
Vanua Levu 145
massage 58

Matacawalevu 115
Matava 170, 174
Matei 31, 163–5, **163**
accommodation 165
Bouma National Park 164
Civa Pearl Farm 165
food 164
islands 164
itineraries 31
Laucala 164
Lavena Coastal Walk 164
Matagi 164
Qamea 164
Tavoro Waterfalls 164
travel within 165
Wainibau Waterfall 165
missionaries 83
Lakeba 181
Marist Convent School 129
St Francis Xavier Catholic Mission 89
Wairiki Catholic Mission 158
Moala 183
Modriki 103
Momi Battery Historical Park, 62
Momi Bay 62, 63
money 188
monuments 20, 124
Moon Reef 33, 41, 85
accommodation 85
itineraries 33
Morris Hedstrom 128
motorboating 27
essentials 119
Moturiki 125, 138
movies 37
Mt Batilamu 59
Mt Tomanivi 33
murals 53
museums 20, 66–7, 128
Fiji Museum 66–7
Levuka 128–9
music 37
Musket Cove Marina 35

**N**

Nabalasere Waterfall 33, 83, 85
Nabogiono Farms 31, 157
Nabutautau 86
packing essentials 85
Nadi 26, 33, 46–93 **48–9**
activities 54–6
beyond Nadi 57–60
festivals & events 53, 55
food 56
Naga Village 86
Naikorokoro Waterfalls 171, 179
Naililili Catholic Mission 83

Nakama Hot Springs 144, 148
Nakauvadra Range 88
Namena Marine Reserve 30, 144, 153
Namosi Highlands 74, 83
Nananu-i-Ra 33
Nanuya Balavu 113–4
Nasilai 83
Nasova House 128
Natadola 28, 40, 61–8, **61**
travel within 63
Natalei Village 85
Natewa Bay 30, 145, 154
national parks **42–3**
Bouma National Park 164
Koroyanitu National Heritage Park 59
Sigatoka Sand Dunes National Park 65
natural medicines 131
Nausori 84
nautical tourism 34, 150
Navala 60
Navini 101
Navua River 28, 41, 73
Navunikabi village 74
nightlife, *see also individual destinations* 26–7, 30, 39, 102, 192, 215
Nukubolu Ruins 145, 155
nurse shark 107

**O**

ocean conditions 35
oceanic patterns 217
Oneta 170
opening hours 199
orchids 26, 58
outdoor activities **42–3**
outrigger canoes 136
Ovalau 120–39, **122–3**
activities 124–5
Arovudi 131
climate 124
holidays 125
itineraries 124–5
Leleuvia 133–9
Levuka 126–132
shipwreck 131
travel within 122
Vatukalo 131
Wainaloka 131
weather 124

**P**

Pacific Harbour 28, 32, 69–74, **70**
itineraries 28, 32
travel within 71, 74
Pacific Harbour Arts Village 69

Map Pages **000**

paddleboarding 114, 136
Panguni Uthiram 53
parasailing 102
parks & gardens
  Flora Tropica Gardens
  145, 149
  Garden of the Sleeping
  Giant 26, 58
pearl farm 31, 144, 151
people 208, 210, 212–3,
  Chinese Fijians 208, 213
  Indo-Fijians 208, 212
  iTaukei 208, 210
performance arts 55
petrol 187
pharmacies 191
photography 19, 60, 79,
  86, 179
planning 36
plants 26, 58, 60, 78,
  83, 149
population 199
Port Denarau 55
postal services 199
pottery 66, 76, 83
prices 188
private islands 10
Provincial Bure 128
public holidays 199

Q

Qaraniqio River 69
Qilaqila 181
quad-bike 54
quarantine 186

R

rafting 28, 73
Rainbow Reef 31, 145, 160–1
rainfall 34–5
rainforests 30, 72, 83, 195
Rakiraki 33, 88
  itineraries 33
Ratua Finau 76
reef sharks 108
religion 35, 117
resorts, *see*
  *accommodation,*
  *individual locations*
resource management 216
responsible travel 194
Rewa River 81, 83
river rafting 41
river tubing 73
rock climbing 83
ROC Market 79
romantic 10
ropewalks 74
Royal Suva Yacht Club 80
rugby 32, 35
Rukuruku 124, 131–2

S

Sabeto Hot springs 26, 58
safe travel 8, 12, 19, 191
Salt Lake 30, 145, 154
Sandbank 132
sand dunes 19, 28
Savusavu 30, 40, 146–55,
  accommodation 147, 148
  Copra Shed Marina 150
  drinking 150
  Flora Tropica Gardens
  149
  itineraries 30
  KokoMana 151
  Korovatu Beach 153
  Marinas 150
  Nakama Hot Springs 148
  Natewa Bay 154
  Naweni Village 153
  Nukubolu, ruins 155
  Salt Lake 154
  travel within 151, 155
  Waisali Forest Walk 154
  Waitui Marina 150
  Wasavula 153
Savusavu Bay 144, 147
Sawa-i-Lau 27, 119
scenic drives 83–4
  Burenitu to Nabalasere
  83
  Nabutautau to Sigatoka
  84
  Nausori to Natovi 83
  Sawani to Naga 84
  Silana to Volivoli 83
  Suva to Colo-i-Suva 84
scuba diving *see dive sites*
sea kayaking 40
sea routes 186
sea wall 80
seismology 149
settlements 20
*sevusevu* 23
sex work 198
Shangri-La Resort 66, 70
Shark Reef Marine Reserve
  70
sharks 26, 28, 32, 70, 107–8
shipwreck 131
shopping 27, 55, 75, 80
  Damodar City 80
  MHCC 80
  Nadi 55
  Suva 75, 80
  Tappoo City 80
Sigatoka 28
Sigatoka River 63
Sigatoka Sand Dunes
  National Park 65
SIM cards 186
skydiving 54
Snake God Cave 84
snorkelling 14, 26–7, 29, 67,
85, 99, 102–3, 107–8, 110,
112, 114, 116, 125, 132, 134,
139, 155, 165, 171, **14**
  Blue Lagoon 114, 116
  Civa Pearl Farm 165
  Drawaqa 114
  Kadavu 171
  Kuata 107
  Lau 171
  Leleuvia 134
  Lomaiviti 112
  manta rays 112
  Ovalau 125
  Picnic Island 139
  Rukuruku 132
  Savusavu 155
  sharks 108, 110
  sunrise 114
  Toberua 139
  Vunabua Beach 67
  Waya 110
sunrise 67, 110, 114, 139
  Toberua 139
  Vunabua Beach 67
  Waya 110
Solomon Islands campaign
  131
solo travel 191
Somosomo 31, 156–161,
  159–161, **156**
  accommodation 157
  bird-watching 157
  Des Voeux Peak 157
  hiking 158
  International Date
  Line 157
  itineraries 31
  Lake Tagimaucia 158
  Rainbow Reef 160
  South Cape Blowhole 157
  travel within 158, 161
  Wairiki
    Catholic
    Mission 158
  Waitavala Water Slide
  157
South Cape Blowhole
  31, 157
Southeastern Vanua
  Levu 145
South Sea Cruises 101
South Sea Island 101
Sovi Bay 65
spinner dolphins 41, 85
sports 56
Sri Siva Subramaniya
  Swami Temple 53
stargazing 27, 41, 117, 136
  Leleuvia 136
  Yaqeta 117
St Francis Xavier Catholic
  Mission 89
Suncoast 88–93, 91–93, **89**
  travel within 90, 93

Sunday services 158
Sunset Strip 66–7
supermarkets 38
surfing 15, 26, 28, 41, 63,
  105, **15, 42–3**
  Cloudbreak 105
  Frigates 63
  lessons 63
  Namotu Left 105
  trips 105
  Wilkes Passage 105
surf sites 175–6
  Board Breaker 176
  Cape Washington 175
  King Kong Left 175
  Naiqoro Passage 176
  Soso Passage 176
  Vesi Passage 175
sustainabililty 194, 216
Suva 28, 32, 46–93, 75–87,
  82–87
  accommodation 76–77
  drives 83
  itineraries 28, 32, 50–51
  Nadi 52
  Natadola 61
  Pacific Harbour 69
  food 78–79
  shopping 80
  Suncoast 88–93
  Suva 75–87
  travel within 81
  walking tours 78
Suva Harbour 80
Suva (m) 75
Suva Municipal Market 79
swimming 18, 26, 65–6, 81,
  85, 102, 105, 110, 131–2, 134
  Shangri-La Resort 66
  Sovi Bay 65
  Waya 110

T

*tagimaucia* 145, 161
Takalana Bay 85
*talanoa* 23
Tanua Levu 144
Tavarua 103
Taveuni 31, 41, 140–165
  dive shops 160
  itineraries 144–45
  markets 145
  Matei 163–165
  Namena Marine Reserve
  145
  navigation 142–143
  Rainbow Reef 144
  Savusavu 146–155,
  Somosomo 156–161,
  travel within 142
  weather 144
Tavoro Waterfalls 31,
  145, 164

taxis 187
television 37
temple 53
tennis 27, 56, 78
Thaipusam 53
Thurston Gardens 78
tiger shark 71, 107
time zone 199
tipping 188
Toberua 29, 125, 139
  itineraries 29
  Totoya 181
  tours 19
  Bula Coffee Tour 67
  cocoa farm 144
  pearl farm 144, 165
transport 102, 187
  buses 187
  car rental 187
  charters 102
  chauffeurs 187
  taxis 187
travel seasons 34–5, 50, 98, 124–5
travel to/from Fiji 186
travel within
  Nadi 48
  Pacific Harbour 74
  Suncoast 90, 93
  Suva 48, 81, 87
  Viti Levu 48
Treasure Island 101

 U

Udre Udre 33
Ului Nakauka 110
Ulutini 119

 V

vaccinations 191
Vanua Balavu 171, 180-3, **180**
  cruises 181
  geology 183
  Lakeba 181
  Moala 183
  travel within 181, 183
Vanua Levu 140-165
  activities 153
  climate 144
  itineraries 144-5
  Matei 163-5
  navigation 142-3
  Rainbow Reef 144
  Savusavu 146-155
  Somosomo 156-61,
  Southeastern Vanua
    Levu 145
  travel seasons 144
  travel within 142
  weather 144
Vatu-i-Ra 33
Vatuvula 26, 110
vegetarian & vegan
  travellers 22, 195
viewpoint 131
villages 20, 23, 36, 57-8,
  60, 138, 153, 155, 215, **23**
  Enadala 117
  Kadavu Koro 178
  Lakeba 181
  Levuka 129
  Nabutautau 86
  Nacula 117
  Naga 86
  Natalei Village 85
  Naweni 153

Nukubolu, ruins 155
*sevusevu 215*
Uluibau 138
Wailotua Village 84
Yaqeta 117
visas 186
Viseisei 58
Viti Levu 28, 32-33, 46-93
  forests 60
  itineraries 28, 32, 50-51
  Nadi 52
  Natadola 61
  Pacific Harbour 69-74
  Suncoast 88-93
  Suva 75-87
volcanoes 19, 32, 83, 110, 131, 148, 155, 158
volleyball 81
Vomo 101
Vou Hub 26, 54
Vuda Marina 58
Vunabua Beach 67
Vunisea 170, 179

 W

Wailagilala 181
Wailotua Village 52, 84
Wainibau Waterfall 165
Wairiki Catholic Mission 31, 158
Waisila Creek 83
Waitabu Marine Park 165
Waitavala Water Slide 157
Waitui Marina 150
Wakaya Club & Spa 139
walking 16–8, 20, 78, 80, 83, **42-43**
waterfalls 18, 32, 59, 72, **18**
  Kila World 74

Nabalasere 85
Naikorokoro Waterfalls 179
Tavoro 164
Wainibau 165
water management 217
water slide, natural 132
waterpark 56
Waya 110–13
Wayasewa 26
weather 20, 34-35, 50, 98
weights & measures 199
whale spotting 139
Whale's Tale 101
whitewater rafting 41, 73
  Navua River 73
World War II 62, 131, 207

 Y

yachting 80, 102
  Blue Lagoon 116
  immigration point 128
  Yaqeta 116
Yanuca 66
Yanuca Lailai 138
Yaqeta 27, 115-19, **115**
  accommodation 116
  activities 116–17
  itineraries 27
  travel within 117, 119
Yasawa 26, 94-119
  day trips 110
  travel within 97
Yasawa Flyer 98

 Z

zip lining 74

Discover Waya Island's (p110) picture-postcard scenery of rugged hills, beautiful lagoons and coastlines featuring long, sandy beaches and rocky headlands.

Embrace Navua River's (p73) impossibly beautiful terrain of interconnected gorges that slice through the highlands like deep knife gashes.

## THIS BOOK

**Design Development**
Marc Backwell

**Content Development**
Mark Jones, Sandie Kestell, Anne Mason, Joana Taborda

**Cartography Development**
Katerina Pavkova

**Production Development**
Sandie Kestell, Fergal Condon

**Series Development Leadership**
Darren O'Connell, Piers Pickard, Chris Zeiher

**Destination Editor**
Amy Lynch

**Production Editor**
Jennifer McCann

**Book Designer**
Megan Cassidy

**Cartographer**
Bohumil Ptacek

**Assisting Editors**
Sarah Bailey, Monique Choy, Brana Vladisavljevic

**Cover Researcher**
Ania Lenihan

**Thanks** Ronan Abayawickrema, Sofie Andersen, Melanie Dankel, Karen Henderson, Karyn Noble